20p

610·694

EDMUNDS. V & SCORER C.G.

ETHICAL RESPONSIBILITY IN
MEDICINE, 1.

ETHICAL RESPONSIBILITY
IN MEDICINE

ETHICAL RESPONSIBILITY IN MEDICINE

A CHRISTIAN APPROACH

EDITED BY

VINCENT EDMUNDS
M.D., M.R.C.P.

C. GORDON SCORER
M.D., F.R.C.S.

E. & S. LIVINGSTONE LTD.
EDINBURGH AND LONDON
1967

Printed in Great Britain

PREFACE

Until the Second World War the ethical problems in Medicine received comparatively little attention from the Profession. There were few authoritative books on the subject and available monographs were negligible. Those which could be unearthed from the stacks of the medical libraries were probably seldom read. In any case, the majority of practitioners did not feel the need to consult them nor were they particularly interested. The reasons are not difficult to see.

In earlier times Christian ethics had pervaded most of the communities of Western Europe and North America, and patterns of conduct derived from this source were firmly embedded in the thinking of most of the practitioners of the medical art. There was general agreement on the topics which were most likely to raise controversy. Similarly, the doctor-patient relationship was usually one of a simple contract between a single practitioner and an individual patient. The diagnostic and therapeutic procedures which were available to the practitioner were relatively uncomplicated and their effects for good or ill were limited. The patient understood that his consent would be obtained before the application of any measures which involved known risk. In short, though the history of Medicine reveals that practice was not always as simple as that, yet in the main professional relationships were comparatively direct and uncomplicated.

The pattern of medical practice has greatly altered in the last twenty-five years. It will most certainly continue to do so—perhaps at an increasing rate. We are living in a collective society. Group practice and hospital team work have to a great extent replaced the gifted individualist. The State's pervasive concern for the care of the sick has undermined the former direct contract between patient and doctor. Most important of all, increasing knowledge of the human body and means of more effective control of its functioning have placed increased power in the hands of the Profession. This power may not always result in good; sometimes harm in unexpected and unwelcome ways comes to the patient.

It is, therefore, not surprising that various problems of ethical responsibility should come to the fore in a new and urgent manner.

It is time to look at them again. Moreover it is not so easy today
to find common agreement amongst the members of the Profession,
for the older standards and conventions are becoming weaker in
their influence. Some of them are not even known to those newly
qualified, who find themselves suddenly confronted by perplexities
and choices which they had not foreseen and for which they are
little prepared. A proportion of members of the Profession no
longer regard Christian principles as relevant to modern man.
Where, then, shall we look for guidance in the realm of morals?
We are sailing into uncharted seas and we need some fixed points
by which to navigate.

Hippocrates falls far short of modern needs. Members of the
public, in any case, are largely mistaken in the popular notion that
all doctors, on qualification, subscribe to the Oath ascribed to him.
Apart from some of the Scottish universities and a few other
institutions, no such undertaking is obtained from those entering
the Profession. Few doctors and fewer medical students have more
than a nodding acquaintance with the Hippocratic Oath; nor have
the pronouncements, and memoranda of medical councils, world
medical organisations or research bodies—valuable as they are—
fared much better at their hands.* Scientific humanism offers
the mirage of a solution, as it pursues its impersonal way. By its
restricted view of man, and its inadequate explanation of his
experience in this universe, it leaves us high and dry.

This book is designed to present the findings of a medical
discussion group. Its members believe that Christian ethics and
the application of Christian principles offer the most reliable and
convincing guidance in the changing responsibilities of this exciting
age. The writers focus attention on two different aspects of
ethical responsibility in Medicine. The first is concerned with
problems arising from the applications of new knowledge and
our increasing power to control life. The second discusses those
attitudes and actions of the Medical Profession which have wider
repercussions for the public and other learned professions.

All the contributors, however, have this in common that they
are interested in Man as a living, reasoning person. They are

*The Declaration of Geneva (International Code of Medical Ethics) 1948;
the Declaration of Helsinki (on Human Experimentation, Code of Ethics of
the World Medical Association) 1964; and the Medical Research Council's
Statement, Responsibility in Investigations on Human Subjects, 1963.

searching for the answers to urgent ethical questions. What is our responsibility as we learn to exercise greater control of certain aspects of human life? What is Man's degree of responsibility for his own conduct? Action based on radical replies to such questions will have far-reaching consequences. It is, therefore, imperative that all concerned—both the advance guard of medical empiricism and the wisest minds of the Legislature—should combine to ensure that the ethical future of the Profession will be established on the surest and best foundation. This, we submit, is 'the Golden Rule' as taught by the One who has remained unrivalled in His concern for His fellow-men.

VINCENT EDMUNDS

C. GORDON SCORER

1967

CONTENTS

		Page
PREFACE		v
I. THE NATURE OF RESPONSIBILITY		1
	Alastair Connell, B.Sc., M.B., Ch.B., M.R.C.P.Ed.	
II. THE ETHICS OF CLINICAL RESEARCH . . .		23
	Douglas MacG. Jackson, M.D., F.R.C.S.	
III. WHY THE PRESERVATION OF LIFE?		43
	Duncan W. Vere, M.D., M.R.C.P.	
IV. THERAPEUTIC PROCEDURES AND THE SANCTITY OF LIFE		75
	John Beattie, M.D., F.R.C.S., F.R.C.O.G.	
V. POPULATION CONTROL		88
	Daniel Andersen, M.B., B.S., F.R.C.S. and Professor Paul W. Brand, C.B.E., M.B., B.S., F.R.C.S.	
VI. THE CONCEPT OF RESPONSIBILITY IN PSYCHIATRIC TREATMENT		100
	F. John Roberts, M.B., B.S., M.R.C.P.Ed., D.P.M.	
VII. ALCOHOLISM AND DRUG ADDICTION . . .		108
	Basil Merriman, M.R.C.S., L.R.C.P.	
VIII. SOCIAL ABERRATIONS—SIN, CRIME OR DISEASE? .		117
	Victor Parsons, D.M., M.R.C.P.	
IX. RESPONSIBILITY IN PREVENTIVE MEDICINE . .		136
	W. George Swann, M.D., B.Sc., D.P.M., D.P.A.	
X. MEETING POINTS OF CHURCH AND MEDICINE . .		148
	The Rev. Hugh Trowell, O.B.E., M.D., F.R.C.P.	
XI. MEDICINE AND THE UNITY OF MAN . . .		169
	André Schlemmer, M.D.	
XII. MAN HIMSELF—THE VITAL FACTOR . . .		181
	Editors	
INDEX		198

CHAPTER I

THE NATURE OF RESPONSIBILITY

ALASTAIR M. CONNELL[1]

" As we get to know more about the complexity of the human mind,
so we try to make our shades of responsibility finer and more complex,
and so I think we get into deeper and deeper muddles.'

BARONESS WOOTTON OF ABINGER,
House of Lords, July, 1962

RESPONSIBILITY

In the flood tide of knowledge unleashed by the first industrial
revolution, engineers and physicists subdued and harnessed nature,
bringing undreamed of prosperity to large areas of the world. On
this wave of unparalleled advance, optimistic philosophers saw the
rapid achievement of man's final destiny, self-sufficient, all powerful,
supreme in nature. All are now beginning to feel the full effects of
the second phase of this advance of knowledge in which the scientific
method has been applied relentlessly to all aspects of the human
situation and has even penetrated the citadel of the mind itself. All
human endeavour and experience has been exposed to its persistent
probing.

The application of chemical and physical principles and methods
has been successful in interpreting some aspects which are fundamental to man's basic existence. Disturbingly, the result has been
that man no longer sees himself as the master of ' things '! ' Things '
have once again become great. Whereas Swinburne in an earlier
age sang ' Glory to the man in the highest,' Aldous Huxley and
George Orwell, the prophets of the present age, see man reduced to
an automaton, twisted and distorted by unfeeling, haunting
external forces. Gone is the old simple account of man's freedom
to choose his own destiny. In its place is the new conception of
the conscious mind as the ' waving sunlit surface of a tropical forest,
beneath which lie the unseen depths of twisted roots and tangled
undergrowth ' (MacNeill Dixon).

In this disturbed confusion the importance and significance of
the individual human personality and its activities have steadily
diminished. Medical opinion has been prominent in relegating man
to his new humbler status. Recently an eminent senior psychiatrist

[1]Alastair M. Connell, B.Sc., M.B., Ch.B., M.R.C.P.(Ed.), Lecturer in Clinical
Science, The Queen's University of Belfast.

has declared that ' There is no place for, and no need of, any factor to explain human behaviour other than the interaction of basic needs with environmental influences, (Maddison, 1959). To those nurtured in a tradition which required the concept of personal responsibility as the keystone of social and legal practice, this appears to be going too far. We instinctively draw back. Yet it is impossible to erase the nagging suspicion that such a conclusion is inevitable and that the overwhelming weight of modern scientific knowledge demands it.

The discomposure is well illustrated by the perplexity of current legal thought. The traditional view of individual responsibility was upheld by the prosecution in the war crime trials after the Second World War. Judge Halevi, summing up in the Eichmann trial, said ' The laws of humanity are binding on individuals. The guilt of Germany does not detract one iota from the personal responsibility of the accused '. On the other hand, the plea of diminished responsibility in a capital charge (first codified in English law in the unlamented Homicide Act of 1957) recognised the changing attitudes. This change has, however, resulted in such difficulties in definition and practice that Wootton (1959) has argued forcibly that it marked the withering away of the whole concept of responsibility in the criminal sense.

In this field of enquiry, as in others, the battle rages, and unhappily partisan attitudes are often struck. Much of what is advanced is opinion and not fact. Fortunately the facts are open to inspection. This chapter, therefore, reviews the nature of the biological data, in various fields, relevant to the discussion. Generalisation is necessary as it is beyond the scope or competence of this chapter to review in detail the extensive literature on the physiology of behaviour. Furthermore, it would be an impertinence to attempt an essay on the doctrines of freewill and determinism. The object is to weigh the nature of the evidence relevant to the discussion of human responsibility, both in the general sense and more particularly in one current point of focus—the court room.

It is important to consider primarily the facts of the situation as it is extraordinary how often sweeping declarations, allegedly scientific, are made with meagre evidence to support them. Maddison, for instance, supports his summary dismissal of human responsibility simply by the claim that ' extensive clinical experience clearly shows that where circumstances appear to offer us several alternative modes of procedure, the path which we in fact take is unswervingly determined by our personality structure '. This is no longer enough in that, as scientists become increasingly aware of the fallibility of simple observation, they demand much more of the doctor than an unsupported appeal to ' clinical experience '.

Facts are the essential matrix of any hypothesis. It was Pavlov who wrote ' Learn the A B C of science before you attempt to scale its peaks. Never try to cover up your knowledge, even by the boldest guesses and hypotheses. No matter how this bubble may delight the eye by its profusion of colours, it is bound to burst and you will be left with nothing but confusion . . . Study, compare, accumulate facts '. Much of the current confusion of thought and practice with regard to responsibility and desert arises out of failure to pay attention to Pavlov's dictum. When facts are stripped of the aura of hypotheses and guesses which enwrap them, they are seen to have a less revolutionary potential than is often assumed.

The biological data relevant to the discussion of human responsibility can be grouped under three headings. These are, firstly, the factors determining and modifying behaviour in biological tissues and animals; secondly, the effect of disease, drugs and trauma in man; and, thirdly, sociological observation and experiment.

ANIMAL EXPERIMENTATION

Studies with isolated tissues

The work of physiologists has given much insight into the nature of the *response* of a tissue or organ to an applied stimulus. Isolated tissues have a characteristic excitability which varies from specimen to specimen and can be altered by environmental factors such as temperature, pH, electrolytes and drugs in a definite and generally predictable way. However, even at these simplest levels, predictability is less than 100 per cent and all experimental physiologists recognise the inherent capriciousness of neuromuscular responses, even when the most elegant and refined techniques are used. Studies, for example, such as the response of the isolated animal gut to nervous or pharmacological stimulation have the frustrating habit of producing unexpected or even paradoxical responses. The older textbooks attribute this, in a nebulous way, to the state of the effector organ at the time of the applied stimulus. Recently the work of Bulbring has shown that these paradoxical responses probably originate in the fundamental instability of the membrane potential of the individual muscle cells of the intestinal wall which not only can be altered by external stimulation but appear to demonstrate a distinct basic rhythm whose control is not yet known. Such basic rhythms are the essential stuff of biology. Variability and unpredictability of biological responses are the essential background to any biological concept of behaviour.

This unpredictability of response is particularly troublesome in studies of the central nervous system. At the spinal level, reflex responses are generally predictable and the factors facilitating or inhibiting the reflex can be closely defined but with ascending order of neuronal and functional complexity, responses become increasingly variable. Another difficulty in the study of the central nervous system is that information has largely to be obtained by deduction from the study of simpler situations experimentally and artificially isolated. As behaviour is the resultant of a large number of complex and interacting neuronal systems its study is attended by formidable difficulties. Even the use of mathematical or physical models can, and probably has, shed only a limited light on these complexities. It is probably for these reasons that many physiologists have abandoned the inductive approach and concentrated on the total response of the animal to applied stimuli.

Studies of behaviour of intact animals

The careful studies of Pavlov and his school have provided a framework for our understanding of behaviour. They showed not only that the behaviour (of animals) could be radically altered in a scientific way but also demonstrated the fundamental mechanism whereby this end could be achieved. By the process of conditioning to appropriate stimuli, complex and permanent behaviour patterns could be established. As Walker noted, Pavlov could be both God and Devil for the dog. Pavlov has also shown how many factors may influence the conditioning process, not least among these being the individual susceptibility of the animals under study. This factor proved so important that in his later work he was obliged to classify dogs according to their constitutional temperament, as different responses to the same experimental situation came from dogs of different character.

The development of this work reveals that the behaviour patterns imposed on animals can be stressed to breaking point. The process of breakdown of behaviour is facilitated by physical deprivation, bodily illness, fatigue, anxiety and other threatening circumstances. In this also there is a broad spectrum of response. In the weak inhibitory type of dog, neurotic patterns can be easily implanted but the breakdown is usually temporary, whereas calm imperturbable animals may need severe interference such as castration before breakdown occurs. In these dogs, however, it is very difficult to eradicate the new behaviour patterns.

These classical studies have been extensively amplified and elaborated, not always, however, with the same scientific impeccability as Pavlov's work. In this field, as in other branches of physiology, increasing specialisation demands finer and finer definitions and isolation of the experimental model from the original area of interest. Thus it is difficult for any single worker or group of workers to have both an informed and comprehensive view of the whole field of study. Therefore fundamental biological studies are in danger of an ever decreasing relevance to the complex interactions of the whole man. The following study is one of many hundreds but it illustrates this criticism. Rats were kept with Elizabethan type collars from birth until just before parturition and so were prevented from exercising normal cleaning movements. Following parturition these rats did not clean and retrieve their young normally and continued placental eating to include the ingestion of the offspring themselves (Birch, 1961). Such a study is a useful addition to our knowledge of the physiology of the rat but the author's claim that it supports the hypothesis that sensory deprivation in infancy results in deviant or undesirable behaviour in the adult human does seem over enthusiastic. This thesis may be true but it cannot be established by experiments of this kind.

Certain principles must be recognised in interpreting these experimental findings. The description of an animal's emotional response are necessarily *interpretations* of its actions on the assumption that the animal experiences the same emotion as would be expected of a normal human being in similar circumstances. This is difficult to establish. Secondly, the final result is usually a statistical one and in most studies wide individual variations in response of different animals occur. Thirdly, there is the more serious problem of differences in animal and human behavioural physiology. If physiological information about the function of an organ obtained from an animal is to be applied to man only with caution, even greater caution is required in transferring information about behaviour from the animal to man. Much human behavioural organisation is not present in any animal.

Behavioural physiology, however, appears to indicate that

mechanisms exist whereby behaviour patterns can be imposed at will, certainly in animals. While these mechanisms clearly exist in the human, it is naive to suppose that one particular mechanism such as the conditioned reflex is the only mechanism of behaviour any more than that the isolated spinal reflex is the only mechanism of locomotion. In order that delicate and complex movements of the limbs may be performed the spinal reflex requires to be modified by other areas of the central nervous system. In the same way, if normal integrated human behaviour is to be achieved the basic patterns must be modified and controlled by other and higher mechanisms. Lastly, these experiments deal with the *responsiveness* of the tissue or the whole organism to an applied or imposed stimulus. They show that responsiveness can be heightened or diminished by appropriate stresses but are equally explicit in indicating that it varies widely, depending on the basic characteristics of the preparation studied. Insofar as they indicate that responsiveness can be altered by forces beyond the control of the individual they are relevant in a discussion of responsibility.

HUMAN STUDIES

Modern society abounds in evidence providing many examples which indicate that man can be conditioned; a fact which Governments, religious bodies and pressure groups the world over have not been slow to recognise (Sargant, 1957). Conditioning techniques have been used to transform the attitudes of whole nations, but the human spectrum of response is wider than the animal. It is also less easy to predict with accuracy the individual reaction to any stress, stimulus or situation. Thus, under the stress of the same military action one soldier may conduct himself with such courage that he is decorated for valour, while another of similar background, with the same training, and under apparently identical stress, will fail to the extent that he faces court martial for cowardice in the face of the enemy.

It is the demonstration that a human being can apparently act in a way opposed to environmental pressures which introduces the concept of responsibility. This has a much wider significance than responsiveness. The first meaning of responsibility in the concise Oxford Dictionary is ' liability to be called to account, including liability to punishment ' and the second meaning is ' capable of rational conduct '. Human beings expect and demand that their fellows be not merely creatures of circumstance, and the structure of society is modelled on the principle that a human being should not follow blindly his instinctive biological drives nor yet be a mere automaton, convenient as that might be for authority. Is this an outmoded and possibly restricting concept? To attempt to answer this we must expand our enquiry beyond the field of animal physiology with its limited relevance to human responsibility to the only proper object of study—man himself.

While undoubtedly the most direct evidence about human responsiveness and responsibility must come from studies of man himself, behind this discussion lies the assumption that it is possible for man to be objective about himself. This assumption is frequently made. For example, psychoanalysis subscribes to the faith principle that the causal relationships prevailing in the sciences of matter also govern the activity of mind. Trueblood (1962) has noted that this assumption was challenged by Pascal ('Man cannot hope to comprehend his own nature by means of the sort of knowledge whereby he apprehends the external world'). However, in recent times certain objective parameters of a chemical and physical nature, which may relate to responsibility, have been used and it is important to be familiar with this evidence.

GENETIC STUDIES

The expansion of genetic studies has indicated that not only are physical characteristics inherited but certain mental characteristics as well. The subject has been reviewed by Kallman (1961). It is now established that certain forms of mental deficiency are genetically determined and, for example, it is known that, in Down's syndrome, patients with their well known abnormalities of intelligence and behaviour have an abnormal chromosomal pattern with non-dysjunction of chromosome 21 (Lejeune et al., 1959). Other diseases are known to be determined by the abnormality of a single enzyme, itself the result of a single gene defect. Thus, phenyl-ketonuria is a hereditary disorder due to an autosomal recessive gene; the affected individual having two such genes. They have typically fair hair and blue eyes and, unless treated at an early age, are stunted in both physical and mental growth. Although rare, it is of interest in that the mental retardation is the result of a genetically determined single biochemical abnormality. These patients are unable to convert phenylalanine to tyrosine and, as a result, phenylpyruvic acid accumulates in the body. If treatment is not instituted the accumulated phenylpyruvate interferes with normal neuronal and mental development. Another familial biochemical abnormality is Hartnup disease, so named after the Hartnup family in whom the disease was originally described. The children described in this pellagra-like syndrome were mentally and socially retarded (Baron *et al.*, 1956) and it has been postulated that the basic abnormality in this condition is a genetically determined failure of absorption of tryptophan (Milne *et al.*, 1960). There is a small number of such conditions in which a mental abnormality appears to be genetically determined. Although the number of persons who have a known genetically determined mental abnormality is small in proportion to the population at risk it seems likely that further study will reveal a more widespread incidence.

There is evidence, too, that in general, intelligent persons have intelligent offspring. Furthermore, families of schizophrenics show a high proportion of members with abnormal personalities— ' formes frustes ' of the disease. Another important study shows that concordance in homosexuality occurred in 37 of 40 pairs of identical twins. While the available evidence is limited, it does indicate that in man intellect and social behaviour can be determined by genetic inheritance.

CLINICAL STUDIES

Every physician can recall examples of alteration of behaviour associated with disease or a disturbance of normal physiology. The influence of abnormality of the endocrine and central nervous systems on behaviour is well known but, in addition, disturbance of organs less commonly associated with behaviour can have profound effects. These effects may be mediated either via the endocrine or central nervous system or may be due to pain, toxaemia or biochemical abnormality. The following case is illustrative. A married man of 42 was admitted to hospital for control of chronic ulcerative colitis. He had a low intermittent pyrexia and troublesome bloody diarrhoea. He was extremely irritable and even abusive. His behaviour became so objectionable that the nurses in the ward refused to attend to him singly. His physical condition deteriorated and he had a sub-total colectomy and ileostomy. Following recovery from surgery it was noted that his personality had altered to the extent that he became one of the most co-operative patients in the ward, leaving with the best wishes of the staff. The effects of disease on the mind have been reviewed by Edmunds (1963) who indicates that behaviour may be profoundly affected by physical changes over which frequently the individual has no control. Clinical usage has shown that behaviour and mood can be modified at will by the use of modern chemotherapeutic agents such as amine oxidase inhibitors or the phenothiazine group of drugs, although reviews (Weatherall, 1962) of the few properly controlled studies of these preparations suggest that their place in therapy is more limited than originally hoped.

The effects of illness, drugs, brain injury or neurosurgery leave no reasonable doubt that behaviour can be profoundly altered by physical agencies beyond the control of the individual and that frequently the changes so produced result in deviant or anti-social conduct. However, considering human behaviour as a whole, it has to be admitted that deviant behaviour often occurs in persons and at times where no clear aetiological factors are apparent. It can be legitimately, if somewhat optimistically argued, that with increasing knowledge, further physical or mental aetiological factors in behaviour will become apparent. Specialists such as Freudian analysts would hold that by invoking their art the proportion of diagnostic successes is increased. From the outside it appears that the mutual recriminations, the semantic disputes, the divergences of thought and practice indicate a lack of confidence in any single approach among the initiated.

DELINQUENCY

Delinquency can be described as a disease only to the extent that the delinquent is out of step with, or deviates from, the norms of behaviour of his society. In so doing, however, we are essentially substituting a new nomenclature for older and more colourful descriptions, which still have widespread acceptance. As Canon Morley has noted: ' The seven deadly sins of the mediaeval Church —Pride, Envy, Anger, Avarice, Sloth, Gluttony and Lust have all been re-named. Now we have turned Pride into Self Fulfilment, Envy into Insecurity, Anger into Stress, Avarice into the Pursuit of Incentives, Sloth into Constitutional Inertia, Gluttony into Defective Metabolism, and Lust into Emotional Tension.'

It may run contrary to the cherished beliefs of many to view delinquency as a disease. Notwithstanding, the facts remain that delinquency as such may be associated with abnormalities of brain function. Hill (1954) studying the electro-encephalogram of normals and delinquents has shown that 84 per cent of young delinquents, 80 per cent of aggressive psychopaths in prison and 75 per cent of motiveless murderers have an abnormal EEG. Hill also showed that 10 per cent of the adult population have variant records which are normal for children and adolescents. These records were found in persons who demonstrated marks of aggressiveness or impulsiveness, and it has been suggested that this indicates a failure of maturing, resulting in a lack of emotional control. These interesting results indicate a statistical association between altered cerebral electrical activity and delinquency, although at present it is not possible to show the nature of the association. It could be that the abnormal behaviour has its origin in the altered cerebral activity. It is, however, equally possible that the abnormal EEG is a reflection of this. These studies illustrate one of the great problems in this field—that of causation.

Human studies, especially those into the effects of injury or disease in the central nervous system, and into genetic endowment, seem to indicate that the delinquent or deviant may be subjected to forces more difficult to control than the normal. These studies, however, deal only with the diseased fringe of the population, and interpolation in the community as a whole is not warranted by present evidence. They show the interaction of physical and mental processes in social health and emphasise the holistic nature of man.

SOCIOLOGICAL STUDIES

The contribution of sociologists to this discussion has been twofold. In the first place they have continued and amplified the work of physiologists and psychiatrists to show that, in the general social setting, early influences profoundly affect later behaviour. At the same time they have established that suitable measures help a proportion of deviant individuals. Properly treated, some persons can be assisted back into the normal bounds of conduct.

The Area of Study of Sociology

There is very little agreement about the exact role of the various factors which make up childhood experience. In review of 21 major studies in this field, Wootton (1959) has exposed the extent of the area of disagreement. After considering in detail 12 criminological hypotheses, including family size, the presence of other criminals in the family, social status, the effect of poverty, the effect of broken homes, poor health and the like, she concludes: ' . . . this collection of studies, although chosen for its comparative methodological merit, produced only the most meagre and dubiously supported generalisations '. Nor can we be surprised. The poor reward of many painstaking sociological studies results from formidable and basic imperfections in the method of scientific sociology. In the first place, the raw data with which the sociologist deals often is not susceptible to scientific treatment. Factors such as love and affection, neglect and cruelty, cannot be measured and can only be assessed very indirectly. Secondly, it is seldom possible to produce an experimental model to test the hypotheses which are advanced.

As the material studied is man in his close personal relationships, it is not possible to impose strict scientific control. The alternative is to study special groups such as institutionalised children, but in so doing a major element of bias is introduced into the study. For example, a number of studies indicate that there is a higher incidence of delinquent children from broken homes than from normal homes. Of necessity, the children studied are usually restricted to those attending local Council Child Guidance Clinics. These are obviously highly selected groups as delinquent children living in a stable home would tend to be dealt with at home and not seen at the clinic. The most serious difficulty, however, in the way of the sociologist is to eliminate personal bias on the part of the observer. Practically all his experimental situations have a high emotional content and he cannot avoid becoming emotionally involved. The intrusion of the beliefs and attitudes of the observer can be minimised only by double blind control of the highest order. Even this is not foolproof.

In the nature of the case, therefore, it is not surprising that in spite of meticulous precautions many studies are less than scientific and other work employing careful scientific methods is less than convincing when applied generally because of the necessarily selected nature of the data. It is probably for these reasons that attempts to predict delinquency have had only limited success.

Prediction and Treatment of Delinquency

One of the better known prediction tables of delinquency is that of Glueck and Glueck (1950) which was constructed from the experience of the later careers of 510 reformatory boys. Evaluations of these prediction tables generally agree that while a high accuracy can be obtained in assessing which boys are unlikely to become delinquent, there is a large error in predicting delinquency. As

the majority of children do not become delinquent, the value of
these predictions is very limited. Even when it is possible to make
an assessment of children likely to become delinquent it is no easy
matter to avert criminality. One of the most ambitious studies
was the Cambridge-Sommerville project reported by McCord
and McCord (1960) which endeavoured to recover potentially
delinquent children by intensive supervision and counselling from
an early age. While the general result was disappointing in that
there was no significant difference in the eventual behaviour of
the experimental group who received counselling, and the control
group who did not, this failure was attributed to difficulties involved
in close counselling of children in difficult social circumstances
over a period of many years, including the period of the Second
World War. However, in 12 children the counselling was believed
to be adequate and in these the results were held to be encouraging.

The existence of our courts, reformatories and schools of all
kinds indicates the common belief that human nature can be
changed and that delinquents with suitable treatment can be brought
within the scale of normal behaviour. Indeed, the dynamic belief
that inspired the Welfare State was that human relations can be
bettered by improved social welfare. Even within the deterministic
framework of their science, sociologists tacitly agree that human
nature can be changed. Even that most deterministic of social and
political philosophies, dialectical materialism of Marx and Engels,
insists that men *can* alter their environment and attitudes by the
determined effort demanded by the call: ' Workers of the world
unite '.

In this way sociologists are at one with the great religions of the
world. All religions emphatically declare that human nature can be
changed and the records of every parish of the Christian Church
attest that this is so. Such evidence often tends to be dismissed as
biassed and not adequately controlled. However, current sociological studies suffer from the same limitations and even if the
religious evidence is unscientific it is impressively strengthened by
the volume of material available for study. It is to our great loss
that it is so little examined.

We have examined the nature of the evidence available for the
discussion of human responsibility from the fields of animal
experiment, clinical experience and sociological study. These three
lines of enquiry agree that responses and behaviour can be changed
experimentally by appropriate stimuli, by adequate therapeutics or

by social change. They agree also that to a large extent normal human behaviour can be, and probably is, moulded and modified by factors in the external environment of the individual. Outstanding in all these studies is the striking variation of the response of individuals, so that the results are statistical in the sense that they express a probability rather than a certainty, and for this reason predictability of behaviour and prognosis is often poor. Owing to the inherent capriciousness of biological material at the cellular level this will probably always be so, even with advances in knowledge and techniques. As Stilpo said, ' Those who speak of men in general speak of nobody '.

RESPONSIBILITY

So far we have dealt with biological responsiveness or the sum of responses of the organism. Responsibility depends in measure on responsiveness, but is, however, something more than the sum of responses. It introduces an intangible element not easily assessed by scientific investigation. It is not possible to define responsibility in absolute terms. Responsibility implies a norm or standard and this introduces us to formidable problems.

The Norm

Social anthropology has uncovered a bewildering variety of customs and behaviour patterns which may be completely contradictory in different places. For instance, natives of Dobie (Melanesia) value highly treacherous conduct, particularly against neighbours and friends and their actions are unmitigated by any ideas of kindness or mercy. In history, communities have exposed children to death or human sacrifice without reproach and even with praise. Even within local areas important differences can be recognised. It is becoming doubtful if there is any value in interpreting recurrent Western social problems on the basis of behaviour of primitive people. To quote John Pringle, ' As I see it, the onus is on the anthropologists to prove that the social and sexual customs of primitive people have any more relevance to the problems of, say, a straphanger in a Piccadilly tube than the situation in Mars. The world is a large place and men are various '. The outstanding lesson of anthropology is that different men behave in different ways and different communities respect entirely different standards. Responsibility can only be considered in terms of the local community and any discussion of responsibility in a universal sense is necessarily abortive unless it has as a background some absolute standard of behaviour.

It is here, in the attempt to define the normal, that difficulties arise. Normal ranges in medicine are often not only difficult to assess (witness the controversy about the nature of hypertension), but frequently surprisingly poorly worked out. The definition of normality in relation to mental health is more illusive. The boundaries between normal, neurotic and psychotic are becoming increasingly blurred and some authors feel that the fences are down altogether (Maddison, 1959). One group of authors is forced back to defining their patients as people who are complaining or are complained of. Wootton (1959) has listed 25 different and some-times contradictory definitions of mental health noted in recent medical literature. Medical opinion is confused and cannot help in the matter of standards.

Group Standards

In spite of this, every community has an accepted minimum code of behaviour usually embodied in the common law of the community which reflects to a greater or lesser degree the assessment by the community of the social capabilities of members within it. While individuals may hold personal convictions on specific matters which differ from the majority view, the community expects, and in fact demands, that the individual can and should conform to the group law and that he is liable to be called to account if he falls short.

This is the critical point in the discussion. Even although it is recognised that human behaviour is affected by external stresses, individuals are expected to conform to the accepted standards even when the ideals, and sometimes the laws, demand behaviour of a type which is different and even opposite to that which would result from raw biological responsiveness. When the Apostle Paul wrote—' The Gentiles—which show the work of the law written in their hearts, their conscience also bearing witness and their thoughts the meanwhile accusing or else excusing one another ' (Rom. ii. 14, 15) this is what he meant. The great religions of the world go a step further and maintain that a universal standard exists towards which all men must aim and in respect of which all men are liable to be called to account, irrespective of the local situation. In the last analysis the lesser standards have no meaning unless a universal standard exists. Without it there is no final answer to the questions ' Why should I? ' or ' Why shouldn't I? '.

THE LEGAL APPLICATION

Turning now to the practical application of this discussion at the point where the debate is most sharp, and considering the specific case of a person who offends against the standards of its society, we have to ask if he is to be considered blameworthy and punished for his act, or if he is to be considered a sick member caught up by forces beyond his control and so excused in part or in whole. Secondly, if we admit that a man's actions may be determined by factors beyond his control, we must decide if it is possible to assess justly the degree of diminution of responsibility.

It is clear that neither criminality, nor any particular form of criminality or deviant behaviour, is in any sense a disease entity. The concept of idiopathic criminality like that of idiopathic epilepsy is gradually being whittled away. The same forms of delinquency are practised by persons whether or not suffering from a recognisable physical or mental condition. It seems a reasonable assumption, however, that if a man is suffering from a defect of mind or body which normally would result in unrestrained behaviour and, if in the course of his illness he commits an offence, he is not fully able to control his actions. On the other hand, should a man who commits an offence while suffering from a condition labelled (possibly loosely) ' manic depressive psychosis ' be held less responsible than another who commits a similar offence while suffering from the nagging pain and irritation of a gastric ulcer (labelled accurately)? As there are no physical, chemical, physiological or pharmacological parameters that can be applied at present to these questions, the answers given can only be expressions of opinion rather than fact. In such circumstances there is always a danger of a circular argument.

The problem of deciding whether a man is sick or wicked is well illustrated in relation to the group of persistent and incorrigible offenders who have been labelled psychopaths. The psychopath has been defined by the Royal Medical Psychological Association as a person whose

' daily behaviour shows a want of social responsibility and of consideration for others, of prudence and foresight and of ability to act in their own best interests. Their persistent anti-social mode of conduct may include inefficiency and lack of interest in any form of occupation, pathological lying, swindling and slandering; alcoholism and drug addiction; sexual offences and violent actions with little motivation and entire absence of self-restraint which may go as far as homicide. Punishment or the threat of punishment influences the behaviour only momentarily and its more lasting effect is to intensify their vindictiveness and anti-social attitude '.

As Wootton dryly comments on this definition, ' Psychopaths are extremely selfish persons and no one knows what makes them so.' However, if we call psychopathy a disease, we run the danger of the error into which doctors sometimes fall whereby mental abnormality is inferred from anti-social behaviour, while the same anti-social behaviour is explained on the basis of mental abnormality.

Apart from the logical difficulties, there are other dangers inherent in defining such social misdemeanours as a disease. The most obvious is that it encourages people not to be ashamed of their weaknesses and deficiencies. Speaking in the House of Lords on the subject of delinquent children, Wootton (1962) drew attention to this danger and noted that from her experience in juvenile courts children very quickly come to think of themselves as ' poor little things suffering from some form of disability, and the side effect of attendance at a clinic or of going to the doctor for apparently mental failings are not entirely to be discounted.' A further danger is that it becomes possible to extend the definition of psychopath almost indefinitely to cover any action of which virtuous people disapprove and so it becomes increasingly difficult to make any moral judgments on social behaviour.

Apart from the problem of the psychopath, it is clear that situations may arise which force a man into anti-social behaviour as a result of pressures greater than himself. The community has a responsibility to itself to bring such a man to judgment. It is right and proper that it should do so in order to express its disapproval of an action threatening its own internal security. In this sense he must be held responsible, but at the same time an enlightened community will attempt to assess the gravity of the misdemeanour against a background of the extraneous factors in the situation at the time of the offence. This is not an assessment of responsibility. It is an assessment of blameworthiness. Blameworthiness or culpability, meaning liability to punishment or correction is less ambiguous in this legal context than responsibility which has a primary meaning of ' liability to be called to account '.

English legal opinion has always upheld the doctrine of ' *mens rea* ' whereby for a man to be convicted of a guilty act, he must also be shown to have had guilty intent. In fact, there are no unequivocal medical data which permit clear definition of mental health or illness. Frequently, there are no scientific data which assist in assessing blameworthiness in an individual case. Where scientific medicine cannot define guilt or innocence of mind, it is doubtful if medical opinion has any greater weight than lay opinion in assessing the guilt of the accused.

Yet medicine has extended its prestige and influence from matters which traditionally have been properly its right into the sphere of morals. Wootton comments,

' In part, the prevailing emphasis upon the medical element in anti-social behaviour must be seen as an expression of the unique prestige enjoyed today by the medical profession. This materialistic age, unable to look with confidence beyond the grave and believing the doctor to hold the keys of life and death, has invested him with the respect and awe once associated with the priesthood. The doctor, like father, knows best '.

For this reason one of the greatest virtues of English law is that guilt is assessed on general grounds by 12 representative and ordinary citizens rather than by a panel of experts who might tend towards doctrinaire judgments.

While it would be a revolutionary move, it would greatly simplify the process of law, if a man were held to be guilty of an action against the community if it could be proved to satisfaction only that he had in fact committed the act. The state of his mind at the time of the offence would then be irrelevant to the verdict but, of course, would become of supreme importance in assessing the sentence. The criminal law could still operate without the concept of responsibility and would still be effective in restraining evil and protecting society.

In the Liège thalidomide trial, it would seem that the jury brought in a verdict of ' Not Guilty ', not because they considered that the accused had not in fact taken the life of the child, but because they realised that if a verdict of ' Guilty ' was given there was no alternative in law to the death sentence. In this case, it appears that they felt that the circumstances of the alleged offence did not justify such a severe penalty. If this were so, as seems likely, the law was brought into disrepute in respect of its verdict on the facts of this alleged crime. However, if the system of differentiating between responsibility and culpability were accepted, such an anomaly at law would be avoided.

Subsequent to guilt having been determined, the doctor with his special interest and knowledge of the mechanisms affecting and controlling behaviour, would have a part to play in assessing blameworthiness. In a number of cases his experience would be critical, in others he would have no more to offer than the intelligent layman. At a further stage, when the degree of culpability has been

c

determined, medical evidence would play a part in determining the nature of the sentence. In a number of cases, unhappily very few, the doctor has the means to effect the necessary changes in behaviour which can restore the offender to a useful place in society. In such cases, this seems the only proper course for the community to take. In the majority of cases, however, with medical knowledge in its present state, no definite evidence will be submitted which would in any way reduce the culpability of the accused or offer any hope of altering his behaviour. For this majority, other measures must be taken which help to condition the offender against further misdemeanours and at the same time protect society from his activities, even if the conditioning stimuli necessary are disagreeable.

With further knowledge our appreciation of the causes of crime and deviant behaviour may be finer and more sensitive and our ability to help the mentally and spiritually sick members of society greater. But we live in the present and must act within the limitations of present knowledge. Therefore in relation to the law, the doctor has to admit the serious limitations of his knowledge. However, in the few cases where his specialist understanding is critical he can contribute to equitable administration of the law by urging the fitting of the punishment not only to the crime but also the individual.

CONCLUSION

There can be no reasonable doubt that the application of the scientific method to the study of behaviour has been heuristically valuable. Not only has it given insight into hitherto undreamt of aspects of man's mind and personality—exposing and charting the dark undercurrents of emotion and tension—but it has also helped in a small measure in our ordering of and control of society. Providing the nature and limitations of scientific knowledge are recognised, such benefits can be expected to multiply. We transgress these limits if, as doctors and scientists, our pride makes us exceed our brief.

There are vast tracts of human experience which the scientific method cannot explore and distant horizons of appreciation and understanding which it is not equipped to approach because no parameters of measurement exist in these areas. The scientific method condescends to recognise no world save that which can be perceived, analysed and interpreted by sensory experience. If phenomena cannot be reduced to material terms, science cannot deal with them. ' There is no scale in physics for determining the value of a poem, or the aspiration of a saint. No instruments for the measurement of Milton's imagination or Rembrandt's soul ' (McNeill Dixon). At present human responsibility defies quanti- tation. Like a sense of decency, appreciation of art, even tears and laughter, human responsibility cannot be defined solely in physico-chemical terms. Thus if aspects of behaviour exist which cannot be reduced to physical terms, science can know nothing of them; we must search elsewhere for understanding.

It should not be thought surprising that the application of the scientific method of the study of behaviour should provide an answer in materialistic terms. From the outset, such an explanation is inevitable. A physical enquiry can only end in a physical explanation. As Merskey and Clarke (1962) have noted, scientific determinism is the basis for the practice of medicine. Now that the scientific method has been applied to the study of behaviour, the practice of psychological medicine must become increasingly based on determinism.

If scientific determinism is pushed to its logical conclusion, and made the basis for all behaviour, many of our accepted norms of behaviour would be destroyed. If all our activities and choices are the result of predetermined stimuli, it follows that the doctrine of freewill as a useful, necessary, or even desirable explanation of human behaviour must be rejected. The corollary is that it is as meaningless to blame a man for his failures as it is to praise him for his successes. Individual responsibility in a moral, social or criminal sense does not exist and absolute values of morality and the theological view of man are denied. While most persons would draw back instinctively and feel that this is too much, a minority would accept that such a price must be paid for scientific progress.

However, the determinist's position is not only destructive but in the end is self-destructive. We are unable to step outside of ourselves and observe dispassionately the operation of our own minds. Both the instrument studied and the instruments of study are one and the same. Thus, in the end, thought and reason them- selves become empty and sterile and only the results of rigid determinism. ' In proportion, as you lower the status of the mind, the greater, one should conclude, should be your hesitation in accepting its deliverances ' (MacNeill Dixon, 1937). Freudians and Pavlovians have used their arguments in a devastating way against almost anything and anybody. The victims of the assaults, however, would seem to be justified in replying in kind to their would-be mentors that their own conclusions ex-hypothesi, must be the result not of independent and fair judgment but the blind interaction of senseless and unfeeling mechanisms. To quote again MacNeill Dixon, ' We may note that some philosophers, having done their best to saw off the branch upon which they are sitting, continue with supreme confidence to sit upon it '.

The position with respect to psychotherapy has been well put by Walters (1966): ' The principle of psychic determinism applied to the process of psychotherapy leads to a logical impasse. If neurosis is produced by elements of prior experience over which the individual can bring no control, psychotherapeutic intervention is destined to be futile. Moreover, the therapist would have to recognise himself, also, as the puppet of forces beyond his own knowledge and control, with no discretionary latitude either in the choice or in the practice of his vocation. Just as the acceptance of psychic determinism as being true pre-supposes freedom to decide between true and false, as Tillich has pointed out, so the offer of assistance by the therapist pre-supposes his freedom to intervene in the life and thought of another person at a crucial point *of his choosing* '.

Finally, we may note that responsibility is essentially an individual matter. Science necessarily is best equipped to study the group or statistical norms. The variety and profusion of individual variables makes scientific handling of individual data extraordinarily difficult. Science always tends to group, to combine, to classify. Individual responsibility may often appear to defy the statistical laws of biological responsiveness, to the frustration of biologists, sociologists, politicians and the traders in mass media.

It is to the credit of Christians that they have at all times upheld the importance of the individual and stressed the significance of individual choices. ' If any man hear My voice ' seems to reduce the sphere of spiritual enlightenment to the unit. At the same time the individual activity takes place against the background of the ' determinate counsel and foreknowledge of God.'. Within this ordered administration, individual choice remains significant and individual responsibility is upheld. It is only by including such supra-scientific sources that the ultimate issues of human responsibility can be faced.

The concept of freewill, like that of God, is implicit in the teaching of the Bible. From the beginning, in the account of the temptation of Adam and Eve, through the call to the Hebrew patriarchs, the vicissitudes of the Jewish nation, the harangues of the prophets, to the final supreme test in Gethsemane, men are called on to 'choose' in whatever environment of conflicting influences they find themselves.

While many examples of tragic conformity to environmental pressures are cited, the Bible upholds and endorses the example of men of faith who persisted in the path of duty in the face of adversity. For example, Moses is said to have chosen ' rather to suffer adversity . . . than to enjoy pleasures . . .' (Heb. xi. 25). Consistently, the course of responsible action is maintained against the mere hedonism of biological responsiveness.

The greatest example is Christ himself—' Who, when He was abused, did not retort with abuse, when He suffered, He uttered no threats ' (I Pet. ii. 23 N.E.B.). Here is the supreme example of steadfast devotion to responsible action, the sign that human nature has the capacity to act in a way other than that dictated by expediency or self interest, and not merely passively to react to environmental influences.

REFERENCES

BARON, D. N., DENT, C. E., HARRIS, H., HART, E. W. & JEPSON, J. B. (1956). *Lancet*, **2**, 421.

BIRCH, H. C. (1961). *Amer. J. Orthopsychiat.* **31**, 267.

EDMUNDS, V. (1963). In the Service of Medicine. 27. Oct.

GLUECK, S. & GLUECK, E. (1950). *Unravelling Juvenile Delinquency.* Cambridge; Commonwealth Fund.

HILL, J. D. N. (1954). *Brit. Med. J.* **1**, 980.

KALLMANN, F. J. (1961). *Am. J. Orthopsychiat.* **31**, 445.

LEJEUNE, J., GAUTIER, M. & TURPIN, R. (1959). *C. R. Acad. Sci.* **248**, 602.

McCORD, W., McCORD, J. & ZOLA, I. (1959). *Origins of Crime.* New York: Columbia University Press.

MACNEILL DIXON, W. (1937). *Gifford Lectures.* London: Arnold.

MADDISON, D. (1959). *Lancet*, **2**, 103.

MERSKEY, H. & CLARKE, P. R. F. (1962). *Lancet*, **2**, 291.

MILNE, M. D., CRAWFORD, M. A., GIRAO, G. B. & LOUGHBRIDGE, L. W. (1960). Quart. J. Med. **29**, 407.

SARGANT, W. (1957). *Battle for the Mind.* London: Heinemann.

TRUEBLOOD, D. E. (1962). *Contemporary Psychiatry and the Concept of Responsibility in Psychiatry and Responsibility.* New York: Van Nostrand.

WALTERS, O. (1966). In press.

WEATHERALL, M. (1962). *Br. med. J.* **1**, 1219.

WOOTTON, B. (1959). *Social Science and Social Pathology.* London.

WOOTTON, B. (1962). *Hansard*, **241**, 1282.

CHAPTER II

THE ETHICS OF CLINICAL RESEARCH
DOUGLAS McG. JACKSON[1]

In 1930 Sir Thomas Lewis used the term *curative medicine* to describe that activity which ministered to the immediate needs of sick individuals, and *progressive medicine* to signify that activity of which the immediate purpose was to advance knowledge. In the past, progress in Medicine followed two main lines, the method of observation which has separated and defined individual diseases, and the experimental method exemplified in the physiological field by Harvey and Claude Bernard, and in the bacteriological field by Pasteur and Koch. This science which deals primarily with patients, Lewis wrote, ' might be called " experimental medicine " if this term had not come to convey too strongly the idea of experiment on animals. It would be called clinical pathology if the latter were not now fenced around by test-tube and needle. It may be termed clinical science ' (Lewis, 1946). Today *clinical research* is perhaps the commonest all-embracing term for this group of activities.

Curative medicine and clinical research are so closely related in the best practice of the art of healing that it is in some ways artificial to separate them. Increasingly, senior members on the staff of most hospitals are carrying on clinical research alongside their medical practice and, far from resenting this, the general public recognise with satisfaction that this is a sign of a keen, up-to-date medical centre. No longer are funds for research limited to special units; every consultant in our National Health Service may apply for a research grant and have his project given serious consideration by an informed committee. However, because these two aspects of medicine have different aims and disciplines and are sometimes found in conflict with each other, it is worth defining their scope and limitations.

Clinical medicine involves investigation of disease in a sick person with the primary aim of helping him to overcome or endure it; the investigation is for the purpose of diagnosis so that effective treatment may be given. Medicine is not an exact science, and

[1]Douglas McG. Jackson, M.D., F.R.C.S., Surgeon, the Birmingham Accident Hospital. Mr. Jackson is a part-time member of the scientific staff of the Medical Research Council's Burns Unit. The opinions expressed here should not be regarded as necessarily approved by the Council or his colleagues.

even at its best, little is established beyond all doubt. Medical practice is seldom a matter of 'diagnosis, treatment, cure' as a first glance at our text-books would suggest. There are many obscure conditions in which the truth of the dictum that 'every therapeutic procedure is a fresh experiment' can be amply illustrated; every day doctors use the results of their treatment to confirm or contradict their provisional diagnosis, but these experiments are motivated by regard for the patient's benefit; the testing of a hypothesis is a subordinate issue.

On the other hand, clinical research is the application of observation and the experimental method to the study of disease in sick people with the primary aim of acquiring new knowledge about disease and its treatment. There are moral limits to this search but they are discussed later. The skill in this type of work is the ability to perceive what is most worthy of investigation and to review the results in such a way as to obtain a significant result, a true addition to knowledge. The conclusions derived from reviewing past work are often inconclusive, and if data collected by observation are to be of any practical value they may need to be formed into a hypothesis which can be tested by experiment. In this context 'experiment' implies deliberately changing the environment or treatment of a patient, with only limited and uncertain foreknowledge of the results, to observe the outcome of the change. In this way the hypothesis can be confirmed or disproved, and a new fact established. Experiment is a sharper research tool than observation, and it has been compared to 'cross-examining nature rather than merely overhearing her' (Gregg, 1941).

Motive in clinical research is important, and some may disagree with the definition that the primary aim of clinical research is to acquire new knowledge about disease and man's response to it. They might wish to include the phrase 'with a view to healing future patients' because they feel that sick people should not be subjected to investigation without an adequate humane reason to justify it. But the disagreement here is more apparent than real and is resolved by distinguishing between primary and secondary purposes.

Most people deprecate the use of human beings (and perhaps animals also) for the purpose of acquiring knowledge in the abstract. The application or secondary purpose of clinical research is the progress of Medicine for the benefit of mankind, but the immediate aim or primary purpose of an individual experiment is the acquisition of a particular piece of knowledge. Fact-finding or the discovery of truth is the foundation of all medical and scientific progress. To expect progress without the necessary discipline of thought and method is wishful thinking. It is a danger peculiar to clinical research that it may become an end in itself. If it does, the good of the individual will no longer predominate. On the other hand, the idea that clinical research should always have a direct application to preventive and therapeutic needs is too restrictive; the usefulness of new facts about disease and the body is not always anticipated, or even immediately apparent. This was illustrated by Edison when he was asked what possible value one of his abstract inventions could have; ' What is the value of a newborn baby?' was his apt retort.

In some centres of experimental medicine the investigator and the physician are different persons—the first primarily interested in his scientific problem, the second in the welfare of the patient. In other centres the two activities are combined in the same person; and intermediate combinations are also found. Whatever the staff pattern, conflict will at times arise, not between personalities— this should be avoidable with appreciation of each other's difficulties —but between care for the experiment and care for the patient. This is the basic moral problem in clinical research. It is a conflict of loyalties in which the doctor-patient relationship of confidence and trust is challenged by a new loyalty, the loyalty of the investigator to his problem. The question arises, ' Will the patient's welfare remain the predominant concern of the doctor? ' and ' Will investigations and treatment always be carried out for the patient's good; or may his comfort and safety be sacrificed to increasing medical knowledge for the possible benefit of mankind? ' Even ' observation,' the simplest tool of clinical research, may involve the patient in anxiety and discomfort; and if the term is used to include diagnostic procedures such as endoscopy, biopsy and catheterisation there may be risk of injury or even death. Some have even spoken of the patient's need of the physician-friend to protect him from the physician-investigator.

THE IMPORTANCE OF CLINICAL RESEARCH

Research, in the sense of acquiring new knowledge which will enable us to treat tomorrow's patients better than today's, is a moral responsibility of the medical profession. Without research there can be no progress, and as McCance points out, ' without it

knowledge could fall away again as it did in the Middle Ages '
(McCance, 1957). Knowledge requires continual critical assessment: a recent Dean of Harvard Medical School is reported to have
said that in 10 years' time a half of what we now believe will have
been shown to be wrong; but, alas, we do not know which half.
Not all doctors are called to carry out experimental medicine
themselves; some choose to give themselves entirely to clinical
medicine, some to teaching, some to carry contemporary knowledge
and skills to underdeveloped countries, but all doctors undertaking
clinical research 'have a right to expect the fullest co-operation
from their medical colleagues, from nurses and other assistants,
from hospital managements, from patients and relatives, and from
the community at large' (McCance, 1957). Their work is for
the sick—for the patients of tomorrow.

There will always be some who do not appreciate the source of
our medical heritage and do not recognise that standard diagnostic
and therapeutic procedures of today (such as cardiac catheterisation
and hypothermia) would have been regarded as ' unjustifiable experiments ' a few years ago. It is particularly encouraging to recall
the contributions of general practitioners—Budd's observations on
the spread of typhoid in a Devon practice, Jenner's work on vaccination, Withering's discovery of the diuretic effect of digitalis,
Sir James MacKenzie's cardiology and Pickles' study of the
epidemiology of infectious diseases. As Pinsent (1953) points out,
hospital research is on a mere 20 per cent of illness; 80 per cent is
handled in general practice only. The general practitioner is in a
unique position to observe those important and increasingly
common diseases which we associate with stress and environment.
It is reasonable to hope that with the encouragement and facilities
offered by the College of General Practitioners, there will be
increasing clinical research into the management of the common,
crippling diseases which rarely come to hospital and which have
been the object of little study hitherto.

Doctors also have a responsibility to evaluate alternative
treatments for a given condition in order to improve medical
practice. This is an aspect of medicine which it is always difficult
for non-medical people to grasp. According to Green (1954):

' When the value of a treatment, new or old, is doubtful, there may be a
higher moral obligation to test it critically than to continue to prescribe it
year-in-year-out with the support merely of custom or of wishful thinking '.

Bull (1951) writes that:

' It must be remembered that many proposed new treatments are themselves dangerous, and it is unjustifiable to use such treatments unless the maximum of information on their possible deleterious effects can also be extracted '.

Although all doctors should think intelligently about their work—questioning their methods, observing critically, and reviewing their results objectively—it must be recognised that successful experimental medicine requires both a gift and training, and cannot be accomplished without time. Much clinical research can only be undertaken in large centres by teams, which include laymen. Furthermore, however productive in knowledge an experiment may be, an essential ingredient in making it beneficial to mankind is a clear dissemination of the result to those who can use it.

The clearest reason for doing research is that it may improve treatment, and its encouragement in this country is now generally regarded by the lay public as a moral obligation of the medical profession. The discoveries of recent years have set a new standard of progress. A medical profession that is not increasing its knowledge of disease and its proficiency in treating it, is not likely to retain the confidence of the public for long.

THE SANCTITY OF HUMAN LIFE

The root of the moral problem associated with clinical research is Man himself. In no other branch of science, except to a limited degree in animal research, do such problems arise. The difficulties stem from two basic beliefs: one is belief in the sanctity of human life which should not be destroyed or spoiled; the other is in the worth of the individual whose right to life and health should not be sacrificed to the society in which he lives.

What is the authority for these beliefs? They are certainly not universally self-evident or acceptable, and they are not subscribed to by some totalitarian regimes of our time. Moreover, those who hold them loosely have not always stood fast for them in the face of strong propaganda and compulsion in the past (Jackson, 1958).

There is no doubt that Christian and Jewish teaching supports belief in the ' sanctity of human life '. This phrase implies that because God is the Author and Giver of life, it is wrong for man to spoil or destroy it without a divine mandate. The authority for this belief is discussed in detail elsewhere (Jackson, 1962), but it is based on the biblical view of the nature of man. Man was made by God for communion with Himself. He belongs to his Creator and has an individual capacity and responsibility to respond to God by love and obedience. His life is a gift from God, but it is a gift which God intends man to use under His lordship and for the benefit of mankind. This is the meaning and purpose of life taught by Christ in His summary of God's plan for man (Matt. xxii. 37-40). It follows from this that a man may rightly risk his health or lay down his life for another, but he has no right to spoil or destroy human life on his own authority or require another to do so for him. In view of this general duty to preserve human life (we are not concerned here with the divine mandates that have been given in the past to take life for judicial reasons) no man has a right to impair or terminate another's life for research purposes.

Side by side with this teaching on the sanctity of life is the appreciation of the worth of man as an individual.

'Christ's intense care for the most helpless and hopeless in whom the flame of life burned dim—the blind, the deaf, the paralytic, the epileptic, the mentally deranged, the leper—was a new revelation not only of the compassionate heart of God, but of the possibilities which He saw in man (Garlick, 1952).

The individual's essential worth to God is also strikingly described by Dietrich Bonhoeffer (1955) in *Ethics*. In a section entitled ' The Right to Bodily Life ' Bonhoeffer, who was murdered by Himmler's Gestapo in 1945 after two years imprisonment, wrote:

' The fact that God is the Creator, Preserver, and Redeemer of life makes even the most wretched life worth living before God. The beggar, Lazarus, a leper, lay at the rich man's gate and the dogs licked his sores: he was devoid of any social usefulness; yet God held him to be worthy of eternal life ' (Luke xvi. 19-31).

For the non-Christian a significant concensus of humanitarian opinion may perhaps be found in such declarations of rights as the British Bill of Rights (1689) written under the influence of Locke, the American Declaration of Independence drafted by Thomas Jefferson (1776), and the Declaration of the Rights of Man passed by the French National Assembly (1789). More recently, the Declaration of Geneva, adopted by the World Medical Association in 1948, includes, ' I will maintain the utmost respect for human life, from the time of conception: even under threat, I will not use my medical knowledge contrary to the laws of humanity '. And again, ' The health of my patient will be my first consideration '.

From a purely logical point of view, if the life of the individual is not regarded as inviolable, who is fit to assess the worth of his brother man and who is qualified to assess the assessors?

It is the human factor—the sanctity of man's life and his worth as an individual—which makes it so difficult to assess the justifiability of a research procedure which carries risk. Lindeboom (1957), representing the views of the Dutch Calvinists, suggests that the physician should perform an ' experiment ' only when he feels compelled and technically able to do so, and then only when the purpose is important and when the patient gives consent: the risk for the patient should stand in reasonable relation to the possible gain for mankind. Edwards (1959) suggests that the decision to experiment should be shared with others to ensure proper consideration of the risk and the justifiability. Moreover, the procedure should involve considerably less risk than the inherent risks of the disease itself, and it should have a reasonable chance of producing information likely to be useful in reducing the inherent risks of the disease. Often those not closely concerned with the project are best fitted to judge its justifiability: a jury composed of those who are habitually practising the thing of which a prisoner is accused will usually acquit!

THE PATIENT'S CONSENT AND CO-OPERATION

The implicit agreement of the patient or the consent of his parent or guardian if he is a minor or not responsible for himself is required for every procedure in medical practice or clinical research. Without it, the action of the doctor or investigator could be regarded as an offence under Common Law. In medical practice, however, written consent is only formally sought for operations, and is then sometimes loosely recorded as permission for what the surgeon considers necessary when he establishes the true nature of the trouble during an exploratory operation. The fact that the patient comes on his own initiative and puts himself in the doctor's hand is taken as unwritten permission for treatment. This agreement is based on the patient's trust in the doctor's good faith—that the doctor will put the patient's interests first—and it would be rudely shattered if he found masquerading as a doctor, a ruthless scientist intent on investigation. In this doctor-patient relationship there is sometimes a place for pressure and persuasion in the interests of the patient: to leave a difficult choice to a patient, who is mentally or emotionally unable to make it, can be seriously lacking in a sense of responsibility. But where the patient's interests are not at stake, a sense of fitness and regard for the patient's feelings is required in seeking participation in an experiment or even in asking relatives for an autopsy.

In present medical practice many tests and investigations are used to assess the extent and progress of disease, the degree of dysfunction and the patient's fitness for operation. These commonplaces of clinical practice are sometimes an ordeal to children or nervous patients but they are usually accepted without question. 'Experiments', in the sense of taking a little extra blood at the time of a diagnostic or therapeutic venepuncture, are often done without seeking special permission. The patient trusts the doctor to see that he comes to no harm, and the doctor regards the liberty to perform such minor investigations as within that bond. Nevertheless, almost all procedures carry some risk—pricking a finger with a contaminated needle may cause serum hepatitis— although in the hands of an experienced and careful investigator the risk can be made extremely small.

If, however, the experiment is more elaborate and involves any appreciable discomfort or risk, most investigators would agree that an attempt must be made to explain the whole procedure to the patient honestly and fully, and obtain his permission. Sometimes this is difficult due to the technicalities of the experiment; the degree of intelligence of the patient or the ability of the investigator to explain the position simply may be a further obstacle. The experimenter may not know fully, in advance, the result of the procedure. Often it would be easy to get a formal consent from a patient who feels that any other reaction would seem ungrateful, but such consent cannot be taken as the green light. At all times the responsibility for an experiment rests squarely on the investigator and each member of his team, and if there is any doubt the trial should be submitted to independent, informed advisers for their opinion about its value and propriety.

Should consent *always* be sought for an experimental procedure? There is no doubt that on the basis of the two basic beliefs stated above the patient always has a right to know what is being done to him. There is also no question that if he does not wish to be involved in an experimental or therapeutic procedure his wishes should be strictly respected. Moreover, experiments involving risk or discomfort must be fully discussed and consent given. But many people would agree that certain classes of experimental medicine may properly be done without explicit consent: for instance, very few patients with depression or paranoid schizophrenia can be effectively approached, and mental deficiency is another condition which must be studied without the patient's understanding consent. The responsibility upon the investigator and the guardian is correspondingly greater. Those who feel that research should never be carried out on mental defectives and other psychiatric groups seem to have given up all hope of finding the cause and eventually a means of prevention or cure. They should know that parents are often only too grateful that ' the medical profession are *at last* beginning to take an interest in the causes of mental deficiency and disease '.

Another example is the evaluation of orthodox treatments, which is a very large field of clinical research. If two or more orthodox treatments for a certain condition are available, and neither is known to be more effective or safe than the other, this is often a positive indication for a controlled trial. No purpose will be served by increasing the anxiety of the patient with an explanation of comparative risks of alternative treatments. Not only would the patient be unable to make a reasonable and informed choice, but he would be burdened with a decision which it is the doctor's duty to make.

A patient's co-operation in clinical research is sometimes to his advantage even when no therapeutic benefit is expected. The patient is not always giving and the doctor receiving. Sometimes a patient can enter into a research project, such as a metabolic balance study, just because he is ill; if at this point he can see that someone is being helped (and we should try to ensure that he appreciates this), his illness will no longer seem a complete and utter waste.

Having agreed to the principle that the investigator has a duty to obtain valid consent to any research procedure which carries discomfort or risk, it may reasonably be questioned whether the patient has in any sense a duty or responsibility to co-operate in research. Knowledge which would be of value in treating future patients can sometimes only be gained by investigating patients who will not benefit personally from the study. Incurable diseases will remain hopeless unless they are investigated. Chromosome diseases in particular require examination of those who may carry the disease without suffering from it. What should be our attitude in a situation like this?

It may be argued that such a patient has a duty to co-operate in research, at least to some extent. He is probably a beneficiary of previous research and sometimes of great sacrifice made by others. Should he not follow the example of blood donors who submit to venepuncture and give a pint of blood from a sense of responsibility or gratitude, or even, as in some countries, for money? In other spheres of civil life demands may be made on the individual for the good of others. Personal liberty is restricted to a code of accepted social behaviour, a proportion of the wealth of the well-to-do is taken to provide welfare services for the less fortunate, and time is demanded for jury service. Such examples, however, are not relevant. They carry no risk to life or health and are legally binding upon all, whereas participation in medical research is an individual matter between investigator and patient with no automatic safeguards. It is generally accepted in this country that the patient's participation in research should not be sought under duress, either by making him feel ' mean ' if he refuses, or by promising rewards to volunteers, such as the shortening of a prison sentence.

It is tempting to try and simplify the matter by generalisations such as ' Operations must always be in the patient's own interests and never other than for the patient's good ' or ' There must be no question of the individual's loss for the community's gain '; but there are always exceptions. Operations to give skin grafts or a kidney are performed for the sake of another person with consent, and patients in hospital who are carrying important pathogenic bacteria are often investigated and treated for the safety of the local ward community without explicit consent, sometimes with isolation and drugs which carry slight risk of harmful side-effects. Such action has general approval, and to do nothing to safeguard other patients would be negligent; but there is no final compulsion, as the carrier can refuse or leave hospital.

It seems, therefore, there is no single formula, code or approach to the patient which is always suitable. In our planning and practice we can do no better than see that the particular patient's interest predominates where this is involved.

SCIENTIFIC REQUIREMENTS

There is also a discipline in clinical research which must be observed if reliable results are to be obtained. This involves such matters as the choice of experimental material, the knowledge of normal values and the provision of controls.

Human beings are sometimes not the most suitable material for the investigation of a particular problem. Animals may have the advantage that they can be obtained more easily in large numbers and this may be essential for a statistically significant result.

Moreover, their rapid rate of reproduction and shorter life-span, together with the possibility of killing them at set times and examining them without delay, make them more suited for many trials on drugs, foodstuffs, genetics, carcinogenesis and new surgical techniques.

Nevertheless Claude Bernard's remarks are still apt, that as far as direct applicability to medical practice is concerned, it is true that experiments made on man are always the most conclusive. Often, healthy volunteers are the best subjects, and according to McCance (1957) they are the ideal for metabolism studies and physiological experiments in which the 'stress' originates in the environment, e.g. the effects of cold, dehydration and high-speed flight.

With the development of new techniques of observation and sampling in the human body, it has become necessary to know the range of normal human values so that these procedures can be used to investigate disease. A technique which carries a risk, such as liver biopsy or cardiac catheterisation, is justifiable if it may reasonably benefit a patient who is in a more dangerous situation; in this circumstance it is a diagnostic procedure with a risk. But to use the same technique simply to obtain normal values is probably never justifiable in patients (who are neither normal, nor possibly as strong as normal) and it may not be justifiable in volunteers. In this context Edwards (1959) writes:

' In some cases the investigator may decide that the possible rewards do not justify the risk, otherwise he may use only such subjects who fully understand the risk involved, and who, without coercion or undue persuasion, volunteer for the study. In practice, this usually means the investigator himself and his immediate colleagues, as they are the only persons truly able to give intelligent consent '.

This may mean that the technique cannot immediately be perfected and made available for patients. Patience in such a situation and efforts to find a safe way round the difficulty, constitute one of the disciplines of clinical research.

The problems of providing ' untreated human controls ' as a standard of comparison in a clinical trial is often more apparent than real. If a controlled trial is contemplated, there must first be reasonable grounds, probably from animal work or a previous ' pilot ' study, that the treatment is both practical and likely to be beneficial. If this is not so, the time is not yet ripe for a controlled trial. On the other hand, the new treatment will not be of *proved* value, or there would be no point in planning a controlled trial to prove it. It is an integral part of such trials that ' treated ' *or* ' control ' cases may finally turn out to have had the best management. Bull (1951) writing in this context points out that the question of human controls:

' is not important when the disease is a mild one (*e.g.* the common cold), nor in the common situation where the expected improvement is a matter of a few days of treatment-time; in such circumstances the greater certainty of a well-planned trial is much to be preferred to dubious results and possibly repeated inconclusive trials by less effective methods.

Secondly, a new and possibly potent therapy is usually only available in small amounts when just introduced. However effective it may be, there is not sufficient to treat all cases of the appropriate disease. In these circumstances, it is clearly best that the cases which can be treated shall be used to yield the maximum of information by being compared carefully with cases not so treated '.

But there should always be an ' escape clause ' in the plan or every clinical trial, so that the patient may be taken out of the investigation at any time and treated differently if this is indicated for his own benefit.

What constitutes an ' experiment ' is well discussed by McCance (1957) who favours a narrow definition.

' The real distinction is a subtle one and may depend upon the mental approach of the man who makes the tests. Nevertheless, I regard collecting an extra specimen of urine or taking an extra 5 cc. of blood from a vein puncture, made purely for established diagnostic or therapeutic purposes, as falling within the range of the term " experiment "! '

This strict view, which even takes cognisance of those investigations which are generally regarded as trivial, keeps the responsibility squarely on the shoulders of the investigator. If he adopts this attitude, he is unlikely to forget the patient's point of view when risk or discomfort is entailed.

THE INVESTIGATOR AND HIS TRAINING

The relevance of the human factor in clinical research is not confined to the sanctity of the life of the patient or volunteer; the investigator also is Man. The weakness of ethical principles is that they are descriptive and not imperative; they describe the good life, but they give neither the will nor the power to live it. Man is frequently tempted to make himself the exception to his own standards with some rational excuse. It is easy for the investigator to say, ' If I were in the patient's position, this would not worry me ': with his expert knowledge he would not himself be anxious, and in his keenness to solve the problem he might minimise the risk and discomfort. It is not the investigator's

D

mental assent to principles that is the patient's real safeguard, but the character and integrity of the investigator himself.

Aims and Motives

For most of us motives in our daily work are mixed. The worker in pure research finds satisfaction, one may presume, in adding to the sum of human knowledge, the body of discovered truth. If he is a Christian and feels called to explore some aspect of God's creation, his reward may be, as it was with Keppler, that he recognises that he is ' thinking God's thoughts after Him '. However, we are considering applied research here, and a further motive for the clinical investigator will be to discover something which will be of benefit to mankind, and this will influence the planning of his work and the lines of research he follows. Sometimes a well-conceived project, originally motivated by curiosity or altruism, may come under the dominance of an idea which seems to impel the worker to press on through thick and thin, sometimes to the detriment of his critical assessment of evidence. Such an impulse should be made a servant, not a master. Unfortunately, there is always a tendency for ambition to control our motives, so that less worthy influences may become involved. A man may feel that ' a series ' should be studied to satisfy his seniors or ' papers ' written to secure a job. These constraints are not wholly bad or without compensations; they have sometimes opened a man's eyes to see where his future lay, and if done conscientiously they have always provided good training. Regrettably, our motives can sometimes only be described as personal vanity, to increase our own status, to be ' first in the field ', to obtain kudos or impress the Profession.

His Beliefs

If in the final analysis the conduct of clinical research depends on the character and responsibility of the investigator, what he thinks about Man is of vital concern. His beliefs, philosophy or religion are not entirely personal matters; they are very pertinent and may even become of public interest.

In this country at present, as far as can be told, our stated medical ethics are in full accord with orthodox Christian belief. Christianity teaches that man has individual rights, such as the right to life, which it would be wrong, and wronging him to deny. Man has corresponding responsibilities to give other individuals their rights when this is possible. Sometimes, however, these mutual claims are incompatible, and then, after comparing them as best we can, our duty is to support the stronger case and choose the lesser evil.

Another philosophy, usually called utilitarian or totalitarian, holds that the greatest amount of resultant happiness must always override ' rights ', and that it justifies any individual ' injustice '; it is the only ground on which any ' rights ' or 'claims ' to ' justice ' can be maintained. Unfortunately, people of different ideologies are inclined to see happiness only in their own system of thought. To illustrate, the East German Prime Minister, Herr Grotewohl, said on March 23rd, 1959 in a speech to artists and writers in East Berlin that ' all is morally right that serves the cause of socialism '. Replying, Dr. Dibelius, Evangelical Bishop of Berlin and Branden-burg, pointed out that this was the same sort of argument as that used by the Nazis, ' everything is good which benefits the German people ' (Manchester Guardian, 1959).

Again, to take an extreme hypothetical case, the investigator might conceivably be influenced by determinism and have little personal belief in moral responsibility at all. What safeguard would one expect for the patient if the investigator was an extreme adherent of the behaviourist school, regarding all man's thoughts and actions as based on conditioned reflexes arising from environ-ment, heredity and the endocrine glands. In this philosophy conduct carries little responsibility: choice and even an original thought or act are scarcely possible.

Training

The would-be clinical investigator must acquire clinical com-petence and he must gain an understanding of his responsibilities as a professional person. The aim of education is not so much to impart knowledge as to teach the student how to learn for himself, and to criticise and use what he learns.

' Moral exhortation without content or direction is a futile thing, and today the student must be brought to share the problems which face his teacher both as concerning the patient and the profession. He must learn that science, which he must use, searches only after truth and has no humanitarian ends in view ' (Ellis, 1960).

This understanding is not achieved by giving junior workers facilities for research and leaving them to sink or swim; this is costly in time, money and staff, and inconsiderate of ' material ' (patients or animals).

Working at first with an experienced investigator can itself be a lifelong stimulus, as well as the best tuition in methods and thoroughness.   It is from such people one can learn humility and willingness to accept criticism, the need to brood and the discipline of time.   The next stage is supervision by an expert of one's own work—a guiding hand that points but does not do the work: this merges unconsciously, not with the worker being on his own, for this is a sad plight, but into being his own master and discussing his work with colleagues.   If a part of training can be in a good unit abroad without the penalty of forfeiting eventual advancement at home, this can be of the greatest value; but it usually needs courage to take the step.

Some investigators involved in clinical research, and contributing greatly as a result of their specialist knowledge, are not medically trained.   This need raise no difficulty if they are members of a united team.   Clinical research, however, cannot be divorced from clinical responsibility, and the physician or surgeon in charge of the patient must take full responsibility for what procedures are carried out, what specimens are taken and who takes them.

An aspect of training which is sometimes given insufficient attention is the instruction of students, nurses, the public and sometimes even patients themselves in the current and completed research of the hospital.   There is still alarm in some quarters about patients ' being experimented on ', and nurses may feel that on occasions the discomfort of the patient is improper compared with any benefit they can see.   The spread of true information in suitable form to these groups could do much to ease the way for good relations in clinical research in the future.

SAFEGUARDS

From time to time doctors have suggested that the Profession should have some supervisory body (like the Law Society in the legal profession) which would check unreasonable clinical research activity.   At present individual investigators with low standards, who are fortunately rare, could plead ' interference with their rights ' to avoid inspection and criticism, and they could continue easy-going and dangerous practice.   A ' professional conscience ' of medically trained persons or a code of ethics for investigators has been suggested in addition to the individual's conscience if the profession does not want regimentation by the Government or regulation by lay committees, juries or coroners.

The Medical Research Council has given its considered opinion on this possibility in a memorandum (McCance, 1957), from which the following is an extract:

' In any particular case—so specialised has medical knowledge become—only a small group of experienced investigators, who have devoted themselves to this branch of medicine, are likely to be competent to pass an opinion on the advisability of undertaking any particular investigation. But in every branch of medicine such a group of investigators exist. It is upon them, and the specialised scientific societies to which they belong, that the medical profession must mainly rely for the creation of the body of precedents and the climate of opinion which shall guide investigators in clinical research '.

The same memorandum also draws attention to the responsibility of editors and editorial boards to satisfy themselves before accepting any publication, and even to insist that the reader shall be left in no doubt that the investigations described are unobjectionable.

More recently, Sir Austin Bradford Hill's Marc Daniels lecture, entitled ' Medical Ethics and Controlled Trials ' (Hill, 1963), has stimulated a new demand for an ethical code for clinical investigation, this time from within the profession (*British Medical Journal*, 1963). A measure of guidance has been provided by the Medical Research Council (1964), entitled ' Responsibility in Investigations on Human Subjects ', and also by the Declaration of Helsinki, which is a ' Code of Ethics on Human Experimentation ' (World Medical Association, 1964). The latter was based on the Nuremburg Code for Permissible Human Experiments drawn up the War Crimes Commission of the United Nations in 1947. As a general guide or as an assertion of our intended standard, these statements are good. There is no harm in emphasising the Hippocratic Oath which already demands that doctors ' abstain from whatever is deleterious or mischievous '. The objection to a detailed code is that someone, sooner or later, may try to apply it rigidly as law, and this will lead to endless controversy and obstruct research without really protecting the patient (Hamilton, 1963). Every code of principles by its very nature embodies inherent contradictions and man has always found it easy to keep within the letter of the law while breaking its spirit. Law can only set a minimum standard—a lower level of conduct below which we must not fall; it deals with actions. But the problems of human experimentation involve our motives, opinions, judgements and the evaluation of risks; right and wrong depend upon sincerity, trust and mutual understanding. To introduce law at this stage would lower research standards. It is up to the profession to preserve the confidence of the public in this field, for if it is lost, the greatest losers will be the patients of the future whom we are all trying to serve.

The common practice of most investigators, who naturally want to conduct their experiments with the greatest safety, and be known to do so, is to prepare a well thought out plan after becoming fully informed about past work in the field. They then discuss it fully with their team and usually with other interested investigators. Experience with the procedures involved must also be obtained if these are unusual or complicated. A critical review and rearrangement of the experiment may be necessary if the investigator feels he cannot keep reasonable control of factors influencing the patient's safety. Animals, members of the team or healthy volunteers may be used before the procedure is tried on patients. A pilot trial may be run to confirm the safety and practicability of the experiment. On occasions an experiment originally considered safe may appear unwise after further experience. Although it will be disappointing, completion may become quite unjustifiable and the experiment may have to be given up. If an experiment cannot be conducted without risking the life or health of an individual, then this is one of the directions in which the increase of scientific knowledge for the time being should not be pursued. This restraint, this limitation on the search for truth is not peculiar to clinical research. In no other field of study is the accumulation of knowledge given deliberate priority over human life.

In practice, criticism is more often justified on account of haphazard investigations carried out in a disconnected and useless form. A doctor may think it ' scientific ' or does his prestige good ' to do one or two ' of some yet unevaluated procedure. He may forget that research needs careful planning, a clear idea of the criteria of success and careful assessment of the results of an adequate series. In contrast to this, research units frequently offer a standard of care and investigation which it will not be possible to give to the majority of patients in general hospitals in the foreseeable future.

Finally, we should recognise that, in spite of all the care and skill that we can muster, it is unfortunately true that many ' advances ' in the treatment of desperate conditions only prolong suffering and the act of dying *in the early stages of their application.* The modern treatment of shock after burns saves many people from death in one or two days, only to die of infection two or three weeks later. This is tragic, but it is unavoidable at the exploratory fringe of Medicine. For every real advance there has usually been a previous series, not only of failures, but of half-successes, which have sometimes increased suffering.

I am well aware of my presumption in writing on this subject when my experience of it is limited. I have done so, however, partly because of the importance of keeping the subject under review, and partly because I am convinced there is a need to carry its consideration a step further than is customary.

At present the ethical standard of clinical research in Great Britain appears fairly satisfactory, largely due to the lead given in recent years by senior members of the Medical Research Council. If the standards of an individual investigator are low, there are checks which have been mentioned that can and should be used. But our generation has seen the climate of opinion swing away repeatedly and in different ways from previously accepted Christian morality.

If the standard is to be safe in the future we should be sure of the foundation truths on which it is based, and we should recognise the authority for believing these truths—that they are God-given and permanent. It is the compelling sense that we must submit to the Author of these beliefs, when it is neither fashionable nor profitable to do so, that is the real safeguard of the patient, for it is this which gives the will and the power to live up to the standard. Consent to contemporary humanist standards will be no anchor when those standards change, as we have seen them do in the past.

The comment of Dr. Albert Einstein, an observer of unquestioned objectivity and recognised wisdom is significant. Though a profoundly religious man all his life, he had had little use for the institutions of religion. Then National Socialism came. The following is a rendering of his observations in pre-War Germany:

‘ Being a lover of freedom, when the revolution came to Germany, I looked to the universities to defend it, knowing that they had always boasted of their devotion to the cause of truth; but no, the universities were immediately silenced. Then I looked to the great editors of the newspapers whose flaming editorials in days gone by had proclaimed their love of freedom, but they, like the universities, were silenced in a few short weeks. Then I looked to the individual writers who as literary guides of Germany had written much and often concerning the place of freedom in modern life; but they too were mute. Only the Church stood squarely across the path of Hitler’s campaign for suppressing truth. I never had any special interest in the Church before, but now I feel a great affection and admiration because the Church alone has had the courage and persistence to stand for intellectual truth and moral freedom. I am forced thus to confess that what I once despised I now praise unreservedly ' (Van Dusen. 1943).

It is for this reason—to safeguard the contemporary ethical standard—that the subject of clinical research is linked here with a consideration of Responsibility and the Sanctity of Life.

REFERENCES

BONHOEFFER, D. (1955). *Ethics*, p. 119. Transl. Smith, N. H. London: S.C.M. Press.
British Medical Journal (1963). Ethics of human experimentation **2**, 1.
BULL, J. P. (1951). *A Study of the History and Principles of Clinical Therapeutic Trials.* M.D. Thesis. University of Cambridge.
EDWARDS, D. (1959). Ethics and emotion in clinical research. *Univ. Coll. Hosp. Rev.* **43**, 191.
ELLIS, J. (1960). Preparation for the Profession—the present and the future. *Lancet*, **2**, 1041.
GARLICK, P. L. (1952). *Man's Search for Health*, p. 143. London: Highway Press.
GREEN, F. H. K. (1954). The clinical evaluation of remedies. *Lancet*, **2**, 1085.
GREGG, A. (1941). *The Furtherance of Medical Research*, p. 7. New Haven: Yale University Press.
HAMILTON, M. (1963). Ethics of human experimentation. *Br. med. J.* **2**, 177.
HILL, Sir AUSTIN B. (1963). Medical ethics and controlled trials. *Br. med. J.* **1**, 1043.
JACKSON, D. MacG. (1958). *Moral Responsibility in Clinical Research*, pp. 14-18. London: Tyndale Press.
JACKSON, D. MacG. (1962). *The Sanctity of Life*, pp. 12-17. London: Tyndale Press.
LEWIS, Sir T. (1946). *Research in Medicine and other Addresses*, 2nd ed. p. 13. London: Lewis.
LINDEBOOM, G. A. (1957). Amsterdam. Personal Communication. AGO (1960). Medische Ethick, Kok, Kampen, Netherlands.
McCANCE, R. A. (1957). In *Medical Ethics*, pp. 147, 149, 142, 144, 151. ed. Davidson, M. London: Lloyd-Luke.
Manchester Guardian (1959). 30th April.
MEDICAL RESEARCH COUNCIL (1964). *Annual Report for* 1962-63, p. 21-25. Cmnd. 2382. London: H.M.S.O.
PINSENT, R. J. F. H. (1953). *An Approach to General Practice*, pp. 155-157. Edinburgh: Livingstone.
VAN DUSEN, H. P. (1943). *What is the Church doing?*, p. 38. London: S.C.M. Press.
WORLD MEDICAL ASSOCIATION (1964). Human experimentation: Code of ethics on human experimentation. *Br. med. J.* **2**, 177.

Since this chapter was written. the legal and ethical problems of transplantation have been discussed in a Ciba Foundation Conference, and the proceedings are now published in—
Ciba Foundation Symposium (1966). *Ethics in Medical Progress: with special reference to transplantation*, ed. Wolstenholme, G. E. W. & O'Conner, M. London: Churchill.

CHAPTER III

WHY THE PRESERVATION OF LIFE?

DUNCAN W. VERE[1]

Discussions of ethics are often tiresome to the practically minded, seeming to revolve endlessly about premises whose validity or relation to the subject are doubtful. A ' common sense ' approach is more attractive, but often proves even more irritating when there is little agreement about which sense is common. ' Common sense ' also crumbles on close examination, for it is found to be based upon a mass of fragmentary ethical premises. This situation is similar to that which occurs in using a computer. If the data of some problem is presented to a machine, with the instruction that it should use its common sense, nothing useful will emerge. A computer must be given both data and a ' programme ' of instructions before it will work. The ' programme ', which may bear little apparent relation to the data, contains those basic premises which the machine must ' know ', before it can do the sum. Very small flaws in the programme produce widely different answers to the sum.

Similarly, it is necessary in tackling human problems to have both data and a ' basis of ethics '. The same problem can be solved using any one of a series of such bases, but with as many different results as there are ethical premises employed. It is, therefore, impossible to avoid a detailed study of the basis of ' ethics ' in any attempt to solve the problems of life preservation, for the outcome is largely dependent upon them. For example, at a recent conference (*Lancet*, 1966a) it was reported that ' concern for the value of man ' was the ' essence of ethics ', and indispensable for medicine as for the survival of mankind. But what is man, and how can his value be reliably determined? These are the questions which determine the practical outcome of concern for the value of man. Concern is not enough; it is not of itself a basis of ethics. The importance of the subject to both patient and doctor is reason enough for thorough discussion.

What is life and why preserve it?   Some Christian and opposed views

It is usual to approach the problem of life preservation by

[1]Duncan W. Vere, M.D., M.R.C.P., is Consultant Physician and Senior Lecturer in Medicine, The London Hospital.

asking ' What is human life '?   Biologists often offer an answer.
Le Gros Clarke has said, ' Probably the differentiation of man from
ape will ultimately have to rest on a functional rather than an
anatomical basis, the criterion of humanity being the ability to
speak and make tools' (quoted in Oakley, 1958).   Oakley,
following Kohler, goes further to say:

"That apes of the present day are capable of perceiving the solution of a
visible problem, and occasionally of improvising a tool to meet a given
situation; but to conceive the idea of shaping a stone or stick for use in an
imagined future eventuality is beyond the mental capacity of any known apes.
Possession of a great capacity for this conceptual thinking, in contrast to the
mainly perceptual thinking of apes . . . is generally regarded by comparative
psychologists as distinctive of man ".

This is all true, and is very good biology.   But, as a full
definition of man, it is about as satisfying to the Christian as to
define a Rembrandt as so many grammes of oil paint.   ' Personality '
need not be unreal simply because scientists cannot define or
measure it.   Those who favour purely biological definitions do
not always follow their outworking, for the best biological course
might be to leave sick people to die rather than interrupt the
ruthless economics of competition for survival.

For this reason many hope to find further distinctive marks
of human life which will strengthen the reasons for its preservation.
A bold attempt has been made to circumvent this difficulty by
regarding *all* forms of life as worthy of reverence.   Schweitzer
argued that life in all forms should be conserved as far as possible.
This theory is unique in renouncing degrees of quality of life.
Schweitzer (1934) noted this distinction and contends against the
majority view.

' Objection is made to this ethic that it sets too high a value on natural life . . .
The ethic of Reverence for life is found particularly strange because it establishes
no dividing line between higher and lower, between more valuable and less
valuable life.   For this omission it has its reasons.   To undertake to lay down
universally valid distinctions of value between differing kinds of life will end
in judging them by the greater or lesser distance at which they seem to stand
from us human beings—as we ourselves judge.   But that is a purely subjective
criterion.   Who among us knows what significance any other kind of life has
in itself, and as a part of the universe? '

Though truly humble and unselfish, this view has limitations
which throw into relief the real nature of our problem.   It is true
that any decisions we may take about the qualities of other lives
will be warped by our egocentricity.   It is not the nature of ' life '
that should concern us first, but the nature of ' reverence '.
Schweitzer is honest, as a man, to refuse to decide which lives are
the more reverend.   But suppose that some external mandate,

some voice of authority outside ourselves, reveals the true nature of reverence? The orthodox Christian position is that the Bible is the source of such authority, for though it relates history from a Jewish cultural background, it contains a commentary on ethical questions which is far from outdated and claims to originate as a divine revelation to man. Thus the authority for the Christian view of reverence for life is held to stem from God rather than from human thought alone, as Schweitzer's view appears to be (Schweitzer, 1934). Commands and directions derived from the Bible in this way will therefore be called ' revealed principle ' in what follows, and we must turn from the problem of life to that of ' reverence '—the question of why any form of life should be thought worthy of preservation.

A CRITICAL REVIEW OF VARIOUS CHRISTIAN VIEWS OF LIFE PRESERVATION.—Many Christians have given interpretations of the Biblical revelation regarding life, its nature and preservation, but whilst there is agreement over many revealed principles, there is little agreement concerning how they should be derived. However, the fault is largely with the variety of ill-conceived approaches to the derivation of a basis of ethics from the Bible. Most writers approach the problem from arguments about detail derived from expediency, rather than aiming to find a revealed principle which can be applied to specific cases or problems. It will be easiest to make this point by quoting a variety of examples in a critical review. We hope to show that it is possible to derive consistent systems of ideas from an ethical basis of ' revealed principle ' but not from rules of expediency, and will take mercy-killing of incurables as a case in point. It has been the general view of the Church for many centuries that life cannot be taken save by an express mandate. This was the climate of Jewish-Christian opinion at an early date, a view consistent with its clear incorporation in Moslem thought in the Koran (Surah lxvii. 1-2. Surah ii. 258. Surah lxxvi. 28). The main monotheistic faiths agree at this point, yet modern writers have difficulty in showing why this is so.

Willard Sperry (1951) emphasised the value of the individual human life, yet rejected the merciful killing of incurably sick persons on the ' wedge ' principle, i.e. that what is wrong for a whole society is wrong for the individual. It seems weak to argue that the ' individual ' counts for most, but then to legislate for him on the basis of society. Sperry quotes but one Bible reference (2 Kings

vi. 32) as an illustrative story, not a source of principle, and therefore argues from expedience rather than revealed principle.

Canon Peter Green (1937) uses similar methods but arrived at the opposite view. ' I have found it impossible to discover any really conclusive arguments against suicide[1] under due restrictions '. Since he made no Biblical quotations it is impossible to tell how far he has looked for arguments in favour of preservation of life. It seems that he did not pursue this approach, for he added ' one might, of course, argue that, as God alone confers life, God alone may decree its end. That argument, however, is impossible while we permit war and capital punishment.' His argument falls down as a Christian view, since it is not grounded in Christian thought, but in expedience. For example, he failed to discuss what seems to be the mandate to take life judicially which is given in Romans xiii and elsewhere.

Canon T. C. Hammond (1938) follows Driver in deriving the idea of human life from Genesis ix. 6.

' Man bears in himself God's image; he therefore who destroys a man does violence to God's image. In other words a man is a *person* with a rational soul, the image of God's personality which must be treated as sacred '.

He pursues his view that the essence of man's life and relationship to God is in his personality by quoting ' He that loveth not his brother whom he hath seen, how can he love God whom he hath not seen? ' But it seems desirable to base so important a principle as life preservation on a broader base than the Divine image doctrine which, though very relevant, is somewhat obscure—particularly to the non-theological reader.

Two particularly thoughtful accounts exist, one Roman Catholic in view, by N. St. John Stevas (1961) and another Protestant by John Murray (1959), which aim to relate theological principle to practical issues. Stevas begins by setting out some useful generalities—that Christian views of morality cannot be enforced upon an unwilling community by legislation, and that theologians often err by mistaking conservatism for morality and ignoring new insights offered by the non-theological sciences. He also points to the main divergences between Roman Catholic and Protestant methods of deriving principle from the Bible. In general, the Roman Catholic looks for abstract rules, the Protestant for concrete problems. He then carefully derives three main arguments, as follows:

[1]In this context he means voluntary mercy-killing.

1. The disposal of life is God's prerogative for it is His gift. Man holds life in trust.
2. There is no Biblical mandate to take innocent human life in any form (Exod. xxiii. 7; Dan. vi. 22).
3. Suffering, though containing evil elements, is not absolute evil, but can have redeeming features and effects.

Stevas has made a very sincere effort to be thoroughly Biblical as well as practical here. However, certain difficulties remain. To what extent has God, by placing in our hands an immense potential to modify the course of life and disease, also delegated decisions to us, which are needed to use this power for Him? Also, while suffering can be the vehicle of good in certain ways, can it be so if it is of such severity as to distort the mind and judgment, crippling our power to use the mind or will?

In the matter of voluntary mercy-killing Stevas unfortunately leaves revealed principle aside to argue from expediency. The ' wedge ' concept is again invoked. Here it is said to mean:

' Once a concession about the disposability of innocent life is made in one sphere it will inevitably spread to others. The recognition of voluntary euthanasia by the law would at once be followed by pressure to extend its scope to deformed persons and imbeciles, and eventually to the old and any who could be shown to be " burdens " to society '.

However true this may be, it is relatively weak since the ' wedge ' argument lacks universal validity, a point which must be held over for further discussion.

Murray (1959) arrives at closely similar theological principles to those of Stevas, but bases his derived principle much more broadly upon the whole Bible, and a study of the contemporary Jewish thought. This gives a convincing Christian statement, and expedient arguments are largely omitted. He examines several scores of passages from both Testaments so that he is above any criticism of text-selection to plead some special cause. Murray takes as his starting point not the fact that God gave life initially, but that it is only by His grace that life is preserved now that man has sinned (Gen. ix. 8-17). This revelation is followed in Genesis by three institutions; life propagation (Gen. ix. 1, 7), life sustenance (Gen. viii. 22; ix. 2, 3) and life protection (Gen. ix. 2a, 6). Again, as shown by Hammond (1938) it is upon the revelation that man was made, ' in the image of God ' that a doctrine of his inviolable personality is based. Man may only be killed by express Divine mandate as in judicial execution.

Murray goes on to examine the sixth commandment, ' Thou shalt do no murder ', but (unfortunately for the present interests) speaks largely of judicial punishment and war rather than of medical difficulties.

It must be said that there is a body of Christian thought which approaches the problem of life preservation quite differently, from the standpoint that love is the highest good. W. R. Matthews (1962) says:

' The advance of medical science has changed the conditions of human life. It is true that the ultimate principles of Christian morals do not change. The root of all Christian morality is the injunction to love God and our neighbour; as St. Paul says, " Love is the fulfilling of the law " '.

Believing from this, that the highest good is the loving and compassionate relief of suffering, Matthews advocates voluntary mercy-killing. ' The great master principle of love and its child compassion should, I urge, impel us to support the legislation of voluntary euthanasia as advocated by the (Euthanasia) Society.' Heading this publication, ' Blessed are the merciful for they shall obtain mercy ', the Society circulates this leaflet with a Christian ethical statement that their views are ' not contrary to the teachings of Christ ' which is signed by some 20 ministers and theologians.

A criticism of this courageous and well-meant view can be made. ' Love is the fulfilling of the law ' can be read with emphasis upon ' love ' or upon ' fulfilling of the law ' and it is the former which is chosen to support mercy-killing—' To *love* (a vague and compassionate term in isolation) is to fulfil the law '. But only that love is appropriate which is consistent with the law, even though it may transcend the law. The law includes the moral duties of the Old Testament which must be seen to accord with any interpretation which we may offer of ' love '. Matthews no doubt believed that mercy-killing did not contravene the moral law, but Murray (1959) adduced strong arguments which could be used to support the contrary view. ' Mercy ' which has been defined as ' a sense of pity plus a desire to relieve the suffering ' (Lloyd-Jones, 1959) or ' inward sympathy and outward acts in relation to the sorrows and sufferings of others ', can be similarly misunderstood. Again, the outcome depends entirely upon the basis of ethics employed to solve the problem. In deriving a revealed principle from the Bible, many feel that it is proper to test it by comparison with the acts of good men in test situations resembling those at which the principle is aimed. For example Job longed for comfort, but refused to accede to any course which involved disobedience to the revealed will of God (Job ii. 9, 10). It was the same with Jesus Christ (Luke xxii. 42), though admittedly in both cases the choice was made by the sufferer for himself. We may infer that a Biblical view cannot support a mercy to man which contravenes a duty to God, though this need not imply that God will require us to be unmerciful. There are different ways of showing mercy, some of which accord with revealed principle and some which do not.

NON-CHRISTIAN AND PHILOSOPHICAL THEORIES OF HUMAN LIFE.— The ideas of those who repudiate religion and argue from materialism or utility must be set against the Christian writers. These ideas have the attraction of avoiding difficulties of Biblical interpretation. ' Logical positivism ' had a great impact until recently, when the pressing realities of life have left this view behind. It regards ethics as inaccessible to analysis and accordingly meaningless, so that a biological definition of life is alone accepted. A. J. Ayer (1958) writes:

' We find that ethical philosophy consists simply in saying that ethical concepts are pseudo-concepts and therefore unanalysable. The further task of describing the different feelings that the different ethical terms are used to express, and the different reactions that they customarily provoke, is a task for the psychologist. There cannot be such a thing as ethical science, if by ethical science one means the elaboration of a " true " system of morals. For we have seen that, as ethical judgments are mere expressions of feeling, there can be no way of determining the validity of any ethical system, and, indeed, no sense in asking whether any such system is true '.

This argument would save us further work were it not fatally weak at both ends. To begin with the assumption that ' only that which may be tested can be accepted as meaningful ' has never been tested or validated, and even if this premise were true and yet some person were to inform me of spiritual values which were also true, I could never demonstrate their truth objectively using my present abilities. This would not make them untrue, as any parent knows who tells his child that the earth is round.

Similarly the utilitarian, who ' defines the rightness of actions and the goodness of ends, in terms of the pleasure or happiness or satisfaction to which they give rise' (Ayer, 1958) gives an insecure foundation. This offers as a basis of ethics that which men agree will provide the most happiness or gain. But which two men agree to the full over this, especially when their personal interests conflict? This is an ethic which can only be prescribed for others. It is too painful to apply to oneself! Indeed it is a sad world where man decides that nothing is of value which does not satisfy self in the majority.

Humanism likewise bears the stamp of weakness produced by its rejection of external authority. If man is to be the origin, end and arbiter of human affairs, he will be pulling himself up by his own shoestrings. Humanism in medicine seems at first to carry ground as a reaction against inconsistent theistic attitudes (Platt, 1961), but does not provide a reliable substitute which can stand apart from Christian ethics. However much the scientific humanist may himself believe in the importance of the individual's welfare, he cannot justify such beliefs on humanistic grounds alone. Only if each individual can be taught to agree that human progress exceeds his own welfare in importance can it be truly said that humanism provides an ethical basis for dealing with the individual, as Huxley (1961) seems to advocate. The individual should regard his life well spent if he has furthered human evolution. Thus the only ethical goal for the individual is to ' contribute his own personal quality to the fulfilment of human destiny; and he has assurance of his own significance in the vaster and more enduring whole of which he is a part '. When Huxley stresses the importance of the individual he accords to him no value in and of himself—he is of value only in terms of what he can contribute to humanity; indeed only to that kind of human progress which Huxley advocates.

THE REASONS FOR DISAGREEMENT, AND A SUGGESTED SOLUTION.—
Those who support a Christian basis of ethics have deep differences, but these differences are not hopeless and can be reduced once their causes are distinguished. A major source of difference is neglect of simple principles of Bible interpretation, the incorporation of extra-Biblical with Biblical views and the stretching of Biblical statements to accord with human ideas. For example, single texts are often used to found a doctrine, but a text can only be understood in its context, especially its time context. Another common mistake is to take what applies to a class and to stretch it to include all mankind. The Bible is set in various ancient cultures, and it is pointless to press detailed instructions for living in the Old Testament to fit modern problems. In deriving a principle it may be necessary to interpolate between Biblical statements, or to distinguish the underlying principle from its detailed application in ancient times. However, this does not allow us to *extrapolate*,

or go beyond such Biblical insights. A principle can only be derived with reference to the whole, not part of the Bible.

Some have added metaphysical ideas to their views of life which lead to such absurdities that they are condemned by their fellow Churchmen. For example, the extra-Biblical doctrine of 'immediate animation of the foetus' is exposed by Miss Alice Jenkins (1960). If 'life' begins at conception, as some argued, every product of miscarriage should be baptised *sub conditione*. It is our belief that there are many similar extra-Biblical doctrines which may contain truth, or even be true in some situations, but confuse in others. They may be regarded as rules of expediency.[1] However useful these may be in some situations, dangers may arise if they are regarded as universally applicable. To take a rather light example, the 'wedge' principle so often invoked by Roman Catholics (that something which is wrong for society is wrong for the individual) might be taken to argue against a celibate priesthood! Such rules are open to the winds of discussion and argument, for few can agree upon what is or is not expedient. The precepts to be found, for example, in the ten commandments and elsewhere in the Bible are in a higher class and should not be intermixed with dogma of human devising.

The various sources of principle must therefore be distinguished. They may be classified under four heads. Two are derived from the Bible—'commandments', which are expressly stated regulations of general validity (*e.g.* do not steal, do not bear false witness)—and 'inferences', which are interpolated ideas derived from the ethical commentary of the Bible. An example of an 'inference' would be compassion for those who suffer, which is nowhere expressly enjoined in that form but which was an obvious premise of the thought and acts of Christ and his apostles. These two Biblical categories are included in the 'revealed principle' already

[1]Examples are the 'wedge' principle, already discussed, and the doctrine of 'double effect' and of distinction between 'ordinary' and 'extraordinary' remedies. 'Double effect' is the argument that an act may have one of two motives, one licit and one illicit. For example, it may be right to will to 'relieve pain with risk to life' but wrong to 'end life and with it pain' (Stevas, 1961) though the outworking of either motive is to give an identical dose of morphine to the patient. This can degenerate readily into the view that the end justifies the means. 'Ordinary' remedies are all which offer reasonable hope of benefit, which can be used without excessive expense, pain or other inconvenience (Kelly, 1951). 'Extraordinary' remedies are those which 'offer no reasonable hope of benefit' (Osborn, 1940). Most find that such a distinction is impossible to apply to actual remedies, however valuable it might be in idealistic discussions, *e.g.* Rynearson (1959).

mentioned in discussion above. The third category is not Biblical, and comprises the rules of expedience (see footnote p. 49). We will refer to these as human ' devices '. The fourth category is Church tradition. Christ taught that it would be from the Bible, not from human inventions, that God the Spirit would give under-standing of the truth (John xiv-xvii). This demarcates the authority of the first two categories from the others. The Christian has three complementary sources of authority; the Bible, Church tradition and reason. The last is not to be despised as an inter-preter, but is inadequate to provide basic principle. It has too short a reach to compass human problems. Church tradition also is weak, for it is liable to corruption. This has been particularly so with the ethics of life preservation, as Glanville Williams (1958) ably demonstrates in a scholarly and informative way. But it is by an understandable, though unfortunate, error that he identifies tradition with Christianity.

There is a distinction between ' commandments ' and ' inferences ' on one hand, and ' devices ' on the other, which resembles that between Equity and Statute Law. The commandments to which we refer are, like Equity, moral principles of conduct, but are insights given by God Himself, derived from the Bible. They have a universal appeal, but are so broad as to be difficult to apply to certain specific cases. ' Inferences ' are weaker, and provide more cause for disagreement than commands. It is easy for special pleaders to invent inferences of doubtful value. However, many inferences are of established worth and come nearer to solving specific problems than the commands. The ' device ' (as we use the term here) is not Biblical, but often contrived in an attempt to formulate a consistent world-wide view to accord with some philosophical system (Williams, 1958). Indeed, its attempted universal validity makes it a sort of substitute commandment. But however true a ' device ' may be in part it cannot attain the universal appeal of Divine Law. It can only be enforced bluntly upon communities, solving some problems but causing individual hardship in others. It has the properties of some Statute law, such as the law relating to parking offences, which certainly lacks the universal appeal of, for example, laws which protect the rights of the individual. If true Equity is like a circle, Statute Law is like a complex polygon within it, which touches it only at certain points. Christians do not differ over ' commandments ', only over ' devices ' and difficulty arises when these are confused or treated as equals. A writer on Christian ethics, Andrew Osborn (1940), describes this vividly in his first experience of a city church.

'The chief cause of confusion lay in a wrong viewpoint . . . They were looking for rules and regulations which would give specific direction in particular problems instead of seeking universal principles'.

It seems that disagreement arises from attempts to mingle 'devices' and traditions with revealed principle (commands and inferences from the Bible) or from treating inferences as if they were commands and so investing them with too much authority. There is little room for doubt regarding the meaning of 'commands'; but human minds are needed to derive 'inferences' so opening them to possible disagreements. Nevertheless, many inferences are so strong as to permit little difference of opinion.

The derivation of a Christian view of human life and disease

What are the 'commands' and 'inferences' for Christian conduct in the medical setting? With regard to human life and suffering three may be recognised. These are the duty to preserve life, the obligations to relieve suffering and the duty to recognise that life has an end; all are 'inferences'. There is one commandment over all, 'This is my commandment, that you love one another, as I have loved you' (John xv. 12).

THE DUTY TO PRESERVE LIFE.—The discussions given by Hammond (1938), Stevas (1961) and Murray (1959) seem true to the Bible. Man, made in God's image and for His pleasure is given life (Gen. i. 26-28, ix. 2-6, ii. 7). Life-taking in haste or malice, even that of a murderer is strictly forbidden (Gen. iv, 15, ix. 5; Exod. xx. 13). It must especially be noted that human life gains its exalted value, *not* from some intrinsic features, but because it is made so by God. It is precious to *Him*. Similarly, human life is *defined*, not merely *as such*, but by its *relation to God*. Hence the weakness of all ethical systems and definitions which omit God from their reckoning. For the Christian, God is the answer to both questions, 'what is human life'? and 'why preserve it'? Though the sixth commandment cannot be used to prohibit killing generally, for it refers specifically to murder, we may infer from it the high regard in which life is to be held. In addition, though there is a clear mandate to take guilty lives judicially (Gen. ix. 6; Rom. xiii. 1-7; 1 Peter ii, 13-17; Num. xxxv.) none is given to take the innocent (Gen. ix. 5, Exod. xxiii. 7; Dan. vi. 22). The book of Job carries us further towards the practical application of this inference. Job, tormented by mental and physical pain, refuses to accede to his wife's ingeniously wicked suggestion of suicide (Job ii. 9). His reason is most noteworthy: ' Shall we receive good at the hand of God and shall we not receive evil? In all this did not Job sin with his lips ' (Job ii. 10). His faith in God's purpose for him was later vindicated.

These ancient insights into life are not, as some think, abrogated, but amplified in the New Testament. Disease is often discussed, and seen as a rule to be the result of evil in the world (Luke xiii. 16; Cf. 1 Cor. v. 5) rather than as a sign of individual guilt (Luke xiii. 4). It derives ultimately from a personal source of evil, Satan, who is a disorderly influence interfering with God's plan (2 Cor. xii. 7). Life is seen in a wider sense than in the Old Testament, where it is largely physical life which is considered, equated with the presence of circulating blood[1] (Gen. ix. 4). In the later Old Testament period life is that which takes place between birth and death (Ps. xvii. 14; Prov. iii. 2) and the physical and mental abilities which enrich it (Job iii. 20; xxxiii. 20). God is seen as its sustainer (1 Sam. xxv. 29). In the New Testament life is something broader— it is now the means of support of, and the quality of work achieved during existence (Matt. vi. 25; Luke xii. 15; Rom. viii. 6; Gal. ii.20). Life is not rigidly defined as a single property of existence, but an examination of the term reveals a vivid kaleidoscope of man's being, closely interwoven as one entity. The mere extension of physical life is now not regarded as the highest good (John xv. 13). These ideas are clearly seen in Christ's words in Luke vi. 9. A man with *physical* disability (a ' withered hand ') is made the object of the lesson, ' is it lawful on the Sabbath day to do good or to do evil, to save life ($\psi v \chi \eta$, that is the normal constitution, or way of life, the integrity of individual personality) or to destroy it? ' Thus, for Christ to heal a hand was not merely to correct a physical disability but to restore a person. This suggestion is confirmed by the fact that, when He healed those who showed faith in Him, He often seemed to deal with the physical and spiritual problems together, as if they were all of a piece; indeed the word is used in these particular cases for ' heal ' and ' save ' together. We may infer that it is wrong to destroy or injure personality, whether in its physical, mental or spiritual aspect. Our activity should tend

[1]It is hard to see why theologians, eager to fix the moment of incipient life, sometimes choose conception or quickening or birth as the dogmatic milestone. The appearance of the foetal circulation would be more logical, though we have never heard of this suggestion.

to the personal restoration of others, though we cannot 'save' of course, in the sense used of Jesus Christ.

Having resolved to preserve human life, how do we recognise it? What are we to aim to conserve as life? Professor Daniel Lamont is particularly helpful in looking at the biological definition of life through Christian eyes. He shows that human life is essentially indefinable because it is only partly measurable.

'Many definitions of life have been attempted which always bring out certain manifestations of life, but which never help us to a knowledge of what life essentially is. The best that we can say about it is that it is one of God's secrets. It is a datum which we have to accept in order that we may proceed upon it' (Lamont, 1940). He adds, '. . . the experiential view of life. This is the view from the inside. Life is something which is experienced and the inner view is concerned with what it means to have that experience. Here we are not in the detached, scientific attitude. We are *in* the river, not standing as dispassionate spectators on the bank. We may know all that science has to teach us about life, but the experience of being alone introduces new facts and new problems which are beyond our biological knowledge. The inner view is obviously more individual than the outer view. One can only have experience of his own life. What it means for another person to be alive he can only infer from his own experience, the inference being enriched by sympathy. This individual character of the inner view is precisely that which marks it off from the outerview. Science is interested in generality and does not try to penetrate to the individuality of anything'.

Lamont then discusses very clearly the distinction between 'knowledge about' and 'acquaintance with'. This view of personality appears to bear a strong resemblance to some existential insights, for example, Buber's distinction between 'I it' and 'I thou' relationships (Buber, 1959), and leads to the concept that human life can only be distinguished in terms of personality. Yet this leaves a very practical difficulty—if we renounce biological definitions of human life as inadequate yet believe that 'the best that we can say about (life) is that it is one of God's secrets', how are we to recognise 'human life' when we see it, so that we can act properly towards it? Is a hydrocephalic monster or the elderly person who has suffered a dementing stroke 'alive' in this sense? We must find a theory which can lead readily to practice.

We would suggest the following definition, that 'life is possessed by those who have personality, either at present or as a future potential, and that we may recognise personality (which is at root the ability to respond to God) by the ability, however slight, to respond to us.' We may be unable to define or measure personality, but we all know what it means. It is that which we know to be within ourselves and which we use in communicating with one another. The importance of the word *potential* is great. Someone who lacks such 'life' today may gain or regain it tomorrow. Ample room must always be left in medical decisions for the possibility of unsuspected or temporarily suppressed life in the patient.

It now seems possible to answer Schweitzer's dilemma of 'reverence for life'. Unable to regard man as fit to apportion degrees of value to various forms of life, he suggested that all life should be reverenced equally. His premise may be true, but his conclusion is unnecessary if God has revealed suitable value judgments for us to follow. Animal life, though it is to be respected, may be taken in so far as is necessary for human wellbeing (Gen. iii. 21).

The foetus remains a problem. What is the relative value of foetal life? We have already resisted attempts to lay down a rigid moment when life begins, and indeed cannot see that there can be such a moment in the biological sense. There is a progressive development of life with admitted inflexions, to the point of independent existence. Similarly, the life potential or likelihood or emergence of personality, rises through foetal life with sharper increases at conception, quickening, birth or any such landmark we may care to take. Since God has revealed no point at which foetal life becomes sacred we can only respect its potential all along, but increasingly as the probability of separate life becomes stronger.

THE OBLIGATION TO RELIEVE SUFFERING.—Job found that suffering may be the purposeful gift of God; a means of refinement, testing and teaching (Job i. 21, ii. 10; Gen. iii. 16; Rom. xii. 1; 1 Thess. v. 10; 2 Cor. v. 15; 1 Peter iv. 1, 2). Life in all its forms and qualities is never seen to be purposeless in the Bible. However, this idea has been stretched too far by some, who almost advocate a callous indifference to suffering to advance its purifying activity! The point is that there are degrees of suffering, and this is well recognised in the Bible. There is bearable suffering which can teach (Heb. xii. 7), but there is also suffering which is unbearable if unrelieved, which so warps the reason as to have no beneficial effects save to evoke compassionate relief from others. The general attitude towards suffering should be one that aims to relieve (Luke iv. 18; Acts iii. 6)[1]. Lastly, we are taught that to be unmerciful is to damage our own soul (Prov. xi. 17; 1 Peter iii. 8).

[1]Asceticism is nowhere a Biblical idea. Some think that Timothy abstained from medicine (wine) for ascetic reasons, which Paul did not share (1 Tim. v. 23).

LIFE HAS AN END.—Many seem motivated by a thoughtless desire to prolong life indefinitely, despite the obvious impossibility of success, in social if not in physiological terms. Again we are taught to expect an end, the ' threescore years and ten ' (Ps. xc. 10; Job xiv. 5) and that 'it is appointed unto men once to die' (Heb. ix. 27).

These inferences have been elaborated at length to avoid the criticism that the Christian view is based upon a few carefully chosen texts which can be made to mean anything that we wish, (*e.g.* Huxley 1961). How are these inferences to be used? Clearly not as mutually exclusive rules, for there are instances where, in incurable suffering, they overlap. In some cases we cannot preserve life, relieve suffering fully and allow life to end all at once. But these inferences, held in tension and given due respect, will work out in us a true course of action. If there is a rare case where they conflict, let suffering have its full relief at the conscious risk to life, for to allow suffering of such intensity to proceed for long is to ' kill ' the mind and to distort the life to something foreign to the purpose of God. In this we do not say that we should cause death as a discrete, deliberate act or allow anyone to die carelessly. But tension there will be, as in all situations involving the issues of life. This is sent by God to test our obedience, to force us to face real issues and to decide (Cf. Piper, 1960). Are we not then invoking the ' double effect ' device (p. 49) in disguise? No, for our inference is not based upon some *permissive* rule for motivation analysis, but from the positive example of Christ.

The Practical Application of this Attitude to Life

THE CHRISTIAN DOCTOR AND HIS PATIENT.—The Christian doctor cannot feel bound by sentiment, devised rules or Church traditions, the *mores* of his society or those wishes of patients or their relatives which he believes to be ethically wrong. His conduct will be governed by what he believes to be revealed commands and inferences from them. As we have shown, he will in all cases aim to conserve life (a Biblical inference), but will not feel bound ' to conserve life *at all costs* ' (which would be a human ' device '). He is not troubled unduly by the problem, ' How much responsibility to decide about human life has been delegated to men ', because he is aware that if he knows and respects revealed principles from his heart this is enough.

There are no sharply delineated rules which tell him what to do in every case. He must consider most carefully the wishes of society or relatives, particularly his patients' desires, but he is not bound to carry them out if they run counter to revealed principle for he believes that an Authority has claim over the actions of all men. Yet he will not enforce his views on the unwilling (a thing which Christ never did, despite His followers' requests that He would change this principle). These duties give the doctor a heavy responsibility to find out all that he can about his patient as a person—not merely as a ' disease '—and to elaborate from this a plan of treatment, which will best assist the restoration of the patient's life.

PROBLEMS OF PRESERVING THE LIVES OF PATIENTS.

Machine maintained existence.—At a debate in a London medical school the motion was recently carried, ' That it is always right to save life at all costs '. As a conditional aim this is good, but applied as a rule it is worse than nonsense. As a real example, a man of 45 with aplastic anaemia became blind, decerebrate and then contracted pneumonia. Antibiotics were prescribed, yet his respiration failed. Artificial respiration was given by tracheostomy, but the pulse was found to persist only while the machine worked and to cease when the current was switched off. Was this saving life?

The problem has been discussed by Watts (1962) who wrote,

' Every man in this world had surely the right to die in peace and comfort. It would be an invidious contradiction of our honour if pride in technical ability made our patients fear us at death. When is the body dead? If the heart can be restarted the patient is technically still alive, even though the brain can be irretrievably lost to contact with the world again. Sometimes, when one knows the patient will die later anyway, a man should be allowed to die in peace. There is the terrible problem of forcing a person to die twice. Alternatively, one may know the patient can be revived only to face a life of imbecility. The Church should give us leadership on this point. The issues are greater than simple dogma or law '.

How well we agree, but believe that this terrible problem arises because the revealed nature of man is ignored by so many. Up to a point we can get by with purely materialistic medicine, but in face of death this is shown up in all its inadequacy. When personality has gone, in fact and in potential, life is lost. All that remains is a biological preparation. Yet to survive only to recognise a friend may be to have lived again. This does not advocate carelessness with life, for the persistently decerebrate is not alive— a credit to the physiologist maybe, but not to the physician. Indeed, there has been public protest about the tendency of doctors to prolong disease needlessly (Miller, 1962).

The Elderly.—The problem of the elderly, which differs because the process of mental deterioration is longer and the stakes less certain, highlights our ignorance. Omnibus rules are now especially dangerous to the individual. Antibiotics, for example, produce some remarkable recoveries and also many fatal super-infections, yet where they are used patients make surprising recoveries often enough to demonstrate their value. The clinical course of the elderly individual seems less predictable.

Research into the prognosis of groups of elderly sufferers can only give a statistical impression. This is helpful in deciding about the number of beds to be provided and similar problems, but less to the individual with whom we are primarily concerned. It will be objected that the best therapy for the individual can only be that which is best for the group. But where life saving is at stake there is a difference between diseases with high and low recovery rates. With a high recovery rate everyone is willing to fight for life, conscious of the risk of producing an occasional dement. An example is childhood tuberculous meningitis. But where the recovery rate is low we are swayed emotionally the other way, tending to allow the occasional potential life to succumb along with the many who would ' survive ' only as ' preparations '. The burden of this fault is lessened by the obvious fact that the elderly have an ever increasing penalty of multiple degenerations and inadequacies, so that our means of treatment, which succeed in the young, may exact a fatal toll in the elderly. But a burden remains. We can lessen our ignorance of prognosis by more vigorous research. This should be done, but as we have said tends not to be of much help to the individual.

It seems best to adopt positive guides for conduct which are an emotional stimulant, rather than permissive statements. For example, it seems better to say ' efforts will continue to preserve life where there is hope of some recovery ' than ' when so-and-so is true the patient may be allowed to die '. This view was endorsed in a leading article (*Lancet*, 1962a), where the issue of *trust* was emphasised. Patients and their relatives must never lose the sense that the doctors have done all that they can. Nevertheless, the futility of preserving ' preparations ' was also discussed with a reminder that the diagnosis of decerebration can be aided by electro- and pneumo-encephalography, so that blind persistence in treatment is unnecessary.

It seems best to avoid rules, and to consider the personality, actual and potential, in each case. Has the patient those who will care for her properly? It is often unrewarding to preserve ' life ' on the physical plane if the survivor must face it alone. The elderly often relinquish life when they are frustrated and miserable. From whatever angle the problem is approached, we are driven back to the apparent view of Christ that the restoration of personality implies not physical renewal alone, but in such mental and spiritual surroundings as will let it flourish. We can only aim to imitate His holistic approach by striving to understand the patient and his environment, and pay full respect to any potential life which may exist.

Two objections are commonly advanced to this view; one is that we are not called upon to decide whether anyone shall live or die; our treatment only assists natural recovery. To withhold it *may* make no difference. This is, in our view, to underestimate powerful modern therapy. While fully agreeing that the issues of life and death ultimately are God's, we have a delegated responsibility. To withhold penicillin in face of bronchopneumonia *may* make no difference, but in suitable cases penicillin must increase the chance of survival, otherwise there would be no reason to think of it at this point in preference to fresh air and good food. When we do aim to save a desperately sick man, there is a real difference of degree between the decision to kill someone and the decision not to treat. But with modern therapy this distinction should not be given undue weight, which may at times amount to shelving our proper responsibilities.

Another objection is that ' experience ' and ' judgment ' are useful guides. We cannot see that they amount to anything more than an impression of prognosis. Such ' subjective ' assessments are notoriously insecure. Any doctor of experience will have known the embarrassment of struggling to save what he believes to be a ' life ', when others have decided that it is unworthwhile.

It seems, then, that neither rules of thumb nor subjective individual assessments are very helpful. It helps to consult colleagues, though we tend to select those who share our views! The whole personality of the patient must be considered; yet comparison of our estimates of the value of others' lives in society should not affect the issue. We can only try to imagine their own assessment, and to learn God's assessment from what He has revealed to us; but in neither can we expect fully to succeed. Many have lived miserable yet invaluable lives, and even a dement can mean much to someone. Experimental, administrative and financial expediency must not have precedence over individual wellbeing. The elderly provide some real problems where, even when we have done our best, ignorance robs us of success.

Monstrosities.—We have said that we should look for personality as the ability to respond to us or to a relative, in however slight a way. Can this be distinguished from purely reflex activity? Mere responsiveness can trick us. Many mothers of imbecile children claim to recognise response where others cannot, and who is to say who is right? Where there is no clear evidence of personality nature need not be hindered if disease threatens to destroy physical life, but the need to leave room for our ignorance of such patient's personality precludes their use as experimental subjects. This is not mere sentiment, nor only an argument from ' ignorance '. Human life is precious and the only way to ensure its proper respect is to agree that everything like it or close to it shall also be respected.

Euthanasia.—Euthanasia, to die as pleasantly as possible, is the wish of all. The term has unfortunately been purloined by those who advocate mercy-killing or ' the merciful extinction of life ' performed upon a dying patient with his consent and as the only way of relieving his suffering (Kelly, 1951). Mostly this is intended to be voluntary—at the sufferer's wish—but there can be no doubt that some intend to go on to compulsory ' euthanasia ' (*New York Times*, 1939). We have said that we do not wish to pursue expedient arguments, because they are relative and open to wide disagreement. This does not mean that they are unimpressive, particularly the arguments that those in a position to ask for ' euthanasia ' are often those whose wills are distorted by pain, that the method would be open to exploitation for gain by relatives, that doctors should be connected with hope and life preservation and not seen as potential executioners, and that the adjudication of requests would be very difficult. All these grounds are arguable.

A Biblical command would be incontestable, but there is none. As we have shown, the common prohibition of mercy-killing, based on the sixth commandment, is not strictly correct. Euthanasia is thereby stigmatised as self-murder; but essential ingredients of murder are hatred and malice (1 John iii. 15). While adult murder is frequently malicious, the aim of many attempts at mercy-killing, suicide, abortion or even infanticide is merciful. However mistaken the judgment that leads to the act may be, the aim is often the preservation of self or another, from something believed to be worse than death. It would be a most abnormal person who hated himself or his own child, enough to kill. Such an act would be regarded by most as one of madness, and the mad are not punished but given help. Thus, general prohibition of mercy-killing, suicide and abortion cannot be justified on the sixth commandment alone. At times assisted suicide has also been prohibited on the ground that it interferes wtih morally beneficial pain. Suffering is sometimes claimed to have a 'redemptive function'; but it is pointless to invoke this where pain so disintegrates personality that the sufferer's power to contemplate its value is lost, which is presumably the case in many who request assisted suicide.

A Christian objection is rather that the motive which prompts mercy-killing is contrary to the Divine prerogative over human life, even allowing for those responsibilities delegated to men already discussed. This view is well presented by D. M. Jackson (1962) who shows that, while the Bible favours life-giving for others, it deplores life-taking for self.

'But the motive in euthanasia is different: it is self-centred in that the patient, by consent, directs that his life shall be ended to rid him of his suffering. It is this independent attitude towards the gift of God which is the crux of the matter, and which the Christian cannot accept as right for himself and for others'.

In this view euthanasia is destroying God's gift of life to avoid the suffering obedience would entail (Jackson, 1962). The reader is advised to consult Jackson's thoughtful discussion of suffering for himself. It has nothing that is callous or doctrinaire, the aim being the full relief of pain in a manner consistent with the revealed will of God.

But the underlying issue is again entirely a matter of the ethical basis employed. Given a utilitarian basis assisted suicide is very plausible; given a conventional Christian basis the reverse is the case. The real point is not whether mercy-killing can be proved right or wrong, but which basis of ethics is to be given most respect. Either basis gives rise to a self-consistent view. The lack of a distinctive commandment drives the Christian to draw inferences from the Bible, which most find to be sufficiently strong to prohibit euthanasia, though some dissent (p. 46).

The kernel of this problem is that some Christian opposition to mercy-killing is based upon negative rather than positive evidence—the lack of Biblical mandate to take life in this way, though none would be expected since the modern problem could not be in view in Biblical times. By contrast, the strength of Jackson's opposition to mercy-killing (Jackson, 1962) is that it is critical of the motive rather than the act itself, and shows this motive to run counter to the purpose of God for human life, as may clearly be inferred from many Biblical passages. In this way his opposition becomes exempt from the criticism that it is invalidated by the historical differences between our own and Biblical times. Detailed mandates are time dependent, being cast in their own culture and social context, but the purposes of God for mankind are not so confined. It is essential to read the Bible to understand the climate of Christian opinion. Consider in detail, for example, the sentiments expressed in Psalms xxii.-xxviii. and especially xxxi., which show the attitudes of a godly man to life and death in a way which no single text or mandate can do. The present political current in this country, however, favours Bentham's utilitarian principle of ' greatest happiness ' (Robbins, 1965) so that there is strong pressure against the Christian attitude.

It is interesting that the demand for ' euthanasia ' has increased just as the need for it becomes less—a change likely to stem from the decline of formal religiosity in the community, though the increasingly aged population has also been advanced in explanation (Glanville Williams, 1958). Intractable pain can still be truly dreadful but less often than before. Morphine in increasing dosage, with the attendant miseries of vomiting and progressive respiratory depression, need not be used. Not only are there potent alternative drugs with fewer unwanted actions, but their combination with respiratory and mental stimulants has been shown to succeed (Gershon et al., 1958). Our strong impression has been that the plea for ' euthanasia ' comes less from those in severe pain (who are usually heavily sedated), than from those who anticipate it and face death with clearer minds, or whose emotions have been stirred by seeing others in pain. But many such sufferers are helped by encouragement to faith in assistance from God and man, not ' humane killing ' by their doctor. The writer has heard recovered patients say that they would have welcomed death during their painful illness, in one case said to be ' incurable ' by doctors.

In a thoughtful and factual survey of the problem Hinton (1963) has shown that the picture which is so often painted of a death racked with pain may be more common in novels than in reality. In his study, some 12 per cent of patients suffered distressing pain, and 10 per cent had other distress which was difficult to relieve. Of those in pain 82 per cent obtained satisfactory relief. Indeed it was those with nausea (37 per cent relieved) and severe dyspnoea (18 per cent relieved) who had most distress. Of the whole group 45 per cent were said to have positive features of depression and 35 per cent of anxiety; but it was noted that a disconnected state, leading ultimately to unconsciousness, preceded death in a large number.

Death is fearful, but it is those who live with the subconscious conspiracy that ' it will never happen to them ' who break when the illusion shatters. Their need is largely of spiritual help. The atmosphere of some specialised hospitals for the dying gives the lie to the idea that such hopelessness is inevitable (Saunders, 1959). It is often abolished by the strong reassurance that loving help will be freely given when the need comes. Dr. Cicely Saunders (1961) has claimed that, in her experience, it is always possible to control pain due to terminal cancer and only very rarely is it necessary to send patients to sleep. But the thing which often brings them pain is the isolation, which has become known as ' the bereavement of the dying ' where they are deserted by relatives and friends who no longer know what to say or do in their presence. Surely it is here that great things can be done for these sufferers.

For these reasons most Christians agree that they cannot commit or support ' euthanasia '. We are guilty in so far as we theorise without practising our ideals. We must see whether we are doing all that we can to provide for the needs of the dying and those who suffer chronic pain.

Abortion.—Few subjects give rise to so many ethical difficulties, perhaps because at least two individuals are involved of whom one has indefinable personality. The Protestant Christian cannot accept the Roman Catholic dogma that the foetus has a soul; indeed the logical out workings of this view are not pursued even by Catholics (Williams, 1960). It is manifest, as Glanville Williams points out, that were all these potential lives as important to God as actual lives, we would have been urged to undertake strenuous research and therapy to prevent the prodigal waste of foetuses by nature (Williams, 1960). (One in every two or three is said to be lost.) The Bible is concerned with those already born, who can respond as individual persons to God. Its emphasis is that it is *personality* which must not be offended (Mark ix. 37, 42).

The everyday practical problems which surround the practice of abortion are many. There is little point here in repeating the statistics of illegal abortion. We can only accept that they are very common and involve great hardship and distress (Williams, 1961: *British Medical Journal*, 1957; Arkle, 1957; *Lancet*, 1964; Tredgold, 1964; Kelly, 1951). No one would fail to see with compassion the plight of the ' worn out mother ', compelled to add an unwanted child to a large ill-cared-for family; nor would anyone fail to regret the distressing psychological misfits which such children may become. At the other extreme there is the almost equally distressing self-centred person, apparently motivated only by personal convenience, who wishes to lose that which might well enrich her whole life and experience. It is not easy to assess even the ' clear-cut ' for it is quite common to find the ill and harassed mother-to-be who demands abortion vociferously, yet who welcomes the child with delight when it is born. In Ekblad's (1955) Swedish series of legal abortions some 25 per cent of patients at the follow-up visit, expressed some self-reproach for having the abortion, and it may be that some of these on reflection had cause to doubt their motives for action. On the other hand the over-cautious attitude of many honourable doctors drive patients towards ' help ' of another kind.

It seems incredible, that in so difficult a context, an annotation should recently have appeared in a leading journal with the naive view that ' only education can ensure that every child born is wanted, and this will take time ' (*Lancet*, 1966a). It is a common finding that the worst hardship often comes to those so ignorant or unintelligent as to be unable to protect themselves from problems or to avail themselves of social services where these are provided.

Also, these remarks apply only to this country. The position is entirely different elsewhere, and post-partum sterilisation may there become a preferable means for the prevention of hardship. This illustrates an added ethical difficulty. We cannot say that abortion is or is not wrong, for the outcome of every ethical argument depends in part upon the social context. Here, as nowhere else, is the danger of general rules and ' devices ' made clear.

The problem of illegitimate births among juveniles is increasing, and with it must come an increased demand for abortion. Here it is probable that much might be achieved by discouraging the false, commercialised image of ' sex ' which is aiming to take the place of marriage as an ideal in youthful minds and culture. Those who urge 'legal reform' often seem strangely silent on methods of correcting faults in the press, television or commercial advertising. Such a one-sided approach to ethical problems is always unconvincing.

An important point of expedience is that we have no means to decide the quality of the life which we may sacrifice when an abortion is allowed. This is especially a problem with abortion for maternal rubella in early pregnancy where estimates of the incidence of foetal malformation vary from 13 to 80 per cent. It is likely that the incidence varies from epidemic to epidemic. Routine abortion destroys many useful lives, but it is impossible to predict how many will be affected by rubella in any local group (Jeffcoate, 1960; Campbell, 1961; Lancet, 1962b; Fisher, 1963).

The law, up to the present, has permitted therapeutic abortion on the grounds of maternal risk, whether physical or psychiatric, though this was more by a sort of gentlemen's agreement over test cases rather than by explicit legislation. Now new Bills may become law. The new climate of opinion is that physical grounds for termination are becoming increasingly few, and there is an honest realisation that social and psychiatric factors cannot be divorced since one engenders the other (Fox, 1966). Our contention that there are no easily definable 'cut-off points' between conception and birth is now more widely held (Lancet, 1966c). These ideas have introduced at least two new grounds for termination, for the sake of the foetus itself and for society (Lancet, 1966b). Parental fecklessness or irresponsibility is also suggested as a ground (Lancet, 1966b). However, it has been urged that the law must not specify such grounds in detail, but leave the matter to the discretion and integrity of the doctors dealing with the case (British Medical Journal, 1966a). To specify grounds in law would be to invite pressures upon doctors or patients which are equally undesirable (British Medical Journal, 1966a). Clearly such new laws will encounter practical difficulties, not least the shortage of psychiatric and gynaecological services (Lancet, 1966b) and the risks of operation (British Medical Journal, 1966b). Though the risks are small, with increased practice they will affect more people. We think that the Biblical inferences to guide conduct here are:

1. The need to conserve potential life as the gift of God.
2. The need to remove suffering where this may be rightly done.

3. The general ideal of family life as it is contained in the Bible (1 Tim. iii. 4, 12, v. 8, 10, 14; 1 Cor. vii. 14) and our obligation to further this.

4. That it is false to act from motives of pleasure or convenience if higher issues are at stake (Rom. xv. 1-6).

All are inferences rather than commands, and again these partly overlap and must be held in balanced tension.

It is open to doubt whether the law in 1965 imposed any restraint where there were genuine psychiatric distress enough to warrant abortion, or in cases of pregnancy arising from assault (*British Medical Journal*, 1957, Arkle, 1957; *Lancet*, 1964; Tredgold, 1964). With regard to the present pressure to expand the grounds for abortion, it seems preferable to leave the matter to the integrity of the profession.   To specify grounds in detail not only invites pressures of the worst kind, but also provides a precedent of prescribed morality which cannot fit the innumerable shades of individual hardship or injustice.   The real safeguard against abuse cannot be the law, but good public opinion.   The problem cannot be isolated from its social setting of debased moral standards, commercialised ' sex ' and ignorance, and it is pointless to apply law whilst neglecting these aspects.   The attack upon any disease has its preventive as well as its curative elements.

In summary, the author believes that there are convincing Biblical reasons to offer abortion in those cases where it is the lesser of two evils—a qualitative decision of great difficulty which should be taken on grounds of the health of those already alive and their family ties.   Yet every abortion *is* an evil, and many are confessions of failure of individual and social responsibility.

If we permit abortion, but not euthanasia, it will be said either that euthanasia should be allowed on the same grounds as abortion—as the lesser of evils—or abortion disallowed on the same grounds as euthanasia—as an arrogant life destruction.   Further, it may be said that euthanasia is less evil as a voluntary destruction, than abortion which destroys a pre-sentient potential personality.   If it is pressed, in opposition, that there is the mother to think of in abortion, then this is worse for being the forced sacrifice of A for B, not of B for his own sake, as in euthanasia.   For these reasons, then, it seems wrong to place too much emphasis on the idea that potential life is inferior to actual life—this is clearly vitiated by the comparison of euthanasia with abortion.   It seems, therefore, that it is illogical to propose abortion, whilst disallowing

F

euthanasia, save where a continued pregnancy would jeopardise both mother *and* foetus. Then abortion is without doubt the lesser of the two evils. Fortunately this is, in the nature of things, more commonly the case.

THE CHRISTIAN AND SOCIETY.—A view of life, if it is to count, must be applicable to society as well as to the individual. But how far can a Christian attitude, which bears on morals and the law, be pressed in society? It has been said that ' No religious group should seek to maintain the religious and ethical standards of its own members by the imposition of laws applied to the general population ' (Calderone, 1958). Of what use, then, is the Christian ethic in society? Are Christians to try to enforce, or advocate or merely practise their beliefs in private?

Lord Denning (1961) is outspoken on the point, saying ' Without religion there can be no morality; without morality there can be no law '. He seems to argue that since religion is the source of ' morals ' it must be invoked in framing laws. But he is aware that only some members of the community are sensitive to right moral judgment, and is reduced to admitting that only ' right thinking members of the community ' should decide issues of justice. Since almost everyone is of the opinion that he is a right thinking member, this becomes in practice the majority opinion, an outcome which, we suspect, would not satisfy Lord Denning's aim to see Christian morality as the foundation of law. That the Jewish-Christian tradition gives rise in general to excellent laws is beyond doubt, but this tradition is no longer supported by the majority of our society. Lord Denning admits that the law is morally neutral, yet it should be framed so as not to offend right thinking. but rather to support it.

It is also doubtful that there can be no morality without religion. Admittedly, this depends a little upon how one defines religion, but in the sense of a commonly agreed basis of faith, religion is virtually absent in some communities, which nevertheless have morals and effective laws. Perhaps they have copied their codes from others, but the point is at least in doubt. However, it must be conceded that religion gives rise to a strong moral sense which tends to produce powerful and effective legislation. Yet such laws may be repressive and inequitable, and it seems important to distinguish between systems based upon religion, as such, and those derived from Biblical Christianity.

Stevas (1961), also a lawyer, discusses both Roman Catholic and Protestant standpoints. He reminds us that though many still look to the Law to enforce Christian standards of morality and sound behaviour, this is easily carried to excess. Unless supported by the general moral consensus of the community this is doomed to failure. But he shows that there is gain as well as loss in separating moral standards from the direct application of physical sanctions. He points out that motives are not the concern of the Law, which deals with the fact of crime rather than the reasons for it, save in assessing penalties.[1] With regard to mercy-killing, for example, legal and moral sanctions are external and internal respectively and are not co-extensive. Yet Law and morals are connected. The absolute distinction between them (positivism) is as unreal as their metaphysical identification.[2] The positivist view has the advantage that to break a moral sanction need not break Law, but that morally desirable rules are sanctioned by Law. Its weakness is that no one can resist Law on moral grounds. This was the case with the Nazi regime in Germany. Stevas then shows that in this country the Law is obeyed as much because men respect its moral backing as because they fear it. The confusion over the moral backing of the Law stems from an admixture of Roman Catholic and Protestant thought. The former (from Aristotle and Plato) argues that the State is good and ' natural '. The latter (from Augustine) that the State is permeated by human evil, yet is necessary to check vice. The Roman Catholic makes much of ' natural ' law, natural being defined as that which furthers man's life as it ought to be. Thus false teeth are ' natural '—they favour nutrition. Contraceptives are unnatural—they hinder reproduction.

Stevas' analysis is subtly penetrating, but leaves the Protestant Christian dissatisfied. As Lord Denning suggests, those who believe that they know the best for mankind by revelation, cannot rest silent and hope that it will be worked out by God's general providence through the State. But they are equally convinced of the hopelessness of legislating morality upon an unwilling community (as attempted by Calvin in Geneva), which brings the Law into open disrepute. Yet the State has as much a revealed obligation

[1]This is not to say that motives are unimportant in establishing guilt.

[2]There are technical problems here, but largely involve failure to distinguish various types of law. See, *e.g.* Devlin (1965), who shows that there is, ' failure to recognise that there is a fundamental difference between the law that expresses a moral principle and the law that is only a social regulation '.

to support right morals, as we have to obey it (Rom. xiii. 1-10). The answer to this dilemma can only be that the Christian's duty lies only in the personal practice and public proclamation of the values which he knows to be right, so that men's consciences may be stirred towards their acceptance (Prov. xiv. 34; Rom. i. 16, x. 12, 17). These views should be put forward not in our name, but God's. St. Paul's remarks (2 Cor. v. 11-21) though addressed to Christians, carries this general principle of persuasion as opposed to the alternative reactions of apathy or attempted enforcement of the Christian view upon others. In Jesus' words, Christians are to be ' salt ' in a corrupting society (Matt. v. 13).

Again we must contrast the Christian view with the materialist and utilitarian. For the materialist ' morals ' reduce to the norms of human behaviour. All that is needed to determine them is a social survey. This overlooks the fact that even opinion is not equated with behaviour (Hammond, 1938). Most of us are critical of what we do, indeed we regard someone who is not self-critical as unfit to be heard in serious affairs. But even opinion is regarded by most humble minded persons to be weak, and to gain by comparison with, and criticism from, the views of others. The utilitarian may also argue that morals should be divorced from the formulation of the Law (Glanville Williams, 1958, 1960). But in its place he would have the consensus of what is thought best by the community, or by experts in social welfare. We do not think it unduly cynical to ask, when self-interest is the general motive, how many will be able to agree on what is best or in the truest interest of others? We are brought back to the need for external standards, which alone enable a man to give himself to the relief of hardship (Jas. ii. 14-18) knowing that his motives are rejected by most of those whom he serves (John xv. 18-25). He is impelled by the belief that ' Ye shall know the truth and the truth shall make you free '.

However, Professor Glanville Williams believes that utilitarians can speak from an ' intuited premise ' . . . ' that the greatest happiness of the greatest number of human beings is the supreme good ' (1958). While admitting that:

' Even the modern infidel tends to give his full support to the belief that it is our duty to regard all human life as sacred, however disabled, worthless or even repellent the individual may be ' he adds that ' this feeling among those who do not subscribe to any religious faith may sometimes be in fact a legacy of their religious heritage '.

But the Christian suspects that such ideas of ' oughtness ' are deeper than an earthly heritage, and represent a scantily heeded revelation from God Himself (Rom. i, ii.). This restraint, which is reinforced by the Christian voice in the community, is primarily moral and internal. It only results in favourable legislation in so far as the community is willing to support these external restraints.

CONCLUSION

It may be truly said that we have achieved little more than to expound a difficulty. It has been shown that a consistent view of life preservation cannot be made out using sets of rules, for life is too subtle to be categorised in that way. A consistent system of ideas can be derived from various bases of ethics, though each will differ from the others, depending upon which basis is employed. In this country the present rivals for wide acceptance are those idea-systems which reject external Authority (utilitarian, materialist and humanist), and those which invoke such Authority (Christian). Men disagree, which makes both systems weak, but only the former is wholly dependent on man and so is the weaker. Those who reject external Authority fail to cohere among themselves; nor is it easy for them to discover an internal principle from which to derive a worthwhile system of ethics.

Christians might seem to be on stronger ground if there were express commandments regarding life preservation, but (excepting murder) there are none. Inferences can be derived in plenty from the Bible but need men to make them and men, being imperfect, disagree. Such disagreement can be greatly reduced once inference is disentangled from wholly man-made rules and traditions, but some problems remain. This fact proves to some that the Christian faith has no value in framing ethics for today.

The Christian will reply that the reverse is true, and that had the Bible been only a book of rules about preserving life it would have perished with the social cultures in which it arose. It has been noted that ethical problems are doubly difficult since they have no omnibus solution but require as many solutions as there are societies or even individuals involved. Rules seem to make all easy—a kind of ' instant ethics '—but genuine ethical decisions from principle require hard work. The Bible provides a framework of revealed commands of timeless and universal validity, and also a wealth of historical illustration and ethical comment from which we may draw inferences to meet the modern case. It is promised that men will be guided if they are meek. To the arrogant and self-willed the Bible yields nothing, and it is the embarrassment and strength of Christian ethics that the quality of the inference drawn from the Bible depends upon the willingness of the person to submit to God (*e.g.* John v. 30, vii. 17, xv. 7, 20). Hence the wide divergences of opinion found, even among Christians, and the difficulty of others in understanding what they say.

The Christian standpoint is popularly identified with conservatism and reaction, but we have tried to show that this is due to mis-understanding, not least by Christian traditionalists. It is the presumption that man has the right to be free from all inconvenience and is open to manipulate his life purely to suit his own ends which is particularly opposed to the Biblical view. This does not mean that the Christian enjoys suffering in some sado-masochistic way. He is enjoined to mitigate and relieve it, but not in so doing to transgress revealed principle. For him there is always value in life and some point in living. If the ' sanctity of life ' means ' respect for the integrity of human personality because it is the gift of God ', it is right to aim to build and restore personality in accordance with His revealed will. It is also right to show to others the benefits and consistency of so doing.

REFERENCES

ARKLE, J. (1957). Termination of pregnancy on psychiatric grounds. *Br. med. J.* **1**, 558.

AYER, A. J. (1958). Critique of ethics. In *A Modern Introduction to Philosophy* ed. Edwards, P. & Pap, A. Illinois: Free Press.

British Medical Journal (1957). Psychiatric indications for terminating pregnancy. **1**, 457.

British Medical Journal (1966a). Summary of memorandum by R.M.P.A. **2**, 44.

British Medical Journal (1966b). Sequels to therapeutic abortion. **2**, 159.

BUBER, MARTIN (1959). *The I and Thou.* Edinburgh: Clark.

CALDERONE, MARY S. ed. (1958). *Abortion in the U.S.A.* New York Conference on Abortion. New York: Harper.

CAMPBELL, C. (1961). Place of maternal rubella in the aetiology of congenital heart disease. *Br. med. J.* **1**, 691.

DENNING, LORD (1961). Religion, morality and the law. *Moral Welfare,* **50**, 39.

DEVLIN, P. (1965). *The Enforcement of Morals.* London: Oxford University Press.

EKBLAD, M. (1955). Induced abortion on psychiatric grounds. *Acta psychiat. neurol. scand.* Suppl. **99**.

FISHER, E. (1963). Abortion law reform. *Br. med. J.* **1**, 1089.

FOX, R. (1966). The law on abortion. *Lancet,* **1**, 542.

GERSHON, S., BRUCE, D. W., ORCHARD, N. & SHAW, F. H. (1958). Amiphenazole and morphine in the production of analgesia. *Br. med. J.* **2**, 366.

GREEN, PETER (1937). *The Problem of Right Conduct.* London: Longmans.

HAMMOND, T. C. (1938). *Perfect Freedom.* London: I.V.F.

HINTON, J. M. (1963). The physical and mental distress of the dying. *Q.Jl. Med.* **32,** 1.

HUXLEY, SIR JULIAN (1961). *The Humanist Frame,* pp. 23, 57, 58, 127. London: Allen & Unwin.

JACKSON, D. M. (1962). *The Sanctity of Life.* London: Tyndale Press.

JEFFCOATE, T. N. A. (1960). Indications for therapeutic abortion. *Br. med. J.* **1,** 581.

JENKINS, ALICE (1960). *Law for the Rich.* London: Gollancz.

KELLY, GERALD (1951). *Theolog. Stud.* **12,** 30, 31, 90, 210, 211, 277, 550.

LLOYD-JONES, D. MARTYN (1959). *Studies on the Sermon on the Mount.* London: I.V.F.

LAMONT, D. (1940). *The Anchorage of Life.* London: I.V.F.

Lancet (1962a). Prolongation of dying, **2.** 1205.

Lancet (1962b). Annotation. Rubella in pregnancy, **2,** 495.

Lancet (1964). Termination of pregnancy on psychiatric grounds. **2,** 1279.

Lancet (1966a). The doctor and situations of tension. **2,** 221.

Lancet (1966b). Annotation. Psychiatric views on therapeutic abortion, **2,** 156.

MATTHEWS, W. R. (1962). In *Merciful Release.* London: Euthanasia Society.

MILLER, L. M. (1962). Neither life nor death. In *Reader's Digest,* pp. 169-176, Oct. 1962. London: Reader's Digest Association.

MURRAY, JOHN (1959). *Principles of Conduct,* pp. 109, 110. London: Tyndale Press.

New York Times (1939). Jan. 27th.

OAKLEY, K. P. (1958). *Man the Toolmaker,* 4th ed. London: British Museum Publications.

OSBORN, ANDREW (1940). *Christian Ethics.* London: Oxford University Press.

PIPER, O. A. (1960). *The Biblical View of Sex and Marriage.* London: Nisbet.

PLATT, SIR ROBERT (1961). The new medicine and its responsibilities. In *The Humanist Frame,* p. 357. ed. Huxley, Sir Julian. London: Allen & Unwin.

ROBBINS, LORD (1965). *Bentham in the Twentieth Century.* London: Athlone Press.

RYNEARSON, E. H. (1959). You are standing at the bedside of a patient dying of untreatable cancer . . . *CA,* **9,** 85.

SAUNDERS, C. (1959). *Care of the Dying.* London: Macmillan.

SAUNDERS, C. (1961). Euthanasia. *Lancet,* **2,** 548.

SCHWEITZER, ALBERT (1934). *My Life and Thought,* pp. 1-3, 185-192. London: Allen.

SPERRY, WILLARD (1951). *The Ethical Basis of Medical Practice.* London: Cassel.

STEVAS, N. ST. J. (1961). *Life, Death and the Law.* London: Eyre & Spottiswood.

TREDGOLD, R. F. (1964). Psychiatric indications for termination of pregnancy. *Lancet,* **2,** 1251.

WATTS, G. (1962). Editorial, *Midl. med. Rev.* **1,** 327.

WILLIAMS, GLANVILLE (1958). *The Sanctity of Life and the Criminal Law,* pp. 58, 59, 282. London: Faber.

WILLIAMS, GLANVILLE (1960). Foreword. In Jenkins, Alice, *Law for the Rich.* London: Gollancz.

CHAPTER IV

THERAPEUTIC PROCEDURES AND THE SANCTITY OF LIFE

JOHN BEATTIE[1]

There is no other discipline in medicine which carries with it so much moral and ethical responsibility as obstetrics and gynaecology. The two subjects bristle with problems and the onus on the doctor is great, for he has the authority to guide his patients and their families in such fundamental matters as contraception, artificial insemination, therapeutic abortion and sterilisation. The obstetrician is concerned with human life in a way that no other doctor is.

The general ethical standard in British Medicine in relation to these two subjects is high. Careful ethical treatment in the past has always safeguarded the interests of the unborn child as well as the reproductive abilities of the mother. The Christian outlook which has hitherto strongly influenced medical standards is always concerned to support such concepts as the sanctity of life, the intrinsic value and rights of the unborn foetus, the intimate relationship between husband and wife and the individual rights of each member of the partnership. Modern subversive influences are now belittling the old ideals and it is no wonder that earlier concepts have been thrown into the melting pot and who can tell what new versions will emerge? It is right constantly to reconsider old standards in the light of modern discovery. On the other hand, the Christian's faith is in a changeless God and whatever new knowledge may be granted to us, man in his due relation to God, and to his fellow men and women, does not alter. It is our duty to respect what is fundamental in human life, while learning to adapt new discoveries to the good of both the individual and the community at large.

Despite the tremendous pressures brought to bear in obstetrical and gynaecological problems, the Christian doctor is not left to himself in making decisions. In Biblical teaching he has principles to guide him. God made man in His own image, but man possesses within him the fatal tendency to set up his own false

[1]John Beattie, M.D., F.R.C.S., F.R.C.O.G., Consulting Obstetrician and Gynaecologist, St. Bartholomew's Hospital, London.

standards. Marriage was designed to be a lasting and fruitful companionship between one man and one woman who live together in mutual respect and love. Children belong to the home created by husband and wife in which they grow to physiological and psychological maturity. It is such basic concepts as these which have shaped and should continue to shape our views on the control of human life.

ABORTION

The English law with regard to abortion stems from two separate Acts. In 1861, the Offences against Persons Act gave protection in law to the unborn foetus. The Infant Life (Preservation) Act of 1929 states that the act of causing the death of the child must be done in good faith and only for preserving the life of the mother. These Acts were clarified in 1938 by Mr. Justice Macnaughton's summing up in the now renowned case of Rex v. Bourne. This arose from the case of a girl of 14 who became pregnant as a result of rape by a soldier while she was held down by five others. Mr. Bourne, an eminent gynaecologist, considered that the continuation of the pregnancy would result in the girl becoming a mental or physical wreck. The Attorney General suggested at the trial that the Act of 1861 does not permit of the termination of pregnancy except for the purpose of preserving the life of the mother. Mr. Justice Macnaughton said that those words should be construed in a reasonable sense: if the doctor is of the opinion, on reasonable grounds and with adequate knowledge, that the probable consequences of the continuation of pregnancy would make the woman a physical or a mental wreck, then he operates, in that honest belief, for preserving the life of the mother.

It has been upheld in the law courts, since the case of Rex v. Bourne, that, provided the doctor's views about the threat to life are honest, they need not necessarily be correct. It is generally agreed that if two competent medical practitioners decide that the physical or mental health and, therefore, the life itself of a pregnant woman is jeopardised, the termination of her pregnancy will be within the law.

In recent years, considerable pressure has been coming from various bodies to urge clarification of the law with regard to abortion. In this way, it is hoped to make the therapeutic indications more certain so that the reputable medical practitioner may have no doubts at all, if he acts in good faith, that there will be no objection in law to the abortion he performs.

Eugenic Considerations

Since the thalidomide disaster and the discovery that rubella in early pregnancy carries with it a real risk of foetal abnormality, there are many who think the law should be made to allow termination of pregnancy when there is a grave risk of foetal abnormality. At present, there is no legal justification for terminating a pregnancy on purely eugenic grounds and, if this is to be allowed, ethical problems arise which are specific to the foetus and not the mother. Many pregnancies have been terminated in this country because of the possibility of an abnormal foetus. Until now it has been done if the mother is greatly distressed at knowing that the risk of congenital abnormality exists. It is then considered that her health and therefore her life are threatened. This psychological trauma is usually a sum of fear for the unhappiness of a deformed child, distress at the contemplation of the effect on herself, the father and other members of the family, and also possible financial burdens.

In the case of rubella of a severe type affecting the pregnant woman in the earliest weeks of pregnancy, there is a 20 per cent risk of grave foetal abnormality. This percentage risk decreases rapidly after the eighth week of intra-uterine life. If termination of pregnancy is to be carried out on the basis of a 1 in 5 risk, then four normal babies have to be destroyed to save the birth of a single baby with a congenital abnormality, either mild or severe. This is a sobering thought and the operation should not be undertaken lightly.

The unborn foetus, despite the arguments about when it becomes a living soul or a personality, has a right to survival. If it were possible for the child to decide, it might well prefer to be born deformed than be destroyed in the uterus. It is, therefore, a formidable undertaking to kill the possibly deformed, unconsulted child-to-be, on the grounds that it is in its own interests to be destroyed.

It has been suggested that the law should be altered to allow therapeutic abortion to be carried out when a pregnancy results from intercourse of a criminal nature, such as rape or incest but, if the child or woman thus attacked is physically and psychologically damaged sufficiently to cause a danger to her health or life, the indication is already allowed at the present time. On the other hand, there must be the greatest sympathy for anyone submitted to rape or incest and some propose that a child who has been raped should have prophylactic curettage performed in case she has conceived. If these assaults have occurred upon women of poor intelligence or low mental development, it is hard to assume that they should have to suffer as a result of the act and, in any case, the progeny resulting from incest may be of doubtful genetic stock.

It has also been suggested that pregnancy should be ended if the health of the patient or the social conditions in which she is living (including the social conditions of her existing children) make it unsuitable for her to assume legal and moral responsibility for caring for a child or another child. If this became law, it would certainly make therapeutic abortion much more common but it is very doubtful if this would be right.

Many gynaecologists, who view with apprehension an alteration of the law to make it easier to evacuate the uterus, consider that it should never be done without the opinion of two expert medical practitioners or after review by a panel of experts interested in the subject. If termination must occur as an emergency, it has been suggested that someone in authority, such as the coroner, should be informed. It is the opinion also of some that therapeutic abortion should be done preferably in a National Health Hospital or without the charge of a fee by the surgeon concerned.

Over the last 30 years, the treatment of many conditions which previously were looked upon as a danger to the pregnant woman, has become so successful that the indications for therapeutic abortion are becoming less and less common. The main indication at present is psychiatric illness and the severity of this and the prognosis are very difficult to assess. Some psychiatrists are much more willing to advise termination than others but clinical research on this problem is being carried out in many places and there is little doubt that the subject will be further clarified soon. The experienced doctor knows well that, in the early weeks of an unwanted pregnancy, the mother, who has a low blood pressure, great lassitude and possibly nausea as well, cannot accurately judge her permanent reaction to the pregnancy and many recover in the last five months and then face, with equanimity, the arrival of the baby. It is also now widely recognised that termination of pregnancy, even in a single woman, may produce a guilt complex which will result in psychological damage which is worse than would have occurred if termination had not taken place.

Many psychiatrists, in consultation with the gynaecologist, will agree to admit a distressed, pregnant woman to a hospital and treat her there until after the child is born. This method often produces a most satisfactory result.

The Roman Catholic attitude to therapeutic abortion is well known for it is never allowed *per primam*. The Church of Rome teaches that all unbaptised infants and foetuses are for ever excluded from participation in God's divinity and in the Beatific Vision reserved for those who have been baptised (Healy, 1956. Cf. Marshall, 1960). According to this doctrine, nobody has any right to be instrumental in excluding an unborn infant from participating in God's divinity.

The Protestant Christian approach finds no teaching in the Bible to uphold this doctrine. The birth, crucifixion, resurrection and ascension of Jesus Christ took place in order to save for eternity all those who believe and put their trust in Him. If this is so, it would be a strange and unjust thing if a foetus dying as a result of abortion, spontaneous, therapeutic or criminal, was relegated, before it could have power to reason or make a decision, to some place where it was excluded from the privileges of the Christian whose spirit returns to God.

It is perhaps relevant to consider the vexed question of viability of the foetus. There is no doubt that the child is entirely dependent upon the mother until the umbilical cord is severed, the lungs expand and respiration becomes normal and physiological. The foetal heart is beating long before it can be heard as a transmitted impulse through the mother's abdomen and movements occur before the mother has the sensation known as quickening. Some obstetricians strongly object to removing the foetus after the twelfth week of intra-uterine life when it is becoming more and more to look like a baby. They prefer to destroy the foetus in the early embryonic stage, but there is no difference at all in the act for, in all cases, the foetus is being destroyed and the life taken from it. The legal view is that viability starts at the twenty-eighth week of intra-uterine life, at which time there is a slender chance of survival after birth.

There is no direct teaching in the Bible specifically advising for or against therapeutic abortion. The sixth commandment (Exod. xx. 13)—'Thou shalt not kill'—certainly applies in ordinary life but almost every Christian doctor, other than the Roman Catholic, believes that it is justifiable to destroy a foetus before it is viable, in order to save the life of the mother. The difficulty is to be certain that the mother's life is in jeopardy, and there is no doubt that many therapeutic abortions are done unnecessarily.

There is instruction in Exodus xxi. 22, about what should happen if a pregnant woman was injured accidentally in a fight and a miscarriage occurred. This happening was to be punished with a fine only, whereas, if the woman herself was injured, the punishment varied according to the degree. The law seems to suggest that the life of the mother is of immensely greater importance than that of the foetus.

From time to time measures are brought before Parliament, as in the Bill (Steele, 1966) which is still *sub judice*, which propose the extension of grounds for therapeutic abortion. Experienced gynaecologists have often emphasised that such measures, unless very conservative, may only alter for the worse a situation best left to the responsible practitioner to decide purely on clinical grounds and within the present law.

Criminal Abortion

It is impossible to say what is the incidence of criminal abortion in this country. Figures suggested vary between 50,000 and 100,000 per annum (Goodhead, 1964). This assessment is almost certainly too high, for such abortions are often carried out under poor aseptic technique and yet only 63 registered deaths from criminal abortion occurred in 1958. It is true that very many complicated cases following criminal abortion are treated in reputable surroundings but the unrecorded incidence of pelvic disease, sterility and ill-health as a result of criminal abortion must be high.

There is no justification for doing a therapeutic abortion in reputable surroundings on the ground that, if it were not done, the patient would threaten to go and have it done under other circumstances.

In considering alteration of the law on abortion in order to make it easier for a woman to have her pregnancy terminated for social reasons, it is relevant to consider the results of this action in other countries. In Hungary, legal abortion is allowed before the twelfth week of pregnancy, virtually at the request of the patient. In 1950, before abortion was legalised, 1,700 operations of this nature were performed and, by 1959, the figure had risen to 152,000. The birth rate fell by 50,000 a year and the abortion rate became greater than the birth rate. It is also reported that the proven criminal abortion rate was not much reduced and that many women became pregnant again within nine months. The mortality rate was 6 per 100,000 abortions, so that nine women lost their lives in one year. The morbidity rate is not reported. Similar figures can be obtained from other countries and it is obvious that contraceptive techniques are infinitely superior as a method of controlling the birth rate. Somewhat similar laws exist in Sweden, East Germany and other European countries but, in recent years, there has been a move towards a more restrictive policy.

In Japan, in 1948, because of the immense population explosion and the incidence of criminal abortion, a law was passed to legalise abortion for health and social reasons. In this way, the number of legal abortions reported rose to more than a million a year. This, together with propaganda on birth control, reduced the birth rate from 34.3 per thousand of population in 1947 to 16.9 per thousand in 1961 which is, at present, the seventh lowest rate in the world. Thus, liberalisation of existing laws on abortion can carry a grave danger to the age structure of the population of a country, not to mention the flood gates which open as a result of the lowering of the moral standards of society.

With all the data which is now available, it is the opinion of many that the English law as it stands at present should not be greatly liberalised. The possible exception is that, for proven rape and incest. and for eugenic reasons when it can be proved that the risk of congenital abnormality in the baby is extremely high, as in some cases of mongolism, it might be wise to allow termination of pregnancy.

CONTRACEPTION

From the ethical point of view, it is necessary to consider this subject from several aspects. There is the family problem in a society which is affluent and in which the country at least pays lip service to Christian doctrine. There is the fact that starvation in the world is probably the greatest single menace to survival, for 10,000 deaths from this occur daily and it has been calculated that one person in every two in the world is badly nourished and one in three is always hungry. The present population explosion is so great that the spectre of increasing starvation looms large. These factors should have a direct bearing on the question of not only how contraception should be taught in all parts of the world, but also what means should be adopted.

The Family Problem

Apart from the Roman Catholic Church, almost all Christians now consider that there is no contra-indication in the Bible teaching to the controlling of conception by married couples. The Christian ideal of marriage is stated in Genesis and is confirmed by the teaching of Jesus Christ (Matt. xix; Mark x.). It should be a permanent and exclusive companionship between man and woman which is to be blessed by the arrival of children and the responsibilities of parenthood. The sex act is fundamentally the fulfilment of a physical need and to assume that it has no function apart from the procreation of children is to suggest that in man it has only a utilitarian capacity.

The Protestant Church in recent times has begun to encourage family planning in an intelligent way. There are many facets to this subject which are relevant in the ethical approach to it. Selfishness in preventing pregnancy in the first few years of marriage often leads to disappointment and frustration as the wife is becoming less fertile in direct relation to increasing age. On the other hand if, in modern society, a wife becomes pregnant repeatedly, her health and the social structure of the family may well deteriorate. Much marital unhappiness stems from a woman being frightened of repeated pregnancies which may make her frigid and frustrate her husband as well.

In Britain, the replacement of population requires an average of 2.3 children per family. As most women marry under the age of 25, contraception is employed by almost every married couple. The maternal mortality has been reduced greatly in the last 30 years and now stands at 0.25 per thousand live and still-births. In 1963, the maternal mortality was twice the average in women between 35 and 40 and four times the average over the age of 40. Maternal mortality doubles in women having the fifth baby and quadruples at the sixth and subsequent pregnancies. The control of fertility in relation to these classes of women has an important bearing on the overall maternal mortality. This also applies to the figures of perinatal foetal mortality which is highest in the woman pregnant for the fifth time and over.

The World Problem

The present world population is 3,400 million and it is increasing by 70 millions per year, and should be doubled within the next 35 years. This growth is greatest in the less developed countries where there is a fall in mortality, both maternal and foetal, due to improving social and medical standards, but there is still a sustained high level of fertility. This level remains twice as high in Latin America, Africa and Asia compared with the rest of the world.

Because of the tremendous fall in infant mortality, about 40 to 50 per cent of the population are under 15 years old which imposes an impossibly heavy economic burden on the adult community for the provision of food, clothing and housing. In India, the population explosion produces three-quarters of a million new mouths to feed every month.

This presents a real problem in relation to the spread of contraceptive techniques in these highly fertile communities with starvation threatening to produce a huge mortality on its own.   The problem was summed up by Julian Huxley (1958) as follows:
' It is surely the height of immorality to condemn hundreds of millions of human beings existing and yet unborn to a sub-standard existence in the strength of religious convictions and doctrines, when family limitation holds out the only hope of lesser misery and greater possibilities of human fulfilment '.

There is an ethical side in regard to which method of contraception should be employed for it is important to be sure that any method advised should not produce damage to the individual— whether temporary, delayed or permanent.

ARTIFICIAL INSEMINATION

This method of fertilisation by artificial means, when using the husband's semen, presents no real ethical and Christian problem. A.I.H. is used when the husband is impotent and, for some mechanical or psychogenic reason, is unable to ejaculate seminal fluid into the vagina. It may be indicated if normal intercourse causes severe pain to the wife and sometimes the seminal fluid is introduced into the cervical canal if there is evidence of a hostility of the wife's secretion towards an insufficient quantity of the male semen.

The use of A.I.H. in cases of male impotence, due to a psychogenic cause, may in fact produce a complete cure when the husband knows that, as a result of A.I.H., his wife is at last pregnant.   There may be a moral objection to A.I.H. in that the husband's seminal fluid is sometimes produced by masturbation but this is not always necessary. The generally accepted medical view on the evils of masturbation has altered in recent years and it is now believed that this act, on such an occasion, does no psychological or physical harm. The Christian must find it difficult to criticise coitus interruptus or masturbation associated with coitus in order to provide a specimen of seminal fluid for the purpose of A.I.H.

Some may hold, on Christian principle, that, if two are joined together in marriage, in the sight of God, and thus become ' one flesh ', and if they are not blessed with progeny in the ordinary way, they should accept this as God's will. On the other hand, medical science and advancement of knowledge in all matters of health and, in this instance, in problems of infertility, can be looked upon as a gift from a beneficent God, and A.I.H. may be viewed in this regard.

A.I.D.

If a husband is sterile and the married couple desire children, the usual course is to adopt a family which is usually a great success. On the other hand, the couple may much prefer to have a baby which is at least half their own. For this reason, artificial insemination by donor is often desired and frequently proposed by the husband himself who usually enjoys a normal sex life with his wife, but is unable to fertilise her ovum. There is, sometimes, a request for A.I.D. when the husband is likely to hand on a genetic abnormality if he has a child of his own. Those who ask for A.I.D. are usually educated, intelligent and thoughtful people.

It is unwise to use donor semen belonging to a relative or friend of the husband and wife because the offspring produced thereby is liable to cause emotional and psychological reactions on the part of the mother, her husband and the donor, which are dangerous. All who agree with this practice advise that the donor semen should come from a source quite unknown to the husband and wife and which should never be revealed. This immediately brings in an atmosphere of secrecy to the project and the doctor becomes heavily involved. He possesses the key to a secret which might well cause repercussions in future years. When the child is born, the doctor who delivers it must sign the birth certificate and, if he states that the husband is the father of the child, he is committing perjury. For this reason some doctors who agree with A.I.D. will carry out the process and refuse to deliver the child. This is done by another doctor who does not know the facts and, therefore, he signs the birth certificate in good faith but his statement

G

is not correct. This is a calculated deception and obviously unethical.

The Legal Problem

The following statement in British Obstetrical and Gynaecological Practice is made:

' At the moment, there is no general agreement, and there have been few cases in Great Britain when the problem has been tested, and in the United States there have been conflicting decisions '.

In the case of Maclennan and Maclennan in 1958, it was held that A.I.D. did not amount to adultery although the opposite view was given in 1921 in Orford and Orford. It has even been suggested by some that the doctor who performed A.I.D. might be looked upon in law as having committed adultery. He might also be liable on the grounds of conspiracy.

Vaisey and Willink (1948) in considering the legal implications of A.I.D. in its many aspects, write as follows:

' We find a strange inconsistency in the principle that married couples desirous of ostensible issue should be permitted by the law to achieve their object by the insemination of the wife aliunde, but not permitted to do so by the concealed introduction of a child begotten by the husband but born of a woman other than the wife, whether normally or artificially by means of his services as " donor ". We cannot think that the advocates of A.I.D. would consider the latter expedient to be justified. To our minds, it is no better and no worse than the other '.

Sociological and Eugenic Problems

The practice of A.I.D. has been pursued for too short a time to assess accurately the possible sociological effects. Indeed, it may well be impossible to find this out even in the future because the whole subject is necessarily surrounded with secrecy and most experts are adamant that the child, born as a result of A.I.D., should never know that this has occurred.

The eugenic aftermath of A.I.D. depends, in some ways, on how often it is practised and how many children are sired by any one individual donor. There is a remote risk, in the presence of such secrecy, of progeny of A.I.D. marrying, in ignorance, a close relation as they may have stemmed from the same forbear.

If A.I.D. is allowed to become widespread there is another aspect of the eugenic problem which has been considered by Dr. Julian Huxley (1958) who writes as follows:

' The perfection of birth control technique has made the separation (between " love " and " reproduction ") more effective; and the still more recent technique of artificial insemination has opened up new horizons by making it possible to provide different objects for the two functions. It is now open to man and woman to consummate the sexual function with those whom, on perhaps quite other grounds, they admire. This consequence is the opportunity of eugenics. But the opportunity cannot yet be grasped. It is first necessary to overcome the bitter opposition to it on dogmatic theological and moral grounds, and the widespread popular shrinking from it, based on vague but powerful feelings, on the ground that it is unnatural . . . unless we alter the social framework of law and ideas so as to make possible the divorce between sex and reproduction or, if you prefer it, between the individual and the social sides of our sexual functions, our efforts at evolutionary improvement will remain mere tinkering . . .'

Following the same theme, the mind boggles at the possible repercussions consequent upon such freedom in human breeding and the consequences, say, of A.I.D. employed on the unmarried woman, the attempt at raising a race of supermen, or the imbalance which could be produced by alterations of the physiological proportion of the two sexes.

Biological Aspects

Many married couples who are sterile accept the fact and adjust their lives to the disappointment, and thus become greater companions to each other as a result. Others cannot adjust and tension and unhappiness develop which may end in severe incompatibility and divorce.

If A.I.D. is decided upon because the husband is at fault, the practice of mixing the donated semen with that of the husband, in case he should be the father, is unlikely to comfort any intelligent man. With the adopted child, despite an upbringing in a happy family environment, unpleasant traits in character may appear and this produces great stress in the couple concerned. The same may happen in the child produced by A.I.D.

The law in this country, in relation to A.I.D. is so uncertain and unproven that subsequent legislation may well affect adversely the peace of mind at any rate of the wife who has given birth to a child for her husband by this means.

The foregoing brief assessment of the complications which surround childbirth by means of A.I.D. will suffice to emphasise that any deviation from the methods of normal physiological reproduction carries with it grave emotional, psychological and moral risks.

Christian Ethics in Relation to A.I.D.

The great majority of gynaecologists in Great Britain will refuse to take any active part in A.I.D., but, if a married couple demand this, they are usually referred to some expert who is prepared to do it for them. If A.I.D. is thought to be morally wrong, it is inconsistent for such a person to aid and abet in the act by referring the couple elsewhere without first explaining the contrary views. The whole process is so hedged around by secrecy and legal, psychological, sociological and theological problems that the average specialist, even although not a professing Christian, will have nothing to do with it.

Vaisey and Willink (1948) in their final remarks on the legal aspects of artificial insemination produced in the report of the Commission appointed by the Archbishop of Canterbury, make the following statement: ' In our view, the evils necessarily involved in A.I.D. are so grave that early consideration should be given to the framing of legislation to make the practice a criminal offence.'

There remains to be considered the special view of the professing Christian whose desire is to walk in God's law and according to the teaching of the Bible. Although all will have great sympathy with a couple who intelligently request A.I.D. and will, in no way, judge them, it is likely that two married people who are followers of Jesus Christ will quickly realise that the process of A.I.D. is against moral and ethical laws in relation to marriage. If man is body, soul and spirit and the spirit returns to God Who gave it because it is His, then man is not an end in himself. He should try to conform during his life to God's teaching about marriage as about everything else. In marriage the three functions comprise procreation, union and ' society, help and comfort ' and this should be achieved by the granting of reciprocal rights over each other, and they become ' one flesh '.

Other than from the legal viewpoint, it is difficult to argue that adultery is committed in the ordinary sense of the word when a donated semen is inserted into the vagina of a married woman by the request of her husband, but the act is surely contrary to accepted marriage laws based upon the Bible and, if this is so, a Christian cannot accept it as a method of procreation.

STERILISATION

The operation of sterilisation in the human female is carried out by division or removal of the Fallopian tubes with conservation of the ovaries so that the sexual characteristics are not altered in any way. Although there is an operation devised to produce temporary sterility which can be reversed by a second operation, it is not an accurate method and, therefore, all operations for sterilisation are, normally speaking, irrevocable. Because of this the operation should be advised as seldom as possible and only after careful consideration.

The Medical Aspect

The operation of sterilisation in the female is not entirely without risk and carries with it a mortality rate of about 0.13 per cent. It is almost 100 per cent successful in producing absolute sterility and, therefore, it is a safe method of contraception.

If modern methods of contraception were completely safe, there would be almost no need for sterilisation to be performed. The frequency with which it is done varies in different centres in Great Britain. When pregnancy constitutes a considerable danger to the woman as, for example, after repeated Caesarean sections have been performed, sterilisation is often advised to avoid the risk of failure in normal contraceptive technique.

In the city of Aberdeen, in the years 1961 to 1963, the incidence of sterilisation in the post-partum period was 4.5 per cent, which is higher than at most centres in this country. The indications were serious medical conditions which made further pregnancy dangerous, and general debility due to rapid and excessive childbearing. Sterilisation is sometimes indicated when contraception has repeatedly failed and the patient is worn out with childbearing and psychologically disturbed by the fear of further pregnancies.

The Eugenic Aspect

Sterilisation on eugenic grounds is a much more debatable subject. It has been suggested that this treatment should be available for mental defectives, those with mental diseases and carriers of grave physical disabilities. Congenital disorders are often carried by recessive genes so that an abnormal person may have a normal child or the disease may be transmitted by an apparently normal person. This makes a decision as to sterilisation most difficult. The Brook report in 1934 recommended voluntary sterilisation for these patients.

Compulsory and punitive sterilisation has nothing to recommend it either for the protection of society or for genetic improvement of the race.

The Social Aspect

Sterilisation can be employed by a State in an attempt to control a population increase which cannot be dealt with by ordinary contraceptive techniques and which constitutes a menace to the economy and welfare of the nation. Voluntary sterilisation in India has been instituted by the Government in an attempt to control a population which may well grow from 438 millions in 1961 to 625 millions in 1976. If such sterilisation is allowed only after a couple have completed a family of four or more, it is doubtful whether this will solve the general problem of over-population.

The Legal Aspect

In the Offences Against the Person Act of 1861, the operation of sterilisation is probably included, with others, in the warning 'whosoever shall unlawfully and maliciously wound or inflict grievous bodily harm' but, apart from this, the law is silent.

Legal opinion has often been taken on this subject and the general consensus of opinion is as quoted in the Annual Report for 1961 of the Medical Defence Union as follows:

'Having regard to the opinions that have been expressed by English and Scottish Counsel, it would seem that the propriety or otherwise of performing a sterilising operation can be summarised as follows:

1. sterilisation on therapeutic grounds would be upheld by the Court;
2. sterilisation on well founded eugenic grounds would also be upheld by the Court;
3. sterilisation carried out merely on the ground of personal convenience (*e.g.* of a husband or a wife solely as a convenient method of birth control) might not be upheld by the Court, and
4. Where there was a clear element of moral turpitude and damage to the public interest (*e.g.* sterilisation of a prostitute for her convenience) the operation would, in all possibility, be condemned by the Court'.

The Ethical Aspect

The Christian approach to sterilisation is concerned with the fact that, except in special circumstances, it is an irrevocable operation which can well be abused. The operation is not to be entirely condemned although the Roman Catholic teaching will not allow it even if a pregnancy will directly endanger the life of the mother. If, however, hysterectomy is required to eradicate disease, then no objection is raised to the sterilisation which necessarily occurs and which forms an example of the Roman Catholic doctrine of 'double effect'.

It is wise to have two expert opinions before sterilisation is agreed to and both partners of the marriage must not only agree but must thoroughly understand the background, finality and repercussions which surround such a serious therapeutic action.

REFERENCES

GOODHEAD, C. B. (1964). *Eug. Rev.* **55**, 197.

HEALEY, E. F. (1956). *Medical Ethics*, pp. 357, 358. Chicago: Loyola University Press.

HUXLEY, JULIAN (1958). In WILLIAMS G. *Sanctity of Life in the Common Law*, p. 72. London: Faber.

MARSHALL, JOHN (1960). *The Ethics of Medical Practice*, pp. 152, 153. London: Darton, Longman & Todd.

VAISEY, W. *et al.* (1948). *Artificial Human Insemination.* London: S.P.C.K.

CHAPTER V

POPULATION CONTROL

DANIEL A. ANDERSEN and PAUL W. BRAND[1]

Introduction

Professor A. V. Hill in his Presidential Address before the Royal Society some years ago took this theme—'We all agree that we should not do evil that good may come, but I now ask the question should we do good if its predictable consequences are evil?' This is an interesting and very challenging subject and one which was obviously directed very largely at what many people have called 'the do-gooders' around the world, who come into a situation which they do not fully understand and disturb the existing balance of affairs, sometimes correcting one evil but perhaps opening the way to other and greater evils. It may seriously be argued that the next World War will be caused, not by the clash of political ideologies, but by the World Health Organisation and by Medical Missions, and that the war will not be a war of conquest but one of extermination; a hungry and over-populated country will be trying desperately to take over the fertile lands of its neighbours. The reason for the hunger and the reason for the excessive numbers will be that malaria has been eradicated and that preventive medicine has doubled the survival rate of babies without reducing the number that are born.

There are many Christian missionary doctors who think that it is not their business to consider the remote consequences of what they do. They hold that we should make sure that we are doing good and then we can leave the consequences to God. But can we really avoid responsibility? We are missionaries going unasked into a new environment where, over the centuries, an equilibrium has been reached—an equilibrium between life and death and between human needs and the resources of nature. If we by our initiative are going to invade that situation and alter the equilibrium then at the same time we must accept the respon-

[1]Daniel A. Andersen, M.D., F.R.C.S., D.T.M. & H., is Hon. Research Fellow, Institute of Urology & University College, London, Adviser, Medical Missionary Affairs Salvation Army; Professor Paul W. Brand, C.B.E., M.B., B.S., F.R.C.S., is Director of the Surgery of Rehabilitation in the Public Health Hospital, Carville, Louisiana, and formerly Professor of Orthopaedic Surgery and Principal, Christian Medical College, Vellore, India.

sibility for the effect of our actions and also of seeing that secondary harmful results do not follow the good that we seek to do.

If we are working in an over-populated country, this means that we should not significantly decrease the death rate without associating ourselves in some way with an attempt to diminish the birth rate.

There are some who feel that we can evade the immediate responsibility, or at least pass it on to the next generation, by pointing out that there are still such untapped resources of food production, that the world can still support a continuing increase for a few more years. Perhaps this is true, but come with us to Calcutta and to some of the other centres of world over-population and see the squalor and the teeming ant-like existence of millions, and ask yourself the question—' Is food the only problem? ' What is the ideal towards which we are working? What is the ' good life '? Does God want us to aim for a ' standing room only ', multi-purpose food concentrate kind of life? Surely we are not alone in thinking that the world is already vastly over-populated, that in God's good world there should be space as well as food, that it should be possible to escape sometimes and be alone with nature and with God! Men were never meant to live pressed and crowded together without the possibility of escape, where the suffocating pressures of teeming humanity breed squalor even in the absence of hunger and where crime and violence multiply as human dignity and personality decays. No! If we are working towards a better world it is not part of our task to multiply life. We are concerned with the quality of men's lives, not with their quantity.

Now, lest we seem to be critical of medical missionary effort, or even to blame it for the population explosion, we must hasten to say that Christian medical missions by and large have been making a fine and constructive contribution to the problems of the over-populated countries.

For us Christians it is worth noticing that the Lord Jesus Christ Himself never seemed anxious to multiply life or even to eradicate disease. His objective was always to help a person rather than to attack a bacillus. Medical missions are sometimes criticised by International Health Agencies and by Government Health Ministries for spending too much on treating patients and not enough on big schemes of preventive medicine. The very method of the medical missionary, motivated by compassion, makes it unlikely that he will seriously disturb the balance of life where he works. By living in the villages he becomes conscious of all the needs of his patients. He feels not only the pain of their sickness, but the hunger of the children and the poverty of the soil that forces even the infirm to toil beyond their strength. The family that accepts with gratitude the life of the child he has saved, will listen while he explains why they should wait before any more children are born. The same mission that has sent the doctor probably has an agriculturalist nearby to help the villager to make the best of his fields and water. This kind of help is broadly based, and is centred on the felt needs of human individuals. If this changes any equilibrium, it replaces it with a new and better equilibrium.

If the world population equilibrium has been upset, it is not the dedicated physician in the jungle hospital who is to blame, it is the pharmaceutical industry, its research chemists and its salesmen and the high pressure disease eradication campaigns of W.H.O. It is reasonable, therefore, that the world should look to the same sources for the answer to the problem. Chemical fertilisers for the soil, the contraceptive pill, these may be the beginning of an answer, but no physical or chemical agent can be effective until the uneducated people in the village realise their need of it and are willing to accept it. It is here that the missionary working in the village may often be of vital assistance because he, by his passionate and realistic approach, has earned a confidence in the village that no touring team has ever enjoyed.

Some Historical and Economic Considerations

If we are to consider how to deal as effectively as possible with the acute problem which the population explosion now presents in the under-developed countries, we will be well advised to consider its economic origins.

According to the scanty information provided by excavations before 6,000 to 7,000 B.C., the fairly scattered groups of people lived as primitive hunters or fishermen and gathered wild fruit and vegetables. The total population at this time has been variously estimated at between 2 to 20 million and the density of population probably did not exceed 2.5 persons to 2 square miles.

The Agricultural Revolution followed the discovery of agriculture and domestication of animals. The period from the earliest agricultural society up to the beginning of the industrial revolution in 1750 is characterised by a gradual rise of world population. While correct records were not kept, the information available suggests that there was a fairly constant pattern in the structure and movements of birth and death rates. Crude birth rates were high throughout this time, reaching between 35 to 50 per thousand, and crude death rates were also very high, though normally lower than the birth rate, reaching to between 30 to 40 per thousand. This resulted in the growth of the population of 5-10 per thousand (0.5 to 1.0 per cent) per year.

The infant mortality was high and the recurrent catastrophies brought about by war, pestilence and famine all tended to reduce the increase of population. It is estimated that the world population by 1760 was about 750 million, a rise of 730 million in 25 centuries.

The term ' population explosion ' is justified when we compare this figure of 750 million with the rise in the next two centuries to 2,500 million. The present rate of overall increase, unless checked, will result in a population of about 4,000 million by the end of the present century. This extraordinary explosion did not take place simultaneously all over the globe, but started in Europe with the Industrial Revolution.

With the Industrial Revolution came a fairly rapid increase in the economic level of the general population (contrasted with the few rich and the many poor in earlier eras). It initiated the modern era with its rapid advance in agriculture, industry and science, including hygiene and medicine.

The crude death rate was reduced and was gradually pushed down to 15 per thousand. This was associated with a drastic reduction in infant mortality. These factors, combined with the control of many diseases and a higher standard of living, led to a major rise in the average life expectancy from below 30 in the primitive agricultural society to over 60 in modern industrial countries. Such changes inevitably led to major increases in the population at the beginning of the Industrial Revolution as this reached the different countries, the death rate falling while the birth rate remained high.

However, after a ' lag period ' the birth rate has consistently shown a fall in the highly industrial countries (Cipolla, 1963), although with considerable variation in the ' lag period '. For example, in England and Wales the crude birth rate in 1755 was 35.0 while in 1950 it was 15.9. The crude death rate was 30 in

1755 and 11.6 in 1950, so the net result was a lower rate of increase in the population at the end of the period. By this means the population has been 'levelled off' in the developed countries. More recently, as the general economic level has reached still higher, there has been a new rise in the birth rate in highly industrialised countries, but this does not alter the general argument relating to the earlier phases.

The Factors at Work

There are two important practical questions to be considered in seeking to apply this historical knowledge to the present problem of world population in India and other under-developed countries:

1. What factors caused the fall of the birth rate in industrial areas?

2. What factors affected the ' lag period ' before the fall began?

The causes of the reduction of the birth rate are difficult to define and probably multiple, but when we consider that the fall in the birth rate started in England and Wales in 1870 (Cipolla, 1963) it can hardly be due to the modern methods of birth control. It appears probable that a major—perhaps *the* major—factor was the *intention* to have smaller families as standards of living rose and families raised their status in society; that is, they wanted better houses, better amenities and better education for their children. All these desirable things led to the intention to have smaller families. The ' time lag ' before the birth rate began to fall was about 90 years in England—1780 to 1870—and it was the early part of this period which gave rise to the gloomy prognostications of Malthus in 1798—and apparently with good cause, as the death rate fell fairly rapidly from 1780 to 1870, while the birth rate was steady—a state of affairs similar to that in under-developed countries today. Possibly an explanation of the ' time lag ' is the period required for the improvement in the economic level to reach a sufficient number in the population in order to bring about a general effect.

A further study of the causes influencing these two factors could be of major importance in determining the long-term view and correct approach in controlling the present rate of increase in the population.

The Special Problem in the Under-developed Countries

A totally new situation has arisen in the last 150 years affecting the under-developed countries and destroying the balance of the population which had previously been achieved in earlier periods during the gradual development of the present industrial societies.

Modern countries, having acquired the technical ability to control disease and lower the death rate substantially, have felt a humanitarian urge to assist societies still basically agricultural. The accumulated knowledge of disease control slowly acquired in the last 150 years, and the gradual lowering of the death rate of the developing western countries during this time has been, in the relatively short time of the last 50 years, applied widely to the mainly agricultural countries, resulting in the rapid fall in the death rate, most marked in the reduction of infant and child mortality which were previously very high. As fertility and birth rates have not been affected, this had led to an 'agricultural society' type of level in the birth rate of over 40 per thousand, with an 'industrial society' death rate of 15 to 20 per thousand, producing a difference of about 25 per thousand, and an increase in the population of about 2·5 per cent per annum. This has resulted, and will continue to result unless adequate measures are taken, in a phenomenal and dangerous increase in the population at a rate faster than the anticipated increase of food provided by improvement in agriculture.

There is basically only one solution to the problem, as it is not possible for these countries to 'put the clock back', and that is to hurry up the development of the industrial society in under-developed countries, so that the same factors which caused the reduction of the birth rate in the present industrial countries, will have a similar effect as early as possible. This provides the real basis for the long term solution to the population explosion in under-developed countries, and is of fundamental importance. It answers the serious objection, already mentioned, of some critics of the 'do-gooders' of all kinds. The solution is not to stop 'doing good', but to do more good more quickly and in a wider sphere of activity. This certainly includes the maintenance and development of mission and other hospitals and dispensaries, of agricultural colleges and demonstration farm, and educational work of all kinds. However, we realise that this is a long-term solution and leaves a dangerous problem of unknown duration. If the 'time lag' equals that of Great Britain historically, there will still be a period of increasing population for at least 50 years (Cipolla, 1963) which, at the present rate of increase, would more than double the population. Even with an increased tempo of economic advance, the problem cannot be left to be solved by the gradual increase in the economic level.

PROPOSED MEASURES

The immediate problem, therefore, is that short-term measures must be taken to shorten this ' time lag ' and provide the necessary food supplies to meet the increase in population which is already inevitable. These measures can be considered under three headings:

1. Measures to increase the *available food supplies*.
2. Education, especially in the teen-age and young adult groups to inculcate the intention to have smaller-spaced families, as well as to teach appropriate methods.
3. The direct attack on the problem by Family Planning Clinics.

Possibly the first method will bring about the earliest results, as the other two methods have a long latent interval before they can be extensive enough to achieve significant results.

Considering these three methods in order—

Food Supplies

It is the opinion of one of the authors that, in the area of India in which he worked (the Deccan), it will be easier in the next 10 years to increase the agricultural output significantly than to reduce the rise in population. An effort to do this is being made by the major irrigation projects started by the Government; but even when the present plans are completed, only 20 per cent of the arable area will be provided with irrigation. It seems to be of equal importance, therefore, to increase minor and local efforts to conserve and utilise existing water supplies better. This area, which is not obviously over-populated, provides a contrast to the extreme density of population in some other areas, such as the Indo-Gangetic Plain and Kerala. The problem, therefore, evidently needs consideration both at a local, as well as at a national level.

In addition to irrigation, there are many other measures by which the output of the existing arable area can be increased, even if it is not practicable to increase that area to any great extent. Here is a large field of activity for mission and other agricultural demonstration centres to supplement the existing international and national Government efforts. However, it is appreciated that, with the natural conservatism of the agriculturalist, it will take time to achieve the major increase in food supplies which is possible theoretically, and during this time food supplies will certainly need to be supplemented from the surplus countries. The benefits from the efforts of F.A.O. and other international organisations are of increasing importance.

Education

In the field of education we feel that the major emphasis, in the first place, should be upon the need to reduce the size of the family and so to generate a definite *intention* to do so. This can be done through the press, radio and lectures for the general public. Most important probably is the approach to high schools and colleges which can influence the outlook and plans for the future of these young people during a formative stage, and the results of such teaching should be apparent within a period of 10 to 15 years.

In the year 1961, the Christian Medical Association of India issued a statement on Family Planning, which was widely distributed through the National Christian Council, based on accepted Christian standards of morality. However, this approach can only affect a small minority of the people of India, and we suggest that a similar approach be made to other communities, emphasising their own moral teaching. The majority Hindu community has traditionally high moral standards, which have been maintained better probably in the rural areas than in the towns.

Would it not be possible to point back to the early Hindu culture in which a boy, after the thread ceremony at the age of about 12, became a ' Brahmachari ', when he stayed at the home of a Vedic teacher or ' guru ', or wandered around with him up to the age of 24, after which he returned home to take up the responsibility of a ' Grihastha ' or married householder? During this interval he was expected to live a chaste life, and received general moral teaching. In our experience, while this period of tutelage is no longer practised, it is represented in a traditional manner at the time of the thread ceremony, and leaves a strong influence on the minds of many, which can be confirmed and developed by education of the right kind. Such valuable elements in the Hindu tradition would be a safeguard against some of the ' modern views ' of sexual behaviour.

The actual methods of birth control are best considered in relation to the individual case and family needs in the Family Planning Clinic and education should concentrate on the *need* for population control. Already the influence of many books, films and the radio, tend to undermine standards of moral behaviour, and when methods of birth control are publicised and the means made generally available through barbers' shops, and even automatic machines, there is a grave danger of the use of these methods by unmarried young people who have been almost encouraged to reject the accepted standards of pre-marital chastity. The situation which has arisen in some western countries of laxity in sexual morality, and the widespread use of birth control methods outside marriage, gives rise to serious fears as to what would be the result of an extension of such attitudes among the millions of young people of the under-developed countries who have so far been protected by their traditional habits and customs.

Family Planning Clinics

Finally, we come to the question of the direct attack on the problem by family planning or birth control. Centres for this should be established and increased as quickly as possible, but they should in all cases be attached to properly established Family Guidance Clinics, with adequately trained medical and nursing staffs who would give advice on all aspects of family life. In many cases such clinics would be attached to a general clinic or dispensary. This would ensure that advice on family planning was given on the basis of the real needs of the person and the family concerned.

As regards the methods to be employed, there are many grave problems about the wide use of any family planning method in the rural parts of any developing country. Those who have had most experience in this field agree that in these village areas a programme will fail if:

1. It has to depend on the male partner.
2. It demands the kind of preparations by the woman which require privacy at short notice.
3. It demands mathematical calculations.
4. It is expensive, by local standards.

Most methods commonly in use in the West are ruled out on one or more of these scores. All of them are frowned upon by orthodox and cultured leaders of society (in India at least) on the grounds that if made widely available, they might lead to the kind of moral laxity which they see in the West.

There is one method, however, the intra-uterine contraceptive device, which has none of the above objections and is now coming into widespread use. Gynaecologists at first were reluctant to use it, because of memories of the old type of metal devices that occasionally became embedded in the uterus. Extensive trials have, however, confirmed that the new soft plastic spirals and tufts are apparently harmless.[1] It was feared at one time that intra-uterine devices would act by causing abortion; but it is now known that they are true contraceptives, that is, they prevent fertilisation of the ovum. Two International Conferences have been held, sponsored by United Nations, entirely for the purpose of assessment and discussion of trials of the modern plastic intra-uterine contraceptive devices. Leading experts have now advised both the Rockefeller Foundation and the Ford Foundation to make this method the basis of their current contribution to help solve the problems of the population explosion. The reports of these conferences, published by *Exerpta Medica* are available for those who are interested.

The basis of the method is the insertion of a fine spiral of polythene or a tuft of plastic threads, through the cervix into the uterus. Some patterns lie wholly in the uterus; others have a stalk which lies in the cervix and projects a few millimetres below the os.

The great advantages of this method are that it can be under the control of the medical profession, and that it is easy to use only on women who have borne children. The doctor, or trained assistant, can go to a village and call the women together and explain the objectives of the plan. Those women who, after consultation with their husbands and with the doctor, wish to avoid pregnancy for the next year, are then examined and prepared. There is no need for dilatation of the cervix or for anaesthesia, and large numbers of patients can be dealt with in one day. The women are informed that the doctor will be back after six months or other suitable time, and will then advise any others who may want to be fitted, and will remove the device from those who now want to have a child. In the interval, any patient who wants help may call at the Centre from which the doctor and his team are operating.

The cost of the device is about that of a button and it seems to be a very suitable addition to the armamentarium of any doctor working amongst the poor.

To those who may feel that there has not yet been time to

[1] The matter is still being discussed in the medical press.

H

exclude possible long-term harmful effects, we must point out, first that in general plastic materials have already been proved to be innocuous when buried for years in the tissues, and when used as prostheses in the mouth, and, secondly, that we are not selecting this method against other equally effective ones. We have, however, to choose this or the known ills of frequent pregnancy, because we seem to have no other method of contraception that is really applicable in village conditions in countries that need it most.

With reference to male sterilisation, this has been adopted by some states in India, and in one state, at least, a cash bonus has been given to every man presenting himself for sterilisation. We feel there are a great many disadvantages in this method. Perhaps the most important is the irreversibility of the procedure. We know of more than one case where an epidemic or accident has resulted in the death of two or more children in a family, leaving no issue. While the restoration of fertility is possible in the hands of an expert, if this method were used extensively enough to have a real effect on the situation, such operations would not generally be practicable. Another disadvantage that might arise is that should a wife die and the husband desire to remarry, the second marriage would be sterile. As the second wife would often be a young woman, this raises the moral issue whether it would be right for such a sterilised man to remarry without first communicating the fact that he is sterile. In addition, there is sometimes a harmful psychological effect on the male who has been sterilised and when the operation has been carried out under poor conditions, we have seen septic local complications.

With regard to the sterilisation of women, this was at one time adopted by one of us where there were three or more children, where both parents requested it. There seemed no other satisfactory method. However, if the ' coil ' method proves satisfactory, then the need for sterilisation will cease.

No one who has worked in rural India will be inclined to think that the ' pill ' will be a safe method for general use. Perhaps, however, it may prove of value in the future for the more educated part of the population.

CONCLUSION

The Christian can never isolate one aspect of his work and take it as a gift to a new country or people. He has to involve himself in the situation as he finds it, and identify himself with the needs and problems of the people who become his people, and share with them the love of his God until they accept Him as Father.

Thus the Christian Church may today recognise the population explosion as an acute problem, demanding intensive measures— much as yesterday it recognised the problem of high infant mortality. But, to plan new campaigns from armchairs at home will lead only to new problems. The strength of the Church is its compassion, and the effectiveness of its mission lies in the dedication of its members not to a cause but to people. As we go to meet the people of other lands, let us go with all the knowledge and all the equipment at our command. Our first purpose may be to preach or to heal, or to teach, but as we are sensitive to local needs, we feel sure that most of us will feel that we have a responsibility to awaken the people to the need to accept a lower birth rate, if they are to enjoy the blessing of a lower death rate. Placed in its true context as a part of the ministry of the love of God, the hand that helps a tired mother to postpone or to avoid her next pregnancy, is as much a part of Christ's ministry on earth as the hand that helps to bring a child to a previously childless marriage.

REFERENCE

CIPOLLA, CARLO M. (1963). *The Economic History of World Population*, Fig. 7, p. 85. Pelican S., Penguin Books.

CHAPTER VI

THE CONCEPT OF RESPONSIBILITY IN PSYCHIATRIC TREATMENT

F. J. ROBERTS[1]

' An incurably psychotic individual may lose his usefulness but yet
retain the dignity of a human being. This is my psychiatric credo.
Without it I should not think it worthwhile to be a psychiatrist.'

VIKTOR FRANKL (1962)

Underlying the practice of Medicine there are a number of
assumptions which have a marked influence on the way in which
we think about, and behave, towards our patients. This is
particularly true of the assumptions which we make about psychological disorders, because they determine for us the view we take
regarding human responsibility. These assumptions have been
greatly influenced by deterministic ideas which deny man's
responsibility. The main ideas, which we shall consider here,
are strange companions as one talks about such intangible things
as the forces in the mind, while on the other hand there are attempts
to reduce all psychological activity to a physico-chemical level.

Views on Determination of Behaviour

The first of these views developed out of the work of Freud
and his colleagues at the turn of the century. As a result of this
work, it was thought that present behaviour and, even to a certain
extent, experience were determined by events which occurred
within the individual's mind. Inherited impulses and the events
of very early years shaped the child's subsequent conduct.
Although an individual may believe that he is in control of his
actions, he is mistaken. The major part of his mind is quite
outside his surveillance and it is in the ' unconscious ' part that
the important processes which determine behaviour occur. In
order to gain some control, he needs the assistance of a skilled
therapist who reveals for him that which he could never find
unaided.

The second set of ideas, which reduced all psychological
processes to a physico-chemical level, has no possible place in it
for the notion of responsibility. It follows from this view that

[1]F. John Roberts, M.B., B.S., M.R.C.P.Ed., D.P.M., is Lecturer, Department
of Medical Health, University of Bristol.

treatment must be directed to physical methods which will in some way alter the organic processes in the brain. If we were to take this view to its logical conclusion, the patient's thoughts or beliefs need never be taken into account. Indeed, as Brain (1958) says:

'. . . it is by investigating the physical events, especially in terms of biochemistry, that we are likely to arrive at a completer understanding and more effective treatment of the major disorders of the mind.'

There is a third view of psychological disorder which regards the condition as a reaction of a unique individual to his own unique environment. Whatever the history of the individual and whatever his environment, one factor in his behaviour is what he chooses to do and therefore, to this extent, he is responsible. This is not meant to imply that all individuals are competent to act to the same extent in a given situation, but it does imply that all (including those with brain damage) can be regarded as responsible.

Definition of a Responsible Person

When we describe someone as a responsible person we mean that in every area of his life he is able to meet the demands of his world. When analysing a particular responsibility we find that it involves the subject in a decision, which in turn leads to some action for which he must accept the consequences. This obviously could involve ethical and legal considerations, but if we are to understand behaviour we need to keep within a psychological framework.

If we accept this point of view, however, it is quite insufficient to assume that just by declaring that a man is responsible for his behaviour we have an adequate explanation of it. After all, the state of being responsible is just one of the behavioural factors. For example, a young married man may insist that his 2-year old daughter shuts the door and in so doing frightens her into action. Suppose that we now ask him why he insisted, despite the child's fright. He may well reply that he did so because he believes that children should do what they are told. In this instance our subject would claim to be responsible. However, if we knew that he was brought up in a rigid authoritarian Children's Home and that, since the age of $17\frac{1}{2}$, he had been in a Guards' Regiment we would begin to understand more about his treatment of his child.

In the above example, the young man was faced with a decision which he made and acted upon. He accepted the consequences of his action. In seeking to understand his action we could say that his decision and behaviour were constrained by his concept of child-rearing, which in turn was dependent upon his own experiences of life. If his behaviour had been limited, not by his experience but, by some disability such as a hemiplegia, this might have made it impossible for him to shut the door himself, and thus have rendered it likely that he would have insisted on his daughter's being obedient. This, however, in no way alters the argument that he should still be regarded as responsible in the situation in which he was.

The first two sets of ideas about psychological disorders are important as they explain the attitudes of some of the Medical Profession and some members of society to those who are disordered. On the one hand, it is said that until the doctor has sorted out or cured the behaviour disorder, the patient should not be regarded as responsible. On the other hand, we find that many doctors are preoccupied by the search for, and the use of, physical methods of treatment. As a direct consequence of both these attitudes, the patient's thoughts about himself tend to be neglected. In addition, they lead doctors to enter into contracts with relatives behind the patient's back. Others decide what is good for him in matters such as treatment and important legal affairs. The result is he is seldom allowed to express his own views.

The Open Door Policy

As a reaction against this deterministic view a movement has developed in the mental hospitals which has shown in a very practical way, that patients are responsible people. Doors have been opened which had previously been locked to prevent the patients' escape. This revolution—which is still not universally applied in Great Britain—has been accompanied by a change in outlook of those who cared for the patients. Instead of being predominantly concerned with detaining their charges, they have begun to see themselves in a therapeutic role. Ratcliffe (1962), when reviewing 10 years of ' open door ' policy at Dingleton Hospital, showed that early fears had been quite unfounded. In the 10 years under review, there had been no increase in the number of accidents among the patients within the hospital, no change in the suicide rate, fewer than expected left the hospital against the advice of the doctors, and there were no serious offences committed. These were the tangible and measurable effects of opening the doors, but in addition there were the intangible benefits in morale of the staff, the well-being of the patients and relief of the relatives.

The Wider Results

As the open door idea spread through the country, a number of hospitals found that the need to detain patients under a legal order lasting for one year declined dramatically. This was, of course, a very important way in which the hospital staff could both demonstrate their belief in the responsibility of their patients and discover the therapeutic value and effect of their change of attitude.

A change in attitude was also observed in the communities which lived near the hospitals. At first when the doors were opened there was concern for the safety of lonely individuals and property. In some areas representation was made to the hospitals to have the doors locked again. Without exception, within a few months this attitude had changed and the local people began to regard their hospital with pride.

As these changes proceeded there gradually emerged the idea that the whole hospital could be viewed as a therapeutic community. This idea developed in two ways. Firstly, that all patients and staff were involved in the treatment, and not just the doctors and nurses. Secondly, treatment was not limited to conventional psychological and physical methods, but included the whole of the social and service spheres of the hospital.

However, instead of applying the idea to the whole of a large hospital, it was applied to smaller groups such as one ward. In these small groups the conventional role of doctor and patient were avoided as far as possible so that the patient could contribute with the staff to the running of the ward, including some of the treatment. Doctors, nurses and patients met regularly so that the views of all could be discussed and the future planned. In these meetings matters of concern both to the whole group and to individuals could be freely debated. In such a group it was possible to generate an atmosphere of therapeutic intention in which everyone was involved and in which everyone had some responsibility.

The introduction of industrial therapy either within the setting of the therapeutic community or as a separate activity, has now become possible. In most psychiatric organisations this consists of work brought into the hospital which the patient is paid to do. He is paid according to his performance and so he is regarded as being responsible for what he does. The conditions of work and the demands made on the workers can be graded according to the patient's progress and are made to resemble the conditions which would prevail in the outside world. For some patients, this practice at normal living is an essential step to their survival in the community. The Industrial Therapy Organisation, which grew out of the activities at Glenside Hospital, Bristol (Early, 1962) is a good example of a self-sufficient group which is able to pay its workers a living wage so that they can eventually live outside the hospital.

The Concept supported and applied

These empirical observations suggest that it is both reasonable and important to regard those with psychological disorders as responsible people. Even the most disordered can be expected to be responsible within certain areas. If the patient is made to realise that he is responsible, then the expectations are fulfilled. As a result of these recent changes of outlook, a growing body of opinion based on experiment and observation has cast grave doubts on the validity of the deterministic views on psychological disorders which have been so important in the past.

In 1924 Kantor started to formulate his concept of inter-behavioural psychology. In this he demonstrated that what happens in the nervous system is only one small factor amongst many in determining the behaviour of an individual. In addition to what is happening in the nervous system, we need to know what experiences an individual has had in the past, and what are the present environmental influences, if we are to be able to understand his behaviour.

Woodger (1956) demonstrated the philosophical inadequacies of the reductionist view of behaviour which he says have been grossly over-influenced by the successes of theoretical physics. They have wrongly been taken as an adequate model for scientific endeavour in other areas. He has made the suggestion that, in forsaking this limited view, the medical psychologist would have to learn the language of many other disciplines, including those of the moral philosopher and those who study animal behaviour. Woodger's main thesis supports Kantor but, what is more important for our purpose, it acknowledges man as being responsible.

One of the most mechanistic approaches towards the functions of the brain is that which studies it in terms of cybernetics and communication theory. Yet Mackay (1960, 1965a, 1965b) has come to the conclusion that even though this approach may well lead to a fuller understanding of brain and psychological mechanisms, the individual is never fully predictable and has a responsibility in the choice situation.

In the clinical sphere, O. H. Mowrer (1961, 1964) has presented some evidence which supports the idea that psychological disorders are directly related to the way in which an individual exercises his responsibility. He goes on to suggest that recovery from many disorders is dependent upon the individual's being able to accept his responsibility. Russell Davis (1966) has collected the evidence for the psychological factors which are related to the various disorders in the field of psychiatry. Included in these is the removal from the patient of his responsibility in certain areas of his life; in most instances this is effected by other members of his family. In his discussion of the treatment of these disorders, Russell Davis draws attention to the importance of re-establishing the patient as a responsible person.

The Effects in Treatment

These scientific and philosophical differences are reflected in the different treatment of psychological disorders in the two types of practice of those who see man as being irresponsible and those who see him as responsible. This difference can be observed in a number of areas, some of which we will now consider.

For those who take the deterministic view of behaviour, admission to hospital is seen either as an exercise to protect the patient or society, or as a means of having the patient in a situation where 'treatment' can be administered. Although all this might be valid, the most important aspect of the procedure from the non-deterministic point of view is that it is in itself a form of treatment. The act of acknowledging that admission is necessary, and acting upon it, is therapeutic in its own right.

In a similar manner there are two ways of using the sections of the Mental Health Act 1959 which give the hospital power to insist that the patient stays in hospital despite his own wishes to the contrary. On the one hand, they can be used to protect the patient and society and to insist on treatment. On the other they can be seen as a means of limiting the patient's geographical freedom, while he re-develops his competence in being responsible.

In the practical management of patients who seem intent on killing themselves, those who take a deterministic view of psychological disorders find themselves in an incongruous position. Most psychiatrists are well aware of the apparent paradox that if the staff treats ' actively suicidal ' patients by locking them up, by continual supervision, and by removal of all means of doing harm to themselves, then the chances of a suicidal attempt being made is increased. If instead, these patients are treated as if they are expected to recover and to be able to live their own lives again, then the restrictive action becomes unnecessary.

Electroconvulsive therapy is now recognised as an effective method of treatment for patients who are experiencing subjective discomfort. It has been argued that the psychological effect obtained arises out of what the patient thinks about the treatment, but it has been shown that the physiological effect is related in some way to the clinical improvement. Although this fact may appear to support the deterministic position, it in no way alters the patient's responsibility. What the treatment does is to extend the range within which the patient is free to exercise his responsibility.

One of the disasters of psychiatry was the introduction, and widespread use, of leucotomy. This treatment involves a direct assault on the brain, leaving it permanently damaged. The rationale for it leaned heavily on a deterministic view of man and his psychological disorders. For thousands of patients in Great Britain the result of the procedure was not to their benefit. The real problem is that, apart from being largely ineffective, it imposes still other limitations on him so that the range within which he can be responsible is reduced.

In emphasising the responsibility of our patients, no attempt is made to avoid the implications of brain function, but rather to put it into its proper place. It is too easy to become so pre-occupied with the physical events within the brain that the wider aspects of man's cerebral functions become obscured. This is no new problem. In 1747 Jerome Gaub (Rather, 1965), wrote on the subject that ' Physicians should actively engage in a search for new drugs capable of affecting the mind '. He said:

'. . . we discover special regimens, universal therapeutic methods, and particular remedies with which we can awaken, sharpen or strengthen any faculty of the mind whatsoever . . . as needed.   Does the magnitude of the task strike terror? In other situations this is so far from depressing the mind as to enkindle it rather.'

He is saying that physicians can be stimulated by psychological means, while patients will only respond to physical methods.

CONCLUSION

We commenced this chapter with a quotation from Viktor Frankl's account of his experiences in concentration camps. He found his Faith and his practice of psychiatry profoundly extended by what happened to him in Auschwitz, and in his record he says:

' There is nothing conceivable which would so condition a man as to leave him without the slightest freedom.   Therefore, a residue of freedom, however limited it may be, is left to man in neurotic and even psychotic cases.'   And, ' A human being is not one thing among others; things determine each other, but man is ultimately self-determining.   What he becomes—within the limits of endowment and environment—he has made out of himself.'

REFERENCES

BRAIN, SIR RUSSELL (1958).   Hughlings Jackson's ideas of consciousness in the light of today.   In *The Brain and its Functions*, ed. Poynter, F. N. L.   Oxford: Blackwell.

DAVIS, D. RUSSELL (1966).   *An Introduction to Psychopathology*, 2nd ed.   Oxford: Blackwell.

EARLY, DONAL F. (1962).   The industrial therapy organisation (Bristol). The first two years.   *Lancet*, 1, 135.

FRANKL, VIKTOR (1962).   *Man's Search for Meaning*.   London: Hodder & Stoughton.

KANTOR, J. R. (1924).   *Principles of Psychology*.   New York: Knopf.

KANTOR, J. R. (1959).   *Interbehavioural Psychology*.   Bloomington, Ind.: Principle Press Inc.

MACKAY, D. M. (1960).   Logical indeterminacy of freechoice.   *Mind*, 60, 31.

MACKAY, D. M. (1965a),   *Christianity in a Mechanistic Universe*, pp. 51-69.   London: Tyndale Press.

MACKAY, D. M. (1965b).   Mechanism to mind.   In *Brain and Mind*, pp. 163-186.   ed. Smythies, J. R.   London: Routledge & Kegan Paul.

MOWRER, O. H. (1961).   *The Crisis in Psychiatry and Religion*.   U.S.A.: Von Nostrand.

MOWRER, O. H. (1964).   *The New Group Therapy*.   U.S.A.: Von Nostrand.

RATCLIFFE, R. A. W. (1962).   The open door: ten years' experience in Dingleton.   *Lancet*, 2, 188.

RATHER, L. T. (1965).   *Mind and Body in Eighteenth Century Medicine. A study based on Jerome Gaub's ' De regimine mentis '*.

WOODGER, J. H. (1956).   *Physics, Psychology and Medicine*.   London: Cambridge University Press.

CHAPTER VII

ALCOHOLISM AND DRUG ADDICTION

BASIL MERRIMAN[1]

Alcoholism, in all its various forms and manifestations, is probably the greatest single cause of broken homes and marriages, behaviour problems in children, accidents on the road and minor impulsive acts of crime. The tragic overcrowding in our prisons is, in large measure due to the presence of alcoholics who may be there, not because they are basically criminal but because they have made an exhibition of themselves in the street or have committed some quite unpremeditated property offence in order to obtain money for further bouts of drinking. The harm caused to the nation as a whole by the loss of industrial efficiency associated with alcoholism is incalculable. In the United States alcoholics have come to be known as ' half men ', or ' half women ' because of their failure to work or, if working, their frequent periods of absenteeism and loss of efficiency and skill.

Despite all this, however, and despite the fact that the alcoholic spoils every relationship into which he enters, sowing disharmony and misery wherever he goes, alcoholism has been, and still is, largely a neglected problem. It has been called ' the Cinderella of Medicine ', and ' the most neglected disease of our time '. Generally speaking, Medicine has tended to disregard the alcoholic and to consider that he or she is merely a squalid nuisance who has brought his or her own trouble on his or her head. Moreover, it is widely held that the alcoholic is really not worth while treating, since the prognosis is so poor, and, in fact, it is a waste of time to try to do more than ' dry the patient out ' occasionally and mitigate the worst ravages of the disease. This is far from being the truth. The popularly-held image of the alcoholic as a useless lay-about on a park bench can be applied to a relatively few in the chronic and terminal stages, where brain damage prevents their playing any effective part in society.

The truth is that by far the larger number of alcoholics in this country are in the earlier recoverable stages and it is therefore nothing short of a tragedy that there are so few centres where

[1]Basil Merriman, M.R.C.S., L.R.C.P., Director, Carter Foundation and Consultant In Alcoholism, H.M. Prisons.

specialised treatment is available. As things are at the present time, they are more than likely to drift into a chronic state, with progressive medical, psychological, and social deterioration. Far from being useless wasters, many of these patients are among the potentially most useful and creative members of the community. It is, in fact, their very sensitivity and imagination that makes them crave for a chemical screen between themselves and the harsh reality of modern life. Unfortunately for them, alcohol—which for several thousand years before the introduction of the modern tranquillisers and sedatives was the only cerebral depressant available—is of limited value when used as a drug, since the secondary effects outweigh its therapeutic properties. The person who starts by using alcohol for the symptomatic relief of anxiety or stress, and continues to do so, will sooner or later undergo such progressive mental and physical changes as to constitute an autonomous disease. Thus the use of alcohol which begins as a sympton of some underlying psychological abnormality, turns into a sickness with successive stages. Whatever the moral responsibility of the patient when he first began to drink, sooner or later, depending on the intensity of his drinking, he will be found to suffer from a severe and crippling disease which it is surely the ethical responsibility of Medicine to treat.

Yet, just as the doctor mistrusts the alcoholic, so the alcoholic mistrusts the doctor, believing he will not be accepted as such. A situation, therefore, often arises between them, which it is perhaps not unfair to call a conspiracy of silence. The alcoholic comes in by the back door as it were, and is given a certificate with the designation, let us say, ' gastritis ' or some similar condition, to explain his absence from work. But the trouble and waste of time that the patient causes, when he comes to the practitioner in this guise, may be far greater than it would have been if he had been accepted and treated as an alcoholic when first seen.

Magnitude of the Problem

What is the number of true alcoholic addicts in Great Britain at the present time? This is an important question, because the way in which alcoholism has been neglected by successive Ministers of Health has generally been justified by claiming that there was no evidence of a problem sufficiently serious to warrant an extensive programme of rehabilitation of the sort now being embarked upon by most of the industrialised countries. It was held that the Jellinek formula, based on the number of deaths from cirrhosis of the liver recorded in any one year (W.H.O. Report 42), could be applied only to its sphere of origin, namely the North American Continent, and the estimated figures for Great Britain were unrealistically high. Support was given to this contention by a survey carried out by Parr in 1956, with the co-operation of the College of General Practitioners (Parr, 1956).

However, a recent and considerably more extensive survey carried out by the Steering Group of Alcoholism (1965) formed by the Joseph Rowntree Social Service Trust confirmed that the Jellinek formula can be applied to this country with the same relative confidence as it is applied to other North-Western communities. The Report puts the number of obvious, chronic alcoholics in England and Wales alone as at least 70,000, whilst the number of alcoholics in earlier stages of deterioration is probably 200,000 or more. This gives a total of the order of 300,000. It is a significant number of people to be suffering from a single progressive and crippling disease which demands for its mitigation a far less leisurely approach than has been shown by recent governments and a keener awareness by the medical profession generally of its ethical responsibility in this field.

Combination with drugs

Alcoholism is frequently combined with the use of drugs. In Great Britain the tendency is not, as in the U.S.A. (Isbell, 1956) to resort to the major drugs of addiction, but to the minor drugs of habituation, with psychic rather than physical dependence. Early in his drinking career the alcoholic comes to realise that he can get 'high' more swiftly, and with far less expense, if he combines a barbiturate preparation with his alcohol. In fact the symptomatology of barbiturate intoxication is similar to that of intoxication with alcohol, so that it is possible for chronic alcoholics to substitute barbiturates alone for alcohol for a time, if they are low in funds. Even in relatively early cases of alcoholism it is not uncommon to find an associated triple dependence, namely to long acting barbiturates with alcohol during the day, to a quick acting barbiturate at night or the early hours for sleep, and an amphetamine or phenmetrazine during the morning for waking up and as a psychic energiser. It is the ethical responsibility of the doctor to resist the alcoholic's frequent demands for these drugs.

Not only are barbiturates used very freely by alcoholics but also non-barbiturate sedatives, which are likely to be more easily obtained, such a glutethimide, methylpentynol, carbromal, meprobamate, and chloral hydrate. Teenagers are more likely to combine alcohol with marihuana or reefers which are generally available in the jazz clubs and all-night cafés which they frequent. Reefers may have no action or make the user sick when employed for the first time, but if continued a variety of effects depending on the basic personality are observed, including a spurious illusion of mystical experience. Teenagers on the psychopathic fringe may resort to a number of destructive and perverted practices of which ether sniffing or drinking, and ' glue ' sniffing (balsa wood cement) are the commonest.

Chronic alcoholics as they descend the social scale also resort to destructive and perverted forms of achieving intoxication too numerous to mention in detail. Methylated and surgical spirits are, of course, the most widely used, but scents and cosmetic preparations containing alcohol and household preparations with alcohol-like solvents, such as metal polishes, may be pressed into service. The most bizarre combination of which the present writer is aware, is ' scrap iron ' intoxicant, consisting of crude spirit in a metal drum, with the addition of naphthalene or moth balls. Surely it is the ethical responsibility of the doctor to ensure that no case of his reaches this final appalling stage.

Aetiology of the escape reaction

Alcoholism and drug addiction are in essence ' escape reactions ' from reality. In their extreme forms they amount to an evasion of life itself, a form of prolonged suicide. In the eighteenth century when the phrase ' Drunk for a penny, dead drunk for twopence: straw free ' was coined, it might be said to have been the alcoholism of poverty. Today we are confronted by a totally different social situation which has been called the ' alcoholism of affluence '. This is not a good term; it might be better described as the alcoholism of emotional and spiritual (rather than material) poverty.

Alcoholism is an increasing medico-social phenomenon in all the industrialised countries at the present time. Why should this be so? The answer is a complex one. It seems in part to be associated with the mode of life inherent in a highly industrialised and technicological society. This places increasing pressures and strains upon the nervous system that are not found in simpler 'more natural' societies. The brain of modern industrial man is in many cases over-stimulated and functions at an abnormally high logical and critical level. It is suggested that a return to a simpler method of brain functioning is necessary from time to time for the homeostatic mechanism of the brain to work effectively. In other words, in self-defence the individual is forced to protect himself against the deluge of ideas that flood in upon him through the various media of communication day after day, producing in the mind a mass of incompletely digested material and a state of conflict and confusion. This has been called the impact of confused impressions. It leads to the nervous system being continually alert and on guard, which is experienced by the individual principally as a complete inability to relax.

Attempts may be made to achieve this return to a 'simpler method of functioning' in various ways, ranging from the use of sedative and tranquilising drugs or psychotherapy, to a prolonged holiday abroad ('getting away from it all'). Unfortunately, an increasing number of people are turning to alcohol which is certainly effective in reducing the degree of alertness and arousal of the brain. As already pointed out, however, it can bring in its train disastrous consequences in the shape of physical and mental illness and disruption of social relationships. This is probably the explanation of the fact that the type of alcoholism known as 'delta alcoholism', in which the patient exhibits an inability to abstain, rather than loss of control with complete inebriation, as in the classical 'gamma' type, appears to be increasing. A sufferer from delta alcoholism drinks steadily through the day and probably night, constantly 'topping up'. He is never really sober, though never completely drunk. They seek, as it were, to interpose a protective screen between themselves and stark reality. This type of alcoholism is increasingly common among those whose work encourages them 'to live on their nerves'—particularly people in show business, creative artistic activities, advertising, journalism and rapidly expanding businesses.

Years ago William James observed that the power of alcohol over mankind might be due to its ability to stimulate the mystical faculties (defined by James as the floodtide of inner warmth and vital energy) which are usually crushed to earth by the cold facts and dry criticisms of the sober hour. A recently published book dealing with the use of d-lysergic acid diethylamide as an ' escape ' drug in the United States under the title *Utopiates* (Blum *et al.*, 1965) throws some interesting contemporary light on James' theories. Blum and his associates suggests that the effects of any drug ' tend to be in keeping with the values of the culture or sub-culture in which it is used ', and that the same drug may produce different effects in people living in different cultures. More significantly, they suggest that the same effects may be achieved with different substances, and they point out that alcohol may be used in much the same way as L.S.D. They argue that users of L.S.D. have an ideology that accents ' the values of the inner life, of personal freedom, and of mystical experience '. In their opinion this ideology can largely be understood as a reaction against, or even a withdrawal from, major trends in contemporary society. They believe that as life and work become more and more organised and complex there are increasing demands on the individual to try to adapt himself to the social organisation or to the prevailing system of bureaucracy. At the same time, he is offered fewer and fewer opportunities for emotional expression or satisfaction. They see, therefore, in the use of L.S.D. and alcohol an attempt to regain values that tend to be crushed to earth today. But too many people are tending to contract out of modern society by these means, and the authors emphasise, strikingly enough, that they include many of those who have been successful in this society and tasted its so-called rewards.

A similar picture is drawn by Alexander Trocchi (1965) in a recent article ' Why Drugs? ' According to Trocchi, drugs lead to a cleansing of the doors of perception, so that the user is able to live in a kind of absolute multi-relational present full of possibility and surprising conjunctions. Events take on the exciting mystical quality (the Wordsworthian wonder at everyday things) they often have for young children, a quality they no longer possess for adults whose normal vision is highly structured and selective.

For Trocchi, drugs are, as it were, one door on to that other face of reality which has been left behind in the evolution of western civilisation. Of itself, material progress seems to lead only to material progress; meanwhile centuries of technicological advance have brought man further away from himself than he has perhaps ever been.

I

What is the Solution?

There is a need for greatly increased government activity within the National Health Service by the provision of specialised Early Treatment Centres which alcoholics and drug addicts could be encouraged to attend. In the meantime, such facilities as exist for treatment remain, in the words of a memorandum by a joint committee of the British Medical Association and the Magistrates' Association 'grossly inadequate'. The emphasis should be upon early treatment and the prevention of chronic illness. This would ultimately lead to a great saving of money which is now poured out when it is too late. There is no use in the shutting of the stable door after the horse has escaped, after the man is in prison, after the wife is in the mental hospital because she can no longer bear the strain of caring for the family, or after the children are in the care of the local authority.

The provision of Early Treatment Centres on an adequate scale would have to be associated with an intensive educational programme to encourage alcoholics and potential alcoholics to attend at the earliest possible opportunity. This should embrace the education of the student, and even, in so far as the early warning signs may be recognised, the practising doctor. It must include the education of the patient and his family, and the education of the community to understand the social implications of the situation and the urgent need for action.

The Ethical Responsibility of Christians

The craving for alcohol and drugs is born of poverty of the personality, its emptiness and isolation. Essentially the need for the escape provided by alcohol is an expression of the failure to find a meaning and purpose in life. As a result of his experience with alcoholics and drug addicts, the writer is firmly convinced that the answer to the stresses of the twentieth century way of life is primarily a religious one. The reader may already have noticed references to the use of alcohol and drugs to obtain a spurious 'mystical' experience; this is a vague and unformulated attempt to achieve by chemical means a state of mind associated with true religious experience.

The development of the highly industrialised nations is creating a material atmosphere, a *zeitgeist*, that is conducive to the development of alcoholism and other addictions. If it is conceded that the nation's business is not solely material business, then it is also a responsibility to provide a spiritual climate in which men can thrive and fulfil their destiny as creative beings and not, as now, to be subjected to pressures that tend mentally and spiritually to twist them and deform.

As pointed out by Galbraith (1961) the character of the age may be described as a restless striving for material possessions—a pattern of life in which stress has become inherent. Most people inflict upon themselves a state of chronic anxiety over money. They suffer during their working hours from the boredom and frustration imposed by the sort of jobs that have to be done in order to satisfy the artificially stimulated demand for the products of fully mechanised mass production. The Christian knows that the world is not as God desires it to be, and his primary responsibility must be the long term one of striving whenever and wherever possible to transform it more nearly in accordance with the purposes of the Kingdom of God. The short term responsibility is the attempt to succour those who have fallen by the wayside.

The essential element in the rehabilitation of the alcoholic, then, is a religious one. This is recognised by the world-wide movement of Alcoholics Anonymous which has succeeded in transforming so many otherwise useless lives. The therapeutic activities of the movement are outlined in a series of steps. The third step emphasises the importance of commitment to God in the following words—' Make a decision to turn our will and our lives to the care of God '. The fourth step is ' Make a searching and fearless moral inventory of ourselves ': the emphasis here is on the alcoholic's need to examine himself in depth. The fifth step is: ' Admit to God, to ourselves and to another human being the exact nature of our wrongs '. The sixth step ' We are entirely ready to have God remove all these defects of character '.

Recognition of the importance of religion in rehabilitating the alcoholic must not, however, blind the doctor to the ethical responsibility of treating the associated physical sickness. For, as already pointed out, the alcoholic is not simply a case of moral failure—he is a person suffering from a progressive physical disease with clearly recognisable stages. Any practitioner who wishes to know about the various forms of alcoholism and their recognition may profitably read *The Disease Concept of Alcoholism* (Jellinek, 1960). It is the Christian doctor, with a living faith of his own, who is in the long run best able to help the alcoholic and drug addict to find a sense of purpose. Such a purpose is needed to replace the desire to escape, and by means of prayer and meditation to find health, strength and renewal of life.

REFERENCES

BLUM, R. and ASSOCIATES (1965). *Utopiates.* London: Tavistock Publications.

GALBRAITH, J. K. (1961). *The Affluent Society.* London: Hamilton.

ISBELL, H. (1956). Abuse of barbiturates. *J. Am. med. Ass.* **162,** 660.

JELLINEK, E. M., ISBELL, H., LUNDQUIST, H., TIEDBOUT, H. M., DUCHENE, M., NARDONES, J. & MACLEOD, L. D. (1955). The craving for alcohol. A symposium by members of the WHO Expert Committee on Mental Health. *Q. Jl. Stud. Alcohol,* **16,** 34.

JELLINEK, E. M. (1960). *The Disease Concept of Alcoholism.* Newhaven, Conn.; Hillhouse Press.

PARR, DENIS (1956). *Br. J. Addict.,* **54,** 25.

STEERING GROUP ON ALCOHOLISM (1965). *Chronic Alcoholics.* London: Joseph Rowntree Social Service Trust.

TROCCHI, A. (1965). Why Drugs? *New Society,* 20th May, p. 9.

W.H.O. TECHNICAL REPORT No. 42, p.20.

WILLIAMS, E. L. (1956). *Alcoholism.* Edinburgh: Livingstone.

WILLIAMS, E. L. (1958). *Tomorrow we'll be Sober* London: Cassell.

CHAPTER VIII

SOCIAL ABERRATIONS —SIN, CRIME OR DISEASE?

With special reference to Homosexuality, Suicide and Alcoholism

VICTOR PARSONS[1]

The conditions to be discussed in this chapter impinge at many points on the Law, Medicine and Christian action. The law has ceased to be concerned with the majority of suicides, homosexuality is at present under debate, and further legislation concerning some aspects of alcoholism is expected in the near future. These measures have led to an appraisal of the wider problems of how established standards of behaviour can be defined and maintained and deviations prevented. The balance between liberty and licence within common morality has been carefully guarded in the past by a core of Christian belief with its instillation of values and the law with its power of intimidation of the offender. The law has considered itself a custodian of the *mores* of the community but is presently faced with the task of ascertaining moral standards in the absence of a generally recognised spiritual or other authority. Times of rapid social change challenge all varieties of authoritarianism and paternalism; some of the impetus can be traced in part to an extension of the scientific methods of experiment and proof into the social field and to existentialist philosophy with its distrust of dogma and isolated objectivity. In an attempt to withstand an erosion of dogma, certain areas of Christian opinion in the past have seemed to oppose changes in such diverse fields as mental health, analgesia in childbirth and contraception. The Christian community of which a doctor may form a part has the task of showing a balanced concern for the general roots of these social problems and the individuals caught up with their specific needs, working at both ends of the situation. In this way the basis of moral standards can be restated and established in action.

Because these types of behaviour may first bring the individual to a doctor rather than to a lawyer or a minister of religion, the

[1]Victor Parsons, D.M., M.R.C.P., is Senior Lecturer in Medicine, King's College Hospital, London.

117

doctor's first duty will be to treat the patient whether he is to blame for his ill-behaviour or not: wounds are dressed however sustained. On occasion moral judgments may interfere with the doctor's willingness to treat ill patients who have behaved in an immoral or delinquent way! (Merskey & Clarke, 1962). Despair, futility and even anger may colour the doctor's attitude to the patient who hovers over the ' no man's land ' between delinquency and cerebral disease. These tendencies have led psychiatrists to plead for a more deterministic outlook on behaviour in the hope that the scientific method of seeking causal chains, which in organic illness has changed much of modern medicine, will yield measurable causes for abnormal behaviour. An exclusively scientific sociology will, it is hoped, lead to a ' common sense ' view of moral behaviour and responsibility, leading in turn to the ' concept of illness continually expanding at the expense of moral failure ' (Wooton, 1963). This wholehearted determinist viewpoint is tempered by the fact that medicine remains an applied science and what is not known about an individual patient may always exceed what is capable of measurement and analysis, hence making each situation unique. If mental mechanisms are analysed at the physical level Mackay (1958) has shown the impossibility of predicting a decision to be made by someone who, at the same time, is informed of the prediction of what his act will be. It is just at this point that indeterminancy persists; moral freedom of choice remains for good or the less good (defined as evil or, theologically, as sin).

It is often here that the doctor in dealing with the individual patient is challenged by the surrounding attitudes of the relatives or even his colleagues who may either maintain that ' it is not his fault ' or that ' he is not even trying '. On occasion the assessment of the inroads which illness may have made on his freedom of choice has a bearing on his responsibility for a crime of which he is accused.

At the ethical level Nowell Smith (1954) suggests that in analysing the concept of trying, three possibilities emerge when an individual does a wrong thing. First, that the action was not against his moral principles—there was no conflict between duty and inclination (he calls this wickedness); second, that the individual knew it to be wrong and could have resisted the temptation but did not (moral weakness); third, he knew it was wrong but the temptation was too strong for him, he could not overcome it (addiction).

From these concepts or personal responsibility and a mind capable of choice comes the basis for the establishment of guilt in common law. If it be proven that the accused did that which is forbidden in law, then he is guilty unless a defence or exception can be sustained such as mistake of fact, accident, coercion, duress, provocation, insanity or infancy.

Professor Dennis Hill (1962) has discussed at length the important issues both for the Courts and for medical witnesses regarding the assessment of an individual's responsibility for a crime of which he is accused since the advent of the Homicide Act of 1957 and the Mental Health Act of 1959. For an assessment of the individual a profile can be built up incorporating three aspects.

1. *Temperament* is the character of the individual's responses to the environment, their strength and speed, and the quality of his prevailing mood and its intensity. These are closely bound to the organic constitution linked to physique but not to differences in intelligence.

2. *Personality* describes the habitual forms of behaviour which are less dependent upon genetic and physical factors.

3. *Character* describes those features of an individual's behaviour which are the outcome of his control to inhibit and canalise into acceptable forms of expression the instinctive impulses and needs which he has inherited as part of his biological constitution. In the assessment of responsibility it is to this question of the forces operating in the development of character that particular attention must be paid. Thus a devient temperament, low intelligence, a pathological physique or a schizoid personality trait will throw a greater burden on the individual's capacity to develop a normal character.

This profile can be modified again by disease or injury further impairing the individual's responsibility. Among the causes are recent trauma, infection, hypoglycaemia, alcoholism, varieties of encephalopathy and epilepsy. Alcoholism is probably the most frequent state in this group, and it is necessary to show that alcoholism is itself the result of psychiatric abnormality and that a small dose of alcohol induces in the subject a pathological state of mind not encountered in normal subjects.

Dennis Hill argues that if a plea of diminished responsibility is successful, then the right place for such an individual is a place of security within the Mental Health Service. Only then can treatment and the safety of release be realistically assessed.

Inner Moral Compulsion and Outer Legal Coercion

If the relation between medicine and the law is complex, that between the latter and Christian ethics is more so, and it is worthwhile to review a few aspects of the problem before the special subjects under discussion are mentioned later.

St. John Stevas (1961) draws three distinctions between law and morals. Firstly, that legal sanctions are essentially physical, while moral sanctions are interior and inspired by conscience, although on occasion there may be social ostracism. Secondly, the law is not normally concerned with interior attitudes but with external conduct, motives are not the prime concern of the law. Thirdly, law in the Western tradition is limited in scope; it only enforces true standards of morality indispensable for community existence. Morality has no such pragmatic limitation, but calls for conformity with the ideal. Law loses its efficacy if it ceases to correspond with ' the living law ' of society, the underlying beliefs and habits of the people. The nearer the latter are to Christian principles the greater interaction between sin and crime and the moral ' ought ' and the ' legal ought '. It is at this point that a difficult course has to be worked out between the freedom of the individual on the one hand and maintaining the framework of society on the other. The Christian recognises that men should be allowed to exercise a large measure of free will even though it involves some harm to themselves and cost to others (Moore, 1964). At a point when moral offences in private or public become too damaging and challenge the common good, legislation can be invoked so that the law can segregate and punish. However, if the law cannot be enforced equitably and if juries reach their decision on moral issues moved mainly by disgust or indignation or sympathy then greater errors may be the result.

Lord Devlin (1965) has dealt extensively with these problems, first stating that a simple application of Stuart Mills' dictum that ' The only purpose for which power can be rightfully exercised over any member of a civilised community against his will is to prevent harm to others ' is impossible in the making of laws which must and do extend into private morality. At present euthanasia, abortion and incest are crimes done in private without offence to others, even with the consent of the victim. Similarly he argues that the line between drunkenness that creates a social problem of sufficient magnitude to justify the intervention of the law and that which does not cannot be drawn in the distinction between private indulgence and public sobriety.   It is a practical one based on an estimate of what can safely be tolerated, whether in public or in private, and shifting from time to time.   It cannot be said that so much is the law's business but more is not!   He conceives that part of the law's function is to ensure that, as well as carrying out his assignable duties, an individual also maintains some standard of health and morality, preventing the harm that would be done to society by the weakness and vice of too many of its members.   Professor Hart (1963) has in turn challenged this interpretation by questioning the morality of enforcing morals and, commenting on homosexuality between consenting adults, he maintains that ' The misery caused directly and indirectly by legal punishment outweighs any conceivable harm these practices may do '.   He (Hart, 1965) has later dealt with the objection that when the Law does not seem to condemn—it seems to condone—an attitude, he felt, out of touch with contemporary social reality. He challenges the attitude that legal sanctions should be the channel whereby public feelings of hatred and the desire for vengeance are expressed, preferring the free mechanisms of public argument, advice and exhortation.

The Christian in this situation will be loath to see the law when it affects morals, subject to a consensus of public opinion, or to an oligarchy of intellectuals.   He will then be forced to accept the task of showing that Christian morals are best for the individual and for society, even when neither acknowledge the ultimate authority of the Christian revelation with its statements on the origin, nature and end of man.   But, reminded of the Parable of the wheat and the tares (Matt. xiii. 24-30). he may recognise that to root out the tares may be more destructive than to allow them to grow together until the final reckoning.   A large section of the discussion which follows will try to show how public opinion is informed by the profession and where a Christian emphasis is most required.

HOMOSEXUALITY

Homosexuality is a sexual propensity for persons of one's own sex.   This tendency is present to a varying degree and for a short period of time in most people's lives.   It may vary in the same individual when the environment changes and is not necessarily confined to adolescence.   In the majority this tendency may be confined to the thought-life and find expression by exclusively living and working amongst the same sex, there never being any

overt sexual behaviour in these circumstances. The remainder
may indulge in such behaviour with those of their own age or less
commonly with persons of a different age. It is these physical
acts of indecency which constitute homosexual offences against
the law.

The incidence of homosexuality is reviewed by D. J. West
(1959) and he finds nothing to refute the findings of Kinsey which
showed that 4 per cent of a cross section of the whole male population was a ' hard core ' of complete homosexuals who indulged
at some stage in overt behaviour. This contrasts with the frequency
of prosecution in the London Metropolitan Police District (West,
1960) of 0.0074 per cent of the population, which is the highest
area of incidence. Some 2,000 persons are in prison each year
for these offences in the United Kingdom.

There is evidence from psychiatric and twin studies that the homosexual tendency can on occasion be inherited although discordance
may be as common (Parker, 1964). Endocrine studies have shown
disturbances, but whether primary or secondary is difficult to
evaluate. Overtly homosexual behaviour may occur as a symptom
in the course of a recognised mental or physical illness, such as
senile dementia where the self-control of the individual is slowly
disintegrating. Evidence given before the Committee on Homosexual Offences and Prostitution suggested that even where the
individual is normally continent by disposition, self-control may
break down temporarily under the influence of factors like alcohol
or mental disorder. However, they also found that in many cases
symptoms of homosexuality could occur in the absence of any other
mental disease, although such behaviour could lead to psychiatric
abnormalities, a sequel to the strain and conflict of the condition.
They concluded that because a particular person's sexual propensity
happens to be in the direction of his or her own sex, there was no
evidence that it was less controllable, compulsive and irresistible
than that of the heterosexual.

In psychiatric practice homosexuality is regarded more as a
symptom than a condition, and treatment is directed more often
at the underlying psychopathology ranging from group psychotherapy in special units to prolonged aversion therapy and on
occasion to direct physical methods.

The criminal aspects of homosexuality can be traced to antiquity
where in Jewish law (Lev. xx. 13) both male and female homosexuality was punished by death. The Christian Church and Ecclesi-

astical Law adopted these principles and eventually passed them into secular law in 1533 when sodomy was made punishable by death. This penalty remained until the sentence was reduced to life imprisonment, under the influence of Sir Robert Peel. Today the homosexual assault is still a felony and any citizen who knows of such an offence has a legal duty to apprehend the guilty persons and notify the police, which raises ethical problems for the doctor who has access to information about such felonies (West, 1960). The Wolfenden Report (Special Report, 1957) realised the possibility of blackmail under these conditions, but found no real cause for changing the law on this count. Acts of gross indecency committed in private between consenting adults first became a criminal offence in 1885 following a Bill introduced quickly by Mr. Henry Labouchere at the end of an Act dealing mainly with prostitution, and now embodied in Section 13 of the Sexual Offences Act, 1956. It is this last amendment that has caused most controversy. Public opinion still demands that the law concerning the more serious offences should stand, even when immunity from penal sanctions is granted because of psychiatric evidence; the individuals should still be segregated for the sake of society at large. Lord Kilmuir (*Medical News*, 1965) in a debate in the House of Lords in May, 1965, stated that from evidence given to the Home Secretary on 96 imprisoned homosexuals, only 15 were psychiatrically ill; the remaining 81 carried out their homosexual practices for such reasons as boredom with women, desire for sensation and for money. He went on to point out that no legislation can distinguish between the genuine 15 and the 81.

The Wolfenden Committee reviewed the evidence for bringing in an amendment to make homosexual behaviour between consenting adult males (over 21), no longer a criminal offence. At least five main reasons were adduced; they are given in detail because they illustrate the general problems of legislating against immorality.

(*a*) Criminal law was designed to preserve public order and decency, to protect the citizen from what is injurious and offensive and to safeguard him from exploitation and corruption. It was not its function to interfere with the private lives of citizens nor to enforce a pattern of behaviour. There remains a realm of private morality which is not the law's business.

(*b*) The criminal law does not attempt to cover all fields of sexual behaviour, innocence does not begin where crime ends. Adultery, fornication and prostitution as such are not crimes at the present time, although in other circumstances unlawful.

(c) No evidence was found to show that homosexual behaviour between males inflicts any greater damage to family life than adultery, fornication or lesbian behaviour.

(d) Legal enactments cannot be markedly ahead of public opinion or it will fall into disrepute. No attempts are made at the moment in other fields to equate crime with sin.

(e) Although there was absolutely no evidence that the police, in carrying out their duties, acted as *agents provocateurs*, there are occasions when the police officer must resort to a degree of subterfuge in the course of his duty.

One dissentient voice was raised by Mr. James Adair (Special Report, 1957), then procurator fiscal in Scotland. A précis of his objections follow.

(a) Homosexual conduct injures the public in general and young people in particular.

(b) There was a sentimental sympathy for all homosexuals on medical grounds. This obscures the fact that some for monetary and other reasons take up this type of behaviour.

(c) That if legal sanctions are removed, fewer individuals will find themselves in the hands of the police and fewer will be forced to seek a medical opinion. This will also remove the ability of the police to act in a preventative fashion and may give the impression of condoning this conduct.

(d) That the very limited hope held out by the medical profession for improving the homosexual tendency of an individual, the present relaxed moral attitude and the artificial division between ' in private ' and ' in public ' as far as the community is concerned, makes the amendment premature and inopportune.

The amendment has still to be accepted, a private trust[1] continues to press for reform, prosecution rates differ in various parts of the country, while the repercussions of public exposure outweigh the legal sanctions.

[1]The Albany Trust, 32 Shaftesbury Avenue, London, W.1.

The theological approach to this problem is based on Jewish law which identified these practices with pagan idolatrous civilisations characterised in the story of Lot and the men of Sodom (Gen. xix. 1-25). St. Paul (Rom. i. 27) takes up the theme singling out the Roman practices as characteristic of a society which worshipped the creature more than the Creator. Christian thought has been unanimous ever since that such acts are grave sins; however, in some sections of the Church, opinion has been in favour of the Wolfenden Report amendment (Bailey, 1956). Against this D. M. Lloyd-Jones in a lecture delivered before the Christian Medical Fellowship in 1959 emphasised that the tendency to explain every aspect of misbehaviour in terms of disease would abolish standards of right and wrong and lead to the dismissal of the concept of sin, granting that some may be excepted on the basis of mental disease. He argued from an historical point of view that when homosexual practices have flourished Christian influence has been on the wane. He made a strong plea that no fear of totalitarianism should make the Christian hesitate to base the laws of the land on the laws of God. In this ideally theocratic situation the more unnatural the offence the more severe the punishment and segregation. Homosexual behaviour on these grounds is to be distinguished from adultery and fornication as being further removed from natural behaviour. Punishment in these circumstances is seen mainly as a deterrent and for the segregation of the offender. Rehabilitation and remedial action will only succeed when the power of God has been able to work through the acceptance of the Gospel. This latter conclusion raises theological problems on whether any specific spiritual response from the individual is required or can be recognised before remedial action can have any effect. In practice the response may be between persons as the offender realises his situation, regains some perspective and dignity, and senses through the efforts of others that he may be worth a place in society again. Only as this process occurs can forgiveness and redemption have much meaning.

For the Christian doctor his task of caring will continue whether his patient is segregated in a psychiatric unit, faced with a prison sentence or punished by social ostracism. Prison may have worsened his ability to break with habitual behaviour; as Dr. Stanley Jones (1947) has commented 'Imprisonment is as futile from the point of view of treatment as to hope to rehabilitate a chronic alcoholic by giving him occupational therapy in a brewery!'

A close Christian community may have difficulty in accepting those convicted of homosexual behaviour even after sentence and treatment, and a large share of the pastoral care may have to be taken by the individual doctor or minister of religion (Harvey, 1955; Gross, 1962).

ATTEMPTED SUICIDE

Attempted suicide presents one of the common causes for acute admission to the general hospital and doctors occasionally sense the futility and despair of the staff who have to stretch limited facilities for intensive care for what are often recurrent admissions. The suicide rate for England is around one for every two hours of every day of the year; in this time five others will have attempted and failed. Higher rates are found in student populations (Rook, 1959) and the medical profession is far from immune (*British Medical Journal*, 1964).

From clinical studies of attempted suicide a general pattern emerges; Stengel and Cook (1958) emphasised that many suicidal attempts can be regarded more as pleas for help than as failures at suicide. The majority of patients are brought to this action because of severe depression or through environmental stress beyond the individual's personality and character ability to handle; others may have organic, cerebral or other disease. Sainsbury (1955) has shown some of the environmental factors behind the successful suicide act. He demonstrated in the 28 London boroughs how high suicide rates coincided with loneliness, social isolation, enforced mobility with the difficulty of finding accommodation. He found evidence of serious physical disease in nearly a third, previous mental disorder in nearly half, and a twenty times greater incidence of malignant disease than in the general population.

A similar pattern of underlying illness was found in Edinburgh 20 years later. Among the attempted suicides studied, 60 per cent required psychiatric treatment; in the remainder the major cause was either a personality defect or a break-up in the home where little help could be offered (Kessel & MacLee, 1962).

It was this mounting and social evidence that demonstrated that the majority of attempted suicides were sick people and therefore needing medical help; legal sanctions were inappropriate and did not act as deterrent. Of 100 women who were in Holloway

Prison charged with attempted suicide, 11 had been previously charged for a similar offence and nearly half knew that suicide was illegal (Epps, 1957). Until the Suicide Act of 1961, an amendment of the Criminal Justice Act of 1948, attempted suicide was punishable with imprisonment, a fine or probation, and some indication of the application of the law is given by the fact that of 5,436 cases of attempted suicide known to the police in 1957, less than 10% were involved in proceedings and some of these included those who in attempting to kill themselves killed or injured another.

The moral and ethical problems still remain. In tracing the Christian attitude to the suicide act very little comment is contained in the six biblical records of those who took action which could have or did lead to their death. Abimelech (Judges ix. 54) and Saul (1 Sam. xxxi. 4) chose death rather than die at the hands of the enemy. Ahithophel (2 Sam. xvii. 23), Zimri (1 Kings xvi. 18) and Judas (Matt. xxvii. 5) were filled with despair, depression and guilt. Samson's death (Judges xvi. 30) might be classed in the separate category of ' altruistic suicide ' where the motive overrules the act, exemplified by Captain Oates on Scott's last expedition. The early Christian Church condemned suicides on three main grounds (Stevas, 1961), that it violated the commandment ' Thou shalt not kill ', which applied to all innocent lives, one's own as much as another's; that it precluded any opportunity of repentance, and that it was a cowardly act. These principles were formulated under the stress of a barbarian invasion of established Christian communities where the choice was between physical submission or suicide. St. Augustine answered this in stating ' If wickedness is so powerful over us that we have in our choice no innocent acts but only sins, is it not better to elect an uncertain adultery in the future rather than a certain homicide in the present? (Saint Augustine).

This traditional viewpoint has changed in emphasis, now stressing the selfishness of the action, summarised as follows— ' The prohibition of suicide is derived from the doctrine of God as Creator. Man is not the author of his own life, he has received it from God. It is given him for its use and service of God on earth. Suicide is contrary to the ' natural law ' of self-preservation, and by so ending his life a man deprives society and his family of those services and benefits which they have a right to expect from him.' (Mortimer, 1959).

This may well be the attitude of the healthy Christian and the community around him; when the doctor has to deal with the attempted suicide it is just at these points that the person's convictions may have broken down through depression, disease, social pressures and spiritual darkness. The elderly may understandably argue that his life is already hazarded by disease, his service is over, society has no dignity to give him, he is a burden to his family, and life as such has little meaning or value—the ' natural law ' of self-preservation has lost its power.

The Christian community, with notable exceptions, has still to grapple with the part that the increasing number of elderly retired and lonely people have to play in their life together. The degree to which they become cut off and uncared for on simple medical grounds has been reviewed recently by an Edinburgh geriatric team (Williamson *et al.*, 1964). Because of this loneliness in large cities, not confined to the elderly, the inaccessibility of many Christian fellowships to those in acute need, emergency Samaritan services (Varah, 1964) have been set up. First in 1953 at St. Stephen's, Walbrook, and now in other cities and local areas, lay workers with professional supervision and advice have provided counselling for those in acute need. In this way a bridge has been provided between Christian communities who otherwise would be unaware of the need.

Faced with people in acute need in these circumstances or after admission to hospital, the first task is to answer some of the problems of the underlying psychiatric disease and environmental chaos; further comment may be irrelevant because they are so overwhelming. When some of the acute wounds are healed, two questions remain to be answered. ' Is my life worth living? Does it or can it have value? ' In discussing these questions a psychotherapist comments (Whalley, 1964), 'the most significant value that the suicide patient seems to have lost is the unique intrinsic worth and irreplaceability of every individual life; with this diminished sense of their own worth, comes a depreciation of the worth of others. Patients will absorb convictions of their own personal worth from every word, attitude and activity on their behalf. It is the activities engaged to save his life that the patient correctly interprets as the telling evidence that others value his life more than at the moment he does.' This is the continuing challenge to the Christian minister, doctor or social worker.

ALCOHOLISM

Drinking alcohol is a common feature of communal life in this country; as our links with Europe grow it may become a regular feature of family meals. The use of alcohol to celebrate, relax and to break down reserve forms the basis of social drinking with great economic significance. Part of the cost of excessive drinking is found in three major problems; road traffic accidents, recurrent drunkenness, and true compulsive alcoholism.

A review (Harvard, 1963) of three recent surveys relating alcohol intake to Road Traffic Accidents showed that among drivers probably responsible for the accident, 73 per cent had been drinking, compared with 20 per cent of a control group matched from drivers at the same place and day of the week as the accidents. Of those involved in the accidents 46 per cent had blood alcohol concentrations of 250 mg. per cent or above. Of all fatal accidents 18.7 per cent were complicated by alcohol intake compared with 10.4 per cent of those resulting in serious injuries and 6 per cent of those resulting in minor injuries. Similar data are now being collected for accidents in this country, and it is hoped that informed public opinion with careful legislation will bring in an Act prohibiting drinking to an extent above prescribed limits and driving, following continental experience and practice. From the surveys taken, it has also emerged that a proportion of those with high blood alcohol concentrations were alcoholics rather than social drinkers, and that a traffic accident may be the first sign of serious addiction to alcohol. In these situations once the surgical complications of the accident are over, it may be in the patient's interest for a more detailed psychiatric assessment to be offered.

Drunkenness, heavy weekend drinking and relief drinking are common causes for admission to accident services, and owing to the pressure on these services, once physical injury and disease have been excluded, the patients are rapidly discharged with a cautionary smile or less. Some of the tensions aroused between the staff on such services, and the aggressive semi-drunk destitute patient with only minor injuries have been observed by two physicians (Abram & McCourt, 1964) attached to an alcohol unit in Boston. They make a strong plea for specialised help in dealing with these patients, and have noted the frequency of recurrent admissions fall with supervision and follow up in a separate clinic. Some emergency admissions may be the first signs of a neurotic illness, severe family stress or even an organic

K

disease such as temporal lobe epilepsy, making a more detailed psychiatric and social history essential.

A recent survey (Jones, 1963) of the disorganised family background, the intermittent and declining status of the individual's work record and his neurotic tendencies has shown how the environment and personality of the alcoholic seem to prevent any hope of recovery unless he receives considerable outside help. This work also brings into relief the almost casual approach of the doctor whose training has seldom included any systematic training on alcoholism.

Alcoholism, in distinction to social drinking and drunkenness has been defined by the World Health Organisation (Expert Committee on Mental Health, 1955) as follows:—

' Alcoholics are those excessive drinkers whose dependence upon alcohol has attained such a degree that it shows a notable mental disturbance or an interference with their bodily and mental health, their interpersonal relationships and their smooth social and economic functioning; or who show the prodromal signs of such developments.   They therefore require treatment '.

The late Dr. Jellinek (1963) was able to group alcoholics into various types which may have aetiological and prognostic significance.   In the first group, alcohol is used to relieve bodily or emotional pain, drinking is frequent and quite undisciplined and yet there is an ability to abstain when other help is offered. There are no signs of a progressive process and in the majority there is an acute underlying psychiatric illness.   In contrast, in the second group environmental factors predominate; income and social state is low, leading in turn to malnutrition, precipitating the medical complications of alcoholism outlined above earlier. There is little evidence of physical or psychological dependence upon alcohol.   The third group predominates in alcoholic clinics and in such associations as Alcoholics Anonymous.   There is long history of increasing alcoholic intake until there is a high tissue tolerance with adaptive cell metabolism which results in acute withdrawal symptoms leading in turn to the financial and social breakdown of the individual.   However, this may be delayed and disguised for several years, especially in those with positions of responsibility.   A fourth group is more often seen in continental Europe; they are never sober and never drunk, they retain a firm control over intake, and they eat well, cirrhosis being a late complication.   These inveterate drinkers are often found among professions which entail constant emotional pressures with ample opportunity for drinking, such as in advertising, commercial selling and the theatre. A fifth and rare group is reserved for the dipsomaniac who has periodic severe bouts of drinking, associated with aggressive behaviour, damaging himself, others and property. Criminal proceedings are a frequent sequel and detention limits the deterioration.

Surveying the many aspects of alcoholism the British Medical Association and Magistrates Association Joint Committee had three major recommendations to make, namely: (a) The better student and postgraduate training of doctors in the recognition of alcoholism. (b) The education of the public to encourage earlier recourse to medical treatment. (c) The provision of facilities for treatment on a much larger scale than exists at present.

Until such facilities exist the compulsory treatment of alcoholics in 'inebriate institutions' is virtually unenforceable, although the legislation has existed for over 50 years, this might now be incorporated by a suitable amendment to the Mental Health Act of 1959. The lack of an overall N.H.S. plan for the care of the alcoholic is offset by the provision of a few inpatient units[1], usually attached to mental hospitals. A number of voluntary bodies cater for the needs of alcoholics, not only from the psychiatric and medical aspects but also for the social and moral rehabilitation of the individual.

Many authors have stressed the need for the alcoholic to 'hit rock bottom' and the total surrender to the fact that he must not drink again (Williams, 1960). This crisis point has many common features with a religious conversion (Merriman, 1958).

Clinebell has developed a thesis that in drinking the alcoholic has found a temporary answer to three fundamental religious needs. The first is a desire for an experience of the transcendent or luminous, something beyond material existence; the alcoholic finds this in intoxication. The second is the demand for a sense of meaning purpose and value in one's existence; under alcohol some of the pain, emptiness and awareness of mortality is forgotten. Finally, the alcoholic feels desperately the need for deep trust and relatedness in life; when drinking with friends he may have a temporary but highly valued experience of unity. The measure to which a Christian fellowship meets these needs may indicate

[1]List obtainable from Joseph Rowntree Social Service Trust Steering Group on Alcoholism at 3 St. James' Sq., S.W.1.

the help which an alcoholic may obtain if he can gain access to it (Clinebell, 1963).

CONCLUSIONS

In these three sociomedical situations common features have emerged which concern the doctor; in each an expert assessment of the medical and psychiatric aspects must be made and help sought in the appropriate area. Whatever the moral or legal problems these individuals are in need of prolonged follow-up and this may be costly in time and involve the family more extensively than in most situations. Although much of what has been commented upon in previous sections seems to lessen the degree of responsibility in the individual, what remains of his responsibility must be encouraged and fostered within the framework of his illness. A large proportion of supportive psychotherapy is arrived at, slowly allowing the individual more freedom to develop not only insight, but also an increasing responsibility for his own decisions and a return to the family and society. The attitude of ' put them out of sight and out of mind ' to stop the spread or to warn others has only increased their degree of alienation which some see as the basis of much continued mental illness (Davis, 1964).

In these conditions with an increasing incidence and high recurrence rate no one can be content with just patching up the victim, and an effort must be made in the community and by the doctor to anticipate these situations before tragedy overtakes the individual and the family.

On occasion there may be an opportunity for doctor-clergy co-operation, although the lines of communication have to be laid down carefully as there is a poverty of common concepts. Together they may be able to clear away the disgust and revulsion that can be evoked in the community and the Church to such behaviour, and recruit more informed care and understanding. Together they may be aware of circumstances in a family or group where alcoholism or suicide might be anticipated and help given in time. Clinebell (1965) maintained that ' mental health is a central and inescapable concern of any local church that is a healthy redemptive fellowship.' It is hoped that the cursory survey of the problems in this review may show some of the lines which a true Christian concern for medical ethics may follow, as it involves the relationships between erring but sick individuals and society.

Finally, there are five areas where constructive action can be taken:—

(*a*) Information is increasingly available to show the particular areas in the family and the wider environment in which these social deviations are most likely to occur. It is at such points that the practitioner and social worker can anticipate (i) where the family environment may lead to homosexuality (West, 1959); (ii) where social isolation and mobility (coupled with early family break-up) can make the suicidal attempt a likely event, and (iii) the ethnic type, psychiatric instability and poor environment may increase the possibility of alcoholism.

(*b*) Forewarned in this way, that is, in those areas where the incidence of suicide and alcoholism are known to be high, whole-hearted support and direction of the social services together with the provision of clinics and day hospitals could meet the increasing need. This would be particularly true in large cities. Churches can also play a significant role in providing a bridge between some of these social tragedies and their full rehabilitation back into their families and society.

(*c*) Those members of the Profession who are in the public health departments can push forward in such areas of social illness with research on the one hand, and the education of the public on the other. In this way the underlying factors could be freely discussed and accurate data made available for those planning social and legal action. In some cities attempted suicide has reached almost epidemic proportions and yet public health action and public feeling has been singularly unimpressive. In the field of alcoholism Ullman (1958) has provided a thesis, which has, however, yet to be tested—' In any group or society in which drinking customs, values and sanctions—together with the attitudes of all segments of the group or society—are well established, known to and agreed upon by all, and are consistent with the rest of the culture, the rate of alcoholism will be low '. Such a state of affairs, if it be proved, will require a thorough reconsideration of the process of educating families concerning the right place of alcohol in their lives.

(*d*) The provision of accurate data related to the effects of treatment, penal sanctions anf follow-up measures in all sections of the community. In this way the truth can be brought to bear on public opinion, legal planning and the provision of increasingly enlightened social services. It has been observed that when a large enough social threat to a whole community is in action (such as the possibility of imminent physical destruction) the incidence of suicide declines. Whether the provision of a strong communal purpose can achieve the same effect has to be seen. Some means, however, must be found to break down the lack of concern, selfishness and isolation which is so widespread in our present society.

(e) An analysis of the factors which have caused amongst our contemporaries a loss of confidence in the literal truth of the Christian religion reveals a reluctance (in a society which is undergoing a continuing scientific revolution) to accept any truth as absolute or revealed. In all the above examples of social deviation the medical and psychiatric aspects of the situation must be fully assessed and the appropriate action taken. Yet, if this in fact be God's world, the basis of a full and healthy personality can only be found in a divine relationship and in a ' given ' pattern of behaviour. It is the present-day Christian's task to turn the Humanist's statement that ' we no longer ask what is pleasing to God, but what is good for man ' (Wotton, 1961) into a clear demonstration that *what is pleasing to God is good for man.*

REFERENCES

ABRAM, H. S. & McCOURT, W. F. (1954). Interaction of physicians with emergency ward alcoholic patients. *Q. Jl Stud. Alcohol,* **25,** 679.

BAILEY, D. S. (1956). *Sexual Offenders and Social Punishment.* London: Church of England Moral Welfare Council, C.I.O.

British Medical Journal (1964). Suicide among doctors, **1,** 789.

CLINEBELL, H. J. (1963). Philosophical religious factors in the etiology and treatment of alcoholism. *J. Stud. Alcohol,* **23,** 453.

CLINEBELL, H. J. (1965). *Mental Health through Christian Community.* New York: Abingdon Press.

DAVIS, D. RUSSELL (1964). Family processes in mental illness. *Lancet,* **1,** 731.

DEVLIN, LORD (1965). *The Enforcement of Morals,* chap. 6. London: Oxford University Press.

EPPS, P. (1957). Women in prison on ' attempted suicide ' charges. *Lancet,* **2,** 182.

EXPERT COMMITTEE ON MENTAL HEALTH (1955). Report of the 1954 session of the alcoholism sub-committee. *Tech. Rep. Ser. Wld. Hlth. Org.* No. 94.

GROSS, A. A. (1962). *Strangers in our Midst.* Washington: Public Affairs Press.

HART, H. R. A. (1963). *Law, Liberty and Morality.* London: Oxford University Press.

HART, H. R. A. (1965). *The Morality of the Criminal Law.* London: Oxford University Press.

HARVARD, J. D. (1963). Recent developments in the alcohol and road traffic situation. *Br. J. Addict.* **59**, 55.

HARVEY, J. F. (1955). Homosexuality as a pastoral problem. *Theolog. Stud.* **10**, 86.

HILL, D. (1962). Character and personality in relation to criminal responsibility. *Med. Sci. Law,* **2**, 221.

JELLINEK, E. M. (1963). The Disease Concept of Alcoholism. Highland Park, N. Jersey: Hillhouse Press.

JONES, D. STANLEY (1947). Sexual inversion. *Lancet,* **1**, 366.

JONES, H. (1963). *Alcohol, Addiction, a Psychological Approach to Abnormal Drinking.* London: Tavistock Publications.

KESSELL, N. & MACLEE, E. (1962). Attempted suicide in Edinburgh. *Scott. med. J.* **7**, 130.

MACKAY, D. M. (1958). *Faith & Thought,* **90**, 103.

Medical News (1965). June 4th.

MERRIMAN, B. (1958). Some observations on alcoholism. In *The Service of Medicine.* No. 14. London: The Christian Medical Fellowship.

MERSKEY, H. & CLARKE, P. R. F. (1962). Determinism, responsibility and illness. *Lancet,* **2**, 291.

MOORE, E. G. (1964). Moral Approach to Law. London: January Crucible C.I.O. Publication.

MORTIMER, R. C. (1959). *Christian Ethics,* p. 123. London:

PARKER, N. (1964). Homosexuality in twins. *Br. J. Psychiat.* **10**, 489.

ROOK, SIR ALAN (1959). Student suicides. *Br. med. J.* **1**, 599.

SAINSBURY, P. (1955). *Suicide in London.* Maudsley Monograph No. 1. London: Chapman & Hall.

SAINT AUGUSTINE. *The City of God against the Pagans,* Book 1, Section 26, p. 109. Classical Library Edition, 1957. Cambridge, Mass.: Harvard University Press.

SMITH, NOWELL P. H. (1954). *Ethics,* chap. 19. London: Penguin Books.

SPECIAL REPORT BY THE COMMITTEE ON HOMOSEXUALITY AND PROSTITUTION. (1957). *The Wolfenden Report.* London: H.M.S.O. Cmd. 247.

STENGEL, E. & COOK, N. G. (1958). *Attempted Suicide.* Maudsley Monograph No. 4. London: Chapman & Hall.

STEVAS, N. ST. JOHN (1961). *Life, Death and the Law.* London: Eyre & Spottiswoode.

ULLMAN, A. D. (1958). Socio-cultural backgrounds of alcoholism. *Ann. Am. Acad. pol. soc. Sci.* **315**, 48.

VARAH, C. (1964). Care for those without hope. In *The Caring Church,* ed. P. Smith: Derby, England.

WEST, D. J. (1960). *Homosexuality.* London: Penguin Books.

WEST, D. J. (1959). Parental relationships in male homosexuality. *Int. J. Soc. Psychiat.* **5**, 85.

WHALLEY, E. A. (1964). Values and the suicide threat. *J. Relig. Hlth,* **3**, 241.

WILLIAMS, L. (1956). *Alcoholism.* Edinburgh: Livingstone.

WILLIAMS, L. (1960). *Tomorrow will be Sober.* London: Cassel.

WILLIAMSON, J., STOKEO, L. H., GRAY, S., FISHER, M., SMITH, A., MCGREE, A. & STEPHENSON, E. (1964). Old people at home, their unreported needs. *Lancet,* **1**, 1117.

WOOTON, B. (1963). *Crime and the Criminal Law.* London: Stevens.

WOTTON, B. (1961). Humanism and social pathology. In *The Humanist Frame,* p. 347. ed. Huxley, J. London: Allen & Unwin.

CHAPTER IX

RESPONSIBILITY IN PREVENTIVE MEDICINE

W. GEORGE SWANN[1]

The road to achievement in social and preventive medicine is not hard to see; to build it is quite another matter. Not only are there entrenched vested interests bestriding the primitive tracks, there is also the natural unwillingness of human nature to have to take the extra trouble needed. In addition, at some points, political, religious, social and individual freedom may seem to be, or actually is, at stake. Some authority and ultimately some person must take responsibility for the planning and carrying out of such measures as seem desirable. Therefore, before discussing the basic problems it will be necessary to outline some of the varied and complicated tasks which concern environmental and preventive medicine in this country, and to indicate who is primarily responsible for the applications.

The fundamental aim of a reformer in public health is to alter the ' environment ' of the social group whom he seeks to serve. This must be done in such a way as to rid that environment of what is injurious to physical or mental health or, alternatively, to add what will work effectively for health. The varieties and complexities which these alterations may take is best appreciated by summarising the work of a Public Health Department.

THE SPHERE OF PUBLIC HEALTH

Local Government through its many services works to protect people against all that might cause disease. In the environmental division of the Health Department the epidemiological section deals with the notification of disease, preventive immunisation and vaccination, control by quarantine of disease at ports, food hygiene in all its aspects, health aspects of housing and factories, smoke abatement, and such like. This work was traditionally developed in connection with the control of infectious disease, but modern epidemiology is equally concerned with non-communicable diseases in an endeavour to unmask the causative factors in the aetiology of diseases such as bronchitis, cancer and

[1] W. George Swann, M.D., B.Sc., D.P.H., D.P.A., is Medical Officer of Health, Port and City of London.

coronary thrombosis. The environmental work of the Public Health Medical Officer also includes the abatement of ' statutory nuisances ', which means a concern for slum clearance and other housing problems, offensive trades, rodent and insect pest control.

In addition, the Medical Officer of Health has powers and duties (under the Food and Drugs Act and subsidiary regulations) to ensure that food is of the nature, substance and quality demanded by the purchaser and that it is free from contamination and fit for human consumption. This has wide ramifications in the field of food production and technology, and concerns such commodities as meat, home slaughtered and imported; production, transportation, pasteurization and distribution of milk supplies; inspection of catering establishments and, in some instances, their registration; and many other aspects of food control dealing with labelling, preservatives and other permitted additives.

The history of public health discloses many instances of the way in which disease has been controlled by altering the environment. The introduction of a pure water supply and of various water-borne sewage disposal systems led to the eradication of epidemics of cholera and typhoid in this country, even before the bacterial causation of these diseases was known.

In traditional Public Health the practitioner was concerned primarily with material factors in the physical environment which should be eliminated, that is those which were injurious to health. The history of the conquest of infectious diseases in this country illustrates how harmful agents, which were a menace to the health of the public, were at first controlled and later largely conquered. The various statutory provisions for the control of the spread of infectious diseases encroached on the liberty of individuals because the welfare of the community as a whole was the overriding consideration. Doctors by law were and are required to notify certain infectious diseases—a responsibility which a few forget, even in this enlightened age! The Medical Officer of Health may become aware of the outbreak of communicable diseases and he then has the responsibility to determine the source of the infection by epidemiological investigations. He seeks to discover the mode of transmission of the disease and takes adequate measures to prevent its spread in the community. At this point the history of preventive medicine shows how necessary it has been to give powers to local authorities to limit the freedom of individuals. This has been done by restricting the movements in public places of persons suffering from notifiable infectious disease and, if necessary, by compulsorily removing them to, and retaining them in, hospital by a magistrate's order, for their own welfare or to protect the health of the public. This compulsion was extended into the realm of preventive treatment as in the case of vaccination against smallpox. However, where the directive involves the freedom of the individual and his right to refuse medical treatment, safeguards were introduced to allow for genuine conscientious scruples as well as exemptions on medical certification of conditions considered as contra-indications to vaccination.

Growth of Public Health

The manner in which other injurious physical factors in both the social and working environment were dealt with in the early practice of public health and preventive medicine readily come to mind, such as improvement in housing by slum clearance and the planning of redevelopment schemes and improvement of working conditions in factories. So at present it may well be that the elimination of harmful agents from the air we breathe could have a similar beneficial effect in reducing the incidence of lung cancer. Who knows but that the introduction of smoke-controlled or smoke-free areas under the new powers given to Local Authorities by the Clean Air Act may reduce considerably this scourge, even before the research workers have discovered its specific cause?

The evolution of public health measures naturally involves the further encroachment of central and local government by statutory powers into the realm of freedom of the individual. This limitation of freedom has been considered equitable in certain instances for the preservation of the health of the community. In fact, in certain instances this ' police-like ' action has been necessary to save the life of a community when threatened by an epidemic disease with high mortality such as cholera or smallpox. Drastic measures, even those which we would today consider barbarous, were taken in certain instances. In this tercentenary year of the great plague of London one recalls that the Lord Mayor and Magistrates attended to the cleanliness of the city and the relief of the poor so that there was little or no actual want. But the administrative measures, carried out with the best intentions to limit the spread of infection, in fact led to further dissemination of the disease. One house after another was shut up with all its occupants inside. Thus each became a focus for further spread of disease. This was followed by the marking of such houses with a red cross and the legend ' God have mercy on us! '

No one would doubt the necessity for governments to have powers such as are given by the present-day International Sanitary Regulations to control by quarantine the spread to other countries of diseases such as smallpox, cholera, plague, yellow fever and typhus. Thus it is that controls which were at first introduced by individual States for self-preservation or protection have become adopted internationally. This unification of the world by rapid transport has its dangers and so legislative means to protect nations against the importation of dangerous epidemic diseases are justifiable.

THE MEDICAL OFFICER OF HEALTH'S RESPONSIBILITIES

The Medical Officer of Health is appointed by a local authority and he is granted certain statutory powers and given duties to perform. The terms and conditions of his appointment are even to some extent circumscribed by legal requirements. For example, he enjoys security in his tenure of office whereby he cannot be dismissed without the concurrence of the designated central government department and only then after due enquiry. The Public Health Service, in which the Medical Officer of Health holds a full-time salaried appointment, was the first sector of the medical profession to come under State authority as a ' servant '. However, subsequent to 1948 with the introduction of the National Health Service, practically all doctors in this country are engaged in, and receive remuneration to some extent from State appointments. The relationships of a doctor practising in a State-run Health Service give rise to many specific responsibilities which he did not previously encounter when he was engaged in private practice. An attempt will be made to define and illustrate some of these responsibilities in relation to the work of a Medical Officer of Health.

The duties of a Medical Officer of Health are largely laid down in Acts of Parliament or subsidiary rules, orders or byelaws and they determine the functions of the employing authority. So whether it be the abatement of a statutory nuisance, control of an outbreak of smallpox or the provision of a domiciliary midwife for the home confinement of an expectant mother, all stem from statutory powers or duties.

The Medical Officer of Health is not solely responsible for

environmental health. Every doctor to some extent is engaged in this work. A practitioner, as he seeks to treat his patients, may become aware that there are diseases in which the patient's environment constitutes some specific adverse factor. This factor may be physical, psychological, social or spiritual in nature. He may discover an allergen in the home environment which is causing his patient's asthma. The industrial medical officer may find that the worker's dermatitis is due to the irritant effect of the material he handles in the factory. The psychiatrist may discover that the underlying complex of an anxiety neurosis consists in his patient's repressed hatred of someone. How important in our environment are the people whom we meet each day! Maladjustment in personal relationships has been shown to be one of the main causes of mental illness.

The M.O.H. recommends to the local Health Committee how best to help the people in the area. These duties extend beyond the elimination of harmful agents from the environment to the attempt to contribute directly to the health of individuals. An example is the introduction of various schemes of immunisation against specific infectious diseases such as diphtheria, poliomyelitis, whooping-cough, tetanus and tuberculosis. These schemes followed compulsory vaccination against smallpox but were voluntary, both for parents and children. Those immunised obtain active immunity, and if a sufficient number of the population are protected, the disease can be eliminated from the community giving protection to all.

Fluoridation of Water

As an illustration of another measure contributing to the health in the community, the fluoridation of water may be cited. This matter is of great topical interest at the present time. The addition of fluoride to a water supply to bring it to almost 1 ppm. will help to prevent dental caries in children. All evidence, such as it is, recommends it as a desirable measure. Some consider that once the Medical Officer of Health has satisfied himself about its value, this is the end of the matter. He must, of course, be fully convinced that it is a safe procedure. The British Medical Officer of Health is merely a professional adviser on the scientific aspects of the problem.

There are other ways of looking at it. For example, a recent annotation in *The Lancet* stated ' passion has entered into the controversy over fluoridation because it is a measure that restricts the liberty of the individual and none can doubt that this is worth caring for deeply.' The Medical Officer of Health, who is very much aware of this, may consider that his scientific recommendation is inadequate, and feel it is his duty to incorporate other considerations in his report.

At the present time the Medical Officer of Health is besieged by propaganda with such titles as ' M.O.H. morality '. In this it is stated ' it is hoped that this article will cause some M.O.s to examine their own consciences and to decide whether or not they are living up to the high standards of their profession.'

So it is obvious that some consider that there is an ethical factor to be considered and that the recommendation to add fluoride to the public water supplies cannot be based on scientific evidence alone. The opponents of fluoridation complain that the process involves forcing fluoridated water upon them without respect of their personal freedom. This complaint may still be validly made even by those who are convinced that the addition of fluoride to 1 ppm is beneficial to children's teeth and is safe as far as the general public is concerned. They argue that in principle it is wrong to add this substance to a water supply and force the whole community to drink it. By adding it to the water it makes it well nigh impossible for those who wish to refrain from drinking such water to be able to do so. This is a denial of personal freedom, they say. Worse may follow. Some have suggested that since 90 per cent of the community is receiving barbiturates or tranquillisers under the National Health Service, a trace of a suitable drug could be added to the water supply to achieve the same result, irrespective of a minority who object to this encroachment on their personal freedom! Such views are honestly held and, in so far as they are, they deserve respect and rational consideration.

Is it the responsibility of the Medical Officer of Health to incorporate advice in his committee report as to what he considers the correct attitude in this matter? If so, this involves him in taking a personal position in relation to what he considers to be the liberty of the subject, and a definition of his understanding of the rights of free citizens living in a democratic community such as ours.

Some are arguing that though the majority vote must rule in democracy, yet there are realms where the State has no right to intervene and to impose its will on the minority. Most of us will agree that this is so in matters of conscience and religious belief, and that the essence of democracy is the maintenance of personal liberty. There are, however, those who believe that fluoridation of the public water supply is one of those realms, and so should be resisted obstinately. They believe that a surrender in principle means opening the door to the limitation of personal freedom by the State.

Water is essential to life, so they argue that no option is left for the individual but to consume it. It is practically impossible to remove fluoride completely from the public water supply by filtration. There is a great difference between being compelled in some respect and being disturbed or inconvenienced. The freedom of the individual to act as he or she chooses is limited by the interest of the rest of the community. In other words, in the exercise of his freedom he must have regard to the like liberty of others, otherwise there would be disorder and anarchy in society. Freedom is relative and qualified. The individual may do or say what he pleases, provided he does so without transgressing the law or infringing the legal rights of others. Likewise public authority can only do what is legally permitted; it cannot interfere with the subject.

The subject has liberties which are not expressly defined in any code of law, and there are some matters in which he does not possess guaranteed rights. Parliament is the law-making authority where the view of the majority prevails. In the modern world central and local government are taking more and more responsibility in the social and public welfare of the community. This legislative encroachment curtails the action of the individual. In public health, as the knowledge of preventive medicine increases, measures are increasingly enacted which the majority considers to be for the public good. In this way freedom of action of the individual is further curtailed. In the final result only a few fundamental rights may remain as ultimately sacrosanct, such as the peaceful enjoyment of property or freedom from illegal detention.

In the matter of fluoridation of water supplies, some opponents have contended that it compels people to take a form of medication contrary to their religious belief, or that it deprives them of the right (as part of their personal freedom) to safeguard their health in the way they consider best. Religious freedom embraces freedom of belief and freedom to act in accordance with one's belief. Freedom of belief is absolute but the second, that is, freedom of action, can only be exercised in conformity with the law. For example, certain sects may regard polygamy as a religious duty, but the State may punish it as a crime. During prohibition in America, the Federal Government had authority to limit the quantity of wine that could be used for sacramental purposes.

DIRECT AND INDIRECT COMPULSION

Again, in consideration of constitutional rights or freedom it is important to distinguish between *direct* compulsion upon the individual as, for example, the compulsory vaccination against smallpox, with penalties for violation of the law, and those which are *indirect*, such as fluoridation, which is incidental to a publicly provided water supply. A citizen is free to drink whatever water he pleases, but in contrast the law takes action if he drives on the right-hand side of the street. A public utility, such as a water supply, which is provided democratically by law, does not give an individual or a minority the right to dictate how the water authority will provide the supply, so long as it acts within its statutory undertaking. Such persons are not compelled to drink the water supply, though it would be difficult for them to obtain an alternative supply. It must, however, be remembered that it is provided as a public utility service and is not, in this sense, like the air we breathe. Individuals possess an obvious right to water as one of the essentials of life, but that is not to say that they have an *equal* right to receive it from a man-made system or without interruption in unlimited quantities and of the nature and quality to suit their individual requirements or tastes. If some persons in such a community combined to provide a public supply, but they were outvoted, it could not be argued that their rights were not protected because they were deprived of the water supply they wanted. Persons receiving water from a public supply system, whether the water is fluoridated or not, are in no worse position than those who receive none at all in this way.

Other opponents contend that fluoridation of water supplies compels them to take a ' form of medication ' or ' compulsory mass medication '—terms which have gained an emotional content, often irrespective of what they mean. The argument here largely hinges on one's conception of what a medicine or medicament is. According to dosage, mode of administration and other circumstances, a substance can be a nutrient, a medicine or a poison. Amounts of vitamin D are needed as a nutrient to promote health and lack of this vitamin leads to the development of rickets. The rickets can be cured by supplying the appropriate dose of the vitamin as a medicine. This dose is in excess of the minute quantity required as an accessory food factor or nutrient to prevent the condition. In still larger doses vitamin D can be poisonous, causing abnormal calcification of bone, and even be fatal. This can be true even of pure water itself.

Again, small traces of iodine are essential to health. In districts where the water supplies are deficient, goitre occurs. This deficiency can be made good by supplying iodine in minute amounts as an addition to table salt. An appropriate dose of iodine can be used as a medicine, for example, as Lugol's iodine, or as an antiseptic tincture of iodine, whereas the consumption of iodine in still larger doses causes iodine poisoning. Similarly fluoride is an essential of human teeth and bone. In areas where the water supply is naturally deficient in fluoride, dental caries in children is greater than in those with approximately 1 ppm. fluoride in the water. In an area where fluoride occurs naturally, in a higher concentration, for example 8 parts per million, the mottling of dental fluorosis is found in children's teeth. Flouride taken in larger doses would cause acute or chronic poisoning depending on the dosage and mode of administration.

Such a consideration of the matter may well lead to the conclusion that fluoride taken in a water supply of 1 ppm. is more properly described as a nutrient than a medicament. It is found in trace amounts in a number of foods.

Many opponents of fluoridation of the water supply are actually drinking water which contains fluoride naturally. It can be argued with equal validity that if such individuals regard the question as an important one, they should be prepared to seek unfluoridated water rather than impose their preferences of this kind of water on a whole community.

In exactly the same or similar ways the problems of the introduction of smoke control areas, accident prevention, increasing drug addiction, and many other causes of mental and physical ill health in the community are to be analysed.

The detailed problems of adjusting corporate responsibility to personal liberty are legion. They go right to the heart of the matter of how far the State, besides eliminating evils, can promote the positive good of the community. The concept of the State as the source of comprehensive welfare causes to loom large the spectre of " interference " in the family, and other similar ' interferences ', until the Totalitarian State takes over. Any large impersonal concept of welfare easily lends itself to one ' Big Brother ' (or a number of Big Brothers) watching over you to such an extent that they eventually take over everything that matters in shaping the individual's life. It will always be in ways which seem good to themselves.

Preventive and Social Medicine may well prove to be the most innocent—or innocent looking—of all forms of the roads to Totalitarianism.

The question of fluoridation of water supplies is also complicated by the fact that the areas of more than one local health authority are usually supplied by one water undertaking. It will be necessary for all the local health authorities supplied by each undertaking to agree to the procedure before fluoridation is introduced. Alternatively government action by Act of Parliament may enforce fluoridation universally. A Medical Officer of Health may well find himself in a situation, such as in the City of London, where the resident population is about 5,000 and the number of children involved is comparatively small. The answer in this case may be to give fluoride tablets to the small group who will benefit. Some say that mothers cannot be expected to give tablets to young infants and children over a period of years regularly. This raises the question of motivation, a very popular one in the modern world of health education. A woman can be trusted to take contraceptive pills regularly, as she is motivated by fear of pregnancy, but not to give tablets in an endeavour to prevent caries in her child's teeth, out of consideration for her child's well-being in this respect.

THE USE OF MASS MEDIA

This brings us to what many consider the most important aspect of the planning of health programmes. It is true to say that opinions have largely become the facts in health education. Opinion polls are used to assess so-called needs or as measures to evaluate services provided. These opinions obtained by postal or personal questionnaires replace the older objective data of mortality or morbidity statistics of public health. Such sociological enquiries seek to discover causes of motivation. It is considered that one must seek to alter habits, but influencing motives often may be at the expense of reason. Exhortation is considered to be ineffective and the modern advertising techniques by pamphlet or television employ such other devices.

Surely there is a responsibility to ensure that such brain-washing techniques are used honestly and truthfully in the service of health education, and that the means employed are as worthy as the ends to be achieved. Methods should not be used which influence action without the rational consent of the individual and his willing acceptance of the benefit offered. ' Do-gooders ' can be a real menace in public health or social work if they intrude upon the sanctity, right or freedom of the individual against his will. The employment of a mass medium such as television or the methods of mob psychology to sway people to do what authority considers to be for their good opens the door to the misuse of their powers, and the eventual elimination of the freedom of the individual. This is a real danger, especially in the field of mental health.

SOME CRUCIAL CONSIDERATIONS

This whole subject of corporate responsibility in relation to Preventive Medicine involves all the basic principles of the theory of the State, the extent to which it should interfere and the age-long uneasy association between corporate action and individual freedom. Not only so, but it involves also the difficult problem of how far the community may impinge on parental responsibility— even when it seems for their good. It involves the difficult sphere of the extent to which suggestive advertising and educative methods may be utilised to alter (against their will) the people's ways of living.

In the last analysis the Christian doctor is bound to make radical judgments and choices. He believes and would argue that his experience confirms that Christianity in its ideal form offers a solution at every turn. If this be God's world, then the *summum bonum* is God's will for the State, the community, family, and the individual. The more we are able to approximate to the overall beneficent plan, and to extend its benefits to all concerned, the more such problems of individual liberty will be absorbed into the common good. The convinced Christian is compelled therefore to believe that he is working for the best of Medicine, the State, and the family, by seeking to conform to the Biblical Revelation.

The corporate action of the State is then seen to be largely negative. It exists for the restraint of evil and the punishment of the evil-doer so that the individual can live in peace and responsible freedom. The Magistrate bears the sword for this purpose. He is responsible for the protection of persons and property in general. The ordinance of marriage preserves the sanctity of the family. Duties and mutual responsibilities are laid on parents and children, husbands and wives. The creational ordinances of work and appropriate ' Sabbath Rest ' remain mandatory principles. The moral law indicates the priority of God in the life of the individual, the sanctity of human life and the right to property. It must be respected. There are other similar implications. In the Bible the Christian finds revealed to him the principles which are to guide him. In so far as these can be incorporated into modern living, he believes that the good of all will be advanced.

As a member of the Church, the Christian finds that he is taught an ideal which is spiritual and ethical. History demonstrates that progress comes from free voluntary institutions when they are protected by a strong State and inspired by a strong Church, which points to higher things. In so far as the members of the Church can demonstrate in their own lives something of the example of Christ, they are better able corporately to influence the moral standards and ethical ideals of the community in which they are placed. Its exceptional members, acting in the ways which a Shaftesbury or a Wilberforce would have done, may be in the vanguard of reforming movements and philanthropic progress. In this way some of the best service to the community has hitherto been assured. Political and social circles were leavened by those who proved to be the salt of the earth and the light of the world. When such private institutions have grown to strength and influence they have been replaced by the public and the corporate organisations. Hence, the best government and the most beneficent forms of progress are believed to come through gifted individuals, who have learnt the art of leading and governing. They need to be assisted and supervised by a small body of well-informed equals. Ultimately they must be controlled by an elected assembly, which adequately represents the community which is being served.

CHAPTER X

MEETING POINTS OF CHURCH AND MEDICINE

THE REV. DR. HUGH TROWELL[1]

In any approach to this intricate subject, there are four main areas of interest. They may be broadly grouped under the following headings: (1) an examination of the Bible's records of miracles of healing; (2) the meeting point of doctors and clergy; (3) the meeting point of physical disease and (4) the meeting point in mental disorders.

MIRACLES IN THE BIBLE

A general view of miracles, in as far as they are recorded in the Bible, suggests that these characterised eras in Biblical history when there were divinely initiated new religious movements on an extensive scale. Thus, in the Old Testament, wonders and signs accompanied the liberation of the Israelites from Egypt and were continued throughout Israel's pilgrimage in the wilderness and at the passage of Jordan; but then the tempo died down and miracles did not characterise the life of outstanding kings, such as David and Solomon. Signs and wonders accompanied the rise of the prophetic movement. They occurred under Samuel, Elijah and Elisha, and it is then that almost for the first time there were miracles of healing and the dead were raised.

The later prophets, such as Isaiah, Jeremiah and others, seldom performed any miracles. When they were wrought it was more for their significance as a sign from God than merely to heal an individual sick person. Somewhat separate, and not discussed here, were the mystical trances of Ezekiel, books such as that of Jonah, and the miraculous elements contained in the book of Daniel. It was always anticipated that when the day of the Lord was revealed and the Messiah was manifested, signs and wonders would again appear.

[1]The Rev. Dr. Hugh C. Trowell, O.B.E., M.D., F.R.C.P., is Vicar of Stratford-sub-Castle, Hospital Chaplain of Salisbury Infirmary, and Study Secretary of the Institute of Religion and Medicine. Formerly he was Consultant Physician, Uganda Medical Department and Lecturer in Medicine, Makerere College Medical School.

Signs in the New Testament

Such signs are recorded in the Gospels, but their number is not restricted to the healing miracles. There were theophanies as on the Mount of Transfiguration, and the voice from heaven at Christ's baptism; there were miracles of the physical universe as in the feeding of the five thousand and walking on the Lake of Galilee. Angels heralded our Lord's birth and sustained Him after the temptation in the wilderness. Finally, there were miracles of healing, of those sick in body, also exorcisms of demons, and the raising of the dead. Beyond all these were the miracles of His Person, His incarnation, death and resurrection.

There are those who feel that we should still be healing in a similar miraculous manner the sick, all of them or many of them or some of them, at the present time. Such persons seldom seem to face up to the question whether we should be raising the dead, rescuing the shipwrecked by teaching them like Peter to walk on the water, or feeding the many millions in the world who are malnourished by multiplying bread and loaves, as in the Gospel story. Our Lord, however, does not ask us to follow the letter of His example in the Gospels, but its spirit.

The Gospels, and also the Acts of the Apostles, recorded that miracles of healing (at least in any number) characterised the early stages of the ministry of our Lord and of the apostles. They did not cease to occur. But the record becomes much less dramatic and more selective as we reach the climax in the Gospels, or indeed the end of the Acts of the Apostles.

The Synoptic Gospels present us with a picture that suggests that miracles of healing characterised the early portions of Christ's ministry; even then, they always played a subsidiary part to preaching. Thus Mark (Mark i. 21-38) describes a day in the early ministry, one culminating in a crowd who collected towards evening at the house where the Master stayed. They were healed. Early next morning our Lord left this house for prayer in solitude, to be interrupted because His disciples reported that more sick persons had arrived and were waiting for Him. Did our Lord return to heal them? No. He chose to go into other villages to preach the gospel. Preaching always took priority and when it conflicted with healing the sick, the latter was dropped. Those who state, quite erroneously, that our Lord never refused to heal the sick, should reflect upon this early passage in St. Mark, for scholars tells us that it recorded a typical day in the life of our Lord and one presumably repeated many times.

The significance of the temptations

The temptations of our Lord were meditations on the use and the abuse of divine power to perform miracles. In the first miracle the Incarnate Christ refused to use miraculous power to turn stones into bread to satisfy His own hunger. He had accepted the implications of the incarnation in a world where physical laws normally remained constant. He would not lightly or easily ask for any dispensation to override them and certainly not in His own interest. The world was hungry, there was much malnutrition in Judaea in His day, but He did not feel it was His task to use His power of multiplying loaves and fishes to feed the hungry people of the world. On one or two occasions He did feed ' the five thousand ', but this at once attracted crowds who marvelled at the miracle. This He reproved. Too many miracles all the time would certainly not help people into God's kingdom, and it would be the same nowadays, if many occurred.

In another temptation Jesus refused to cast Himself from the Temple to fly in the face of the laws of gravity. Either these forces would have operated and His body would have been destroyed by the law of gravity or else God would have intervened in an arbitrary manner. This was to tempt—to test—God. Here again our Lord rejected any appeal to miraculous help on His own behalf. The action might have drawn the attention of the worshippers at the Temple, but not in ways that He wanted. He always refused to attract persons by miracles; yet His compassion impelled Him to heal the sick. This was a human, if not a divine, dilemma. If God allowed many miracles at the present time we would face the same difficulty.

Certainly the life and action of our Lord showed that in His kingdom—which is both already here and yet has to come in its fullness—all sickness, mental illness and death will be abolished. As portents of this kingdom, the twelve apostles and the seventy, when they were commissioned to travel for our Lord and to proclaim the coming of the kingdom, were instructed to heal the sick. This they accomplished. What is not clear is whether they continued to proclaim the gospel and to heal the sick once they had completed their missionary journeys and returned to be with our Lord. The silence of the Gospels on this point is most perplexing. It is as if, when Jesus was present, He did all the preaching and all the healing. It was only when He was absent (as on the Mount of Transfiguration) that the disciples were expected to heal the epileptic boy. Even then they failed through lack of faith.

Special difficulties will always arise if any person heals many sick. Crowds came to see the wonders and on many occasions our Lord spoke against this attitude. He then started to hide Himself, to evade crowds by crossing the lake in a boat and to travel to foreign parts. It was not His only reason for hiding Himself; the Gospels state that it was one of the reasons. He chose to hide His power, and this because it would confuse the issues and confound His mission. He wished to devote Himself to instructing the twelve.

The events of Passion week

Consider the last week, the Passion week, and bear in mind that this occupied nearly half of the earliest Gospel record, that of St. Mark. In this half of the Gospel only one miracle of healing was recorded. Blind Bartimaeus was cured at Jericho. He had asked to see the Messiah, and this miracle symbolised the answer to his prayer. Matthew recorded the healing of multitudes beyond Jordan; Mark had recorded only that they were taught. In a similar manner, Mark did not record the healing of the beggars, after the cleansing of the Temple; this again was mentioned by Matthew. Finally, we must note that John described the raising of Lazarus as an event immediately preceding the Passion of our Lord; and also, that although all the Gospels record the wounding of Malchus, only Luke reported that his ear was healed.

Let us try to envisage the events of this week. Scholars tell us that there might have been 100,000 or more at Jerusalem. Of that number, by modern standards, 1,000 would be sufficiently ill to be in hospital, a score or so would die in the week and a few thousand would be chronically sick. Was our Lord to raise all these from the dead, to heal all these sick? Was human nature fundamentally different in the time of our Lord? If he healed all who touched His garments on all occasions, how would His life have ended save by being smothered by an avalanche of sick? No, during the Passion week our Lord, on His human side, was to challenge the Pharisees and scribes in the debates in the Temple. He produced neither at that time nor at His trial, cured persons or any raised from the dead to support His claims to be the Messiah. On His human side our Lord was to be arrested and no angels would intervene. He was to be cast into prison and no heavenly messenger would release Him, as occurred later to Peter. He was to heal the wound of Malchus, but not His own wounds. He who refused to cast Himself down from the Temple top at the beginning of His ministry was also to refuse to come down from the cross and confute His tormentors at the end of His earthly life. The crisis of the cross is the absence of the miraculous, that He who saved others did not save Himself. The truth of the gospel is that miracles, as we count them, do not always happen; but that God reigns, albeit from a cross.

The Church's commission

How far did the Risen Lord commission His Church to heal the sick? Or do we rest content with His words of commission to the twelve apostles and the seventy disciples to preach the gospel and *to heal the sick*? Certainly the Canonical Gospels, Acts and the Epistles contain only one reference to the words of our Risen Lord on this matter. It is noteworthy that they occur only in the ' appendix ' to St. Mark's Gospel. They are thus found only in verses which were possibly not part of the original Gospel and were not present in many of the earliest manuscripts. The New English Bible makes this point clear. A further doubt arises because these words of the Marcan appendix introduce an eclectic note found nowhere else in the New Testament. The words exhort us to preach the gospel and to baptise believers. There is no direct exhortation to heal the sick. It is rather a statement that ' Faith will bring with it these miracles: believers will cast out devils in my name and speak in strange tongues; if they handle snakes or drink any deadly poison, they will come to no harm; and the sick on whom they lay their hands will recover ' (Mark xvi. 17, 18. NEB). The words about drinking poison are reflected in no other passage of Scripture, and have been taken literally, as has the handling of poisonous snakes, only by a few heretical sects.

The book of Acts certainly records miracles and signs, especially at Pentecost, when ' the tongues of fire ' appeared, and the early Church spoke with diverse languages. Peter was released from prison. He also raised a fellow-believer from the dead. Paul on his first journeys performed miracles, but these did not always aid the preaching of the gospel, as when he was greeted as an incarnate god at Lystra after curing the man who had been crippled since birth.   Acts, like the Gospels, finishes on a more rigoristic note.   Paul had been ill, probably on several occasions, as the Epistle to the Galatians would seem to imply.   Illness occurred in his followers.   They had to be left behind at various places, as the Epistles narrate.   Not everyone was healed by a miracle. St. Paul had his evil ' thorn in the flesh '.   It was not removed, but he was given grace to bear it.   St. Paul asked Luke ' the beloved physician ' to accompany him, first on his sea voyages.   He may have been a bad sailor and possibly suffered from migraine (his ' thorn in the flesh ') which affected his head and his eyes from time to time.

Like John the Baptist and his Master, Paul, too was cast into prison and not released by any angel.   He was shipwrecked, but did not walk over the water as Peter did.   We do not know how seriously he was bitten on the arm by the snake of Malta, but his Epistles end by telling us that his arms were in chains.   He himself, however, was still believing (as we presume that John the Baptist was) that Jesus was indeed the Messiah, of whom Isaiah prophesied that He should release the captives from prison. He, like John the Baptist, had to accept the gospel and these things by faith, and not by what they saw and experienced.   They had not to be, as Jesus so pointedly said, ' offended at these words '. ' These words ' were addressed to John who remained in prison awaiting death, hearing of other miracles, but receiving none himself.

The Epistles complete the instructions to the Church on this matter.   It is suggested that a believer, who is seriously ill, should ask to be anointed by the presbyter, and he will often, as St. James said, recover.   Ultimately we all have to die.   We must remind ourselves that all old people die of disease, almost no-one dies of pure old age.   Science knows that human life should extend possibly to 120 years and that at a post-mortem on all elderly persons, even those who die peacefully in their sleep, numerous diseased conditions, often chronic and incurable, are nearly always found. With the single exception of these words about anointing and recovery by St. James, the Epistles did not exhort believers to perform miracles of healing.   No church was taken to task because they did not occur.   Very few miracles were alluded to, and illness in believers was reported, but such facts did not raise any theological difficulties. Timothy suffered from indigestion: were hands laid on him? No, he is exhorted to take some wine.

Finally, we have the amazing travelling partnership of Paul and Luke. How did this partnership get on? Did sick persons first come to Luke and then, if not cured by Greek medicine, were they referred to St. Paul? He was an apostle, we must remember, who still appeared to be carrying his uncured ' thorn in the flesh '. The Epistles contain a number of striking passages in which we are exhorted to follow the sufferings of our Lord. Is it too naive to suggest that if every illness in a believer were miraculously cured, and every misfortune corrected by prayer, we should not be following the steps of the Master?

The miracles in the Acts

The Acts of the Apostles does not claim to be a comprehensive account of the early Church, far less of the miracles performed, so that any deductions are tentative in the extreme. From the point of view of the healing miracles, and assuming that the author was Luke, the physician, the record falls into three sections. First there was the early Church in Palestine; miracles were frequently reported and these confirmed the faith of the converts, almost all of whom were Jews. The second portion of Acts—the missionary journeys of St. Paul (unless he was also accompanied by Luke)— carried the preaching of the gospel into the pagan Graeco-Roman world. The story continued to follow the lines that were summarised in the Marcan appendix; the Word was preached and signs followed.

The third portion of Acts is that section of which the author, traditionally Luke, was an eye-witness. The subtle change in emphasis of the recorded healings, noted only on two or three occasions, is instructive. There was the slave-girl medium at Philippi; Paul commanded the spirit to leave her. It is not stated that it was an evil spirit, but one of divination, as in the oracles of the heathen gods. The event was described more in the spirit of the conversion of a spiritualist medium than in terms of exorcism of a demon, although undertones of the latter were present in the narrative. Acts recorded exorcisms on only four possible occasions, and far less frequently than in the Gospels. The second unusual event witnessed by the author of Acts was the resuscitation of Eutychus. He fell from the third floor of a building and was taken up as dead. Paul, however, insisted that he was still alive. The event was reported as if it were the natural recovery of a concussed person.   No word or action of Paul suggested a miracle, though it has been regarded as such by many commentators.

Finally, on the island of Malta, Paul ' healed ' the father of the chief magistrate; subsequently others came and were ' cured ', ' who honoured us with many honours '.   Some have seen in the change of verb, in the introduction of the word ' us ', a probable reference to Luke treating, presumably as a physician, the sick on the island.   For an author who was so self-effacing, no other reasonable explanation can be offered for the use of the word ' us ' immediately after the report of the ' healings ' and ' curings '.

Assuming that Luke is the author of Acts, it is not stated why he joined Paul at Troas.   If the illness that occurred in Galatia (Gal. iv. 13, 14) had taken place just before Paul reached Troas, the answer appears obvious.   Paul needed a physician; he was not in the habit of having useless persons on his travels.   Soon afterwards and upon reaching Philippi, Luke stayed behind; presumably Paul had recovered.   Luke possibly continued to practise medicine in that town until Paul met him there some six years later.   It is possible that illness had occurred shortly before this second meeting (2 Corinthians iv. 10, 16).   Uncertainty over places and dates arises because the movements of the apostle, as recorded in Acts (remembering that the author of the book was in a number of cases absent), do not tally completely with those gleaned from the Epistles.   After this second meeting Luke remained with the apostle until at least the end of the New Testament's record of Paul's life.   Presumably he was needed.

The implication of the apostle's own illness

The Second Epistle to the Corinthians contains the clearest references to the frequent illnesses of the apostle (2 Cor. i. 3-5; iv. 16; v. 4).   It contains the passage on the ' thorn in the flesh ', ' Satan's messenger '.   There have been many conjectures— were these bouts of malaria, attacks of migraine or some ophthalmic disorder?   There is only one certainty; the illness was not healed after repeated prayer.   God's grace was to be perfected in weakness. It is possible, even if unrecorded, that these events and the many conversations with Luke who, like the other of Paul's companions, probably continued to work in his profession, led to the enlargement of the outlook of the apostle.   Previously, as in the Gospels and in the Acts, the sick had been helped exclusively by miracles. Henceforth, there were to be gifts of healing;   these were distinguished from the power to perform miracles. There would be some differentiation in the gifts of the spirit; not all would work miracles, nor have gifts of healing (1 Cor. xii. 28-30).

The reason we are given no details about how St. Paul, who performed miracles on others but not on himself, and St. Luke, the beloved physician, worked closely together, is that every generation must thrash out this problem afresh. Thus in the early Roman Empire there were many healing cults, all claiming to perform miracles, and hundreds of temples to Asclepius. This religion lasted from about 500 B.C. to 500 A.D. and was, some consider, the most formidable rival to Christianity. It certainly claimed hundreds, if not thousands, of miracles at its own temples. I do not think we can dismiss all of these as false. The exorcising of demons was common and even our Lord Himself implied in the Beelzebub controversy that the sons of the Pharisees could cast out devils. Later in the Gospel story the disciples were puzzled by finding someone who cast out demons in the name of Christ. Jesus did not explicitly condemn this.

Christianity was born into a world of healing cults, and peopled with evil spirits. It was one in which miracles were considered to happen not infrequently. It is a very long story which narrates how Christianity eventually and largely won the day, until there arose the cults devoted to the relics of the saints and the healing of the pilgrims at the shrines in the middle ages. This is such a different world from ours that I do not think we could reproduce it at the present time. In considering the medieval times it is necessary to ask: What is 'superstition' and what is 'faith'? It is a difficult question on which to be precise.

DOCTORS AND CLERGY

St. Paul at several places in the Epistles speaks of the whole body of Christ, compounded of its different parts, working together in the plan of salvation. Further than that we must admit of specialisation, into eye and ear, hand and foot. No part must look in contempt on another. This is a far more helpful simile, and far more biblical than the phrase ' Doctor-clergy co-operation '. Indeed I think the latter term is very misleading. It suggests that a doctor and a priest must meet either informally about someone who is sick, or formally in groups (possibly in a combined group at a meeting, or in a course of instruction) and thus co-operate together.

The Pauline concept is that of the body, with very specialised parts, co-operating consciously, but also, I suggest, unconsciously together as a whole. Christ is healing the sick at the present day largely through the laity—doctors, nurses, laboratory technicians, psychiatrists, psychiatric social workers, and all concerned in a modern hospital and the Health Service. Their number will increase, as will their specialisation. Like John the Baptist, the clergy must learn to watch this growth of the others without rancour and jealousy.

Specialisation has certainly proceeded much further than in the days of the apostle Paul. At the present time the right hand (say, the physicians) is unable to confer helpfully with the left (let us call it the surgeons). Neither hand seems sufficiently in touch with the feet (the general practitioners!). Only very occasionally can there be a helpful formal meeting of different groups, say, of physicians and nurses, or surgeons and medical social workers. There is just not enough overlap between these various professions and disciplines.

A broad view of the Christian theology to the sick sees God working and answering our prayers in the created forces of nature, in the knowledge of the physician and the skill of the nurse. Other members of the team are there, but they are largely hidden in the background, e.g., laboratory technicians, hospital administrators, and so forth. All those who meet the patient must be compounded of compassion and informed by charity. This is part of true religion. Relatives may feel quite helpless, but their presence and sympathy means everything to the patient. Just as they may feel helpless, so does the Christian minister visiting his parishioner. But he stands for the love and power of God. The grace of God flows through the appointed means. God's grace also flows through the Christian laity. Sick persons are very sensitive to spiritual matters. In the hospital where I am Chaplain, about the same proportion of patients receive Holy Communion each week as would attend at Easter in any parish. At Evensong on Sunday the attendance in Chapel is often from a quarter to a third of all the mobile patients. The Chaplain is welcomed at almost all the beds, for they know they are in need.

Informal meeting points

There are, however, many areas where doctors and clergy informally can co-operate, both in hospitals and outside. A village practitioner 'phones up the parson to say that someone has only a few more hours of life; a pastor induces an ailing parishioner to see the doctor and stop dosing himself. One could multiply these instances, especially if on the one side one adds to the word doctor, other names of nurse, pharmacist, psychiatric social worker, therapist, cook, hospital administrator, ward maid, district nurse and all who work for the National Health Service. On the other side. to that of the clergy one must add the names of all who pray for the sick, the friends and relatives who care for and visit the sick and those who support the relatives in their anxiety. All this is our area of co-operation; in a sense it is almost all informal, it cannot be regularised or made the object of any formal study.

Areas of formal study and concern

Can there be any formal co-operation between doctors and clergy? By this I mean anything more informal than a doctor and a priest meeting to discuss an individual. Can there be formal meetings of doctors and clergy to study how they can help one another in the treatment of physical disease of the body? There can, of course, be an occasional service as at St. Luke's tide. There can be occasional meetings between some doctors and some clergy in any one district; these have their value. It is good to meet and know one another; apart from these, clergy and doctors seldom meet, especially in a large town. There are a few subjects which interest both of them—theological ones like miracles and prayers for the sick, ethical ones like the prolongation of life, even euthanasia, and informing dying persons of their true condition. There are also pastoral and medical problems such as suicide, venereal disease, alcoholism and pregnancy in an unmarried girl, but the number of such topics is limited.

There are few books or journals which both groups can study and this is a commentary on the gulf between our mental disciplines. The whole spirit of the two subjects does not mix easily. Medicine is rationalistic, scientific; it attempts to find underlying scientific laws and mechanisms. It is not, as a science, interested in the individual. It is deeply sceptical of all that cannot be seen and demonstrated. Theology must always be rooted in the super-natural, in revelation, in what is not seen and can never rationally be proved, and in the eternal. In any case the active and committed Church is really a small minority movement at the present time.

It is almost a miracle that any doctor has any faith at all. Those who survive best are usually the Evangelical doctor, for nothing can gainsay his spiritual experience of Christ, or the Catholic doctor, who finds that his Church means everything to him—it is ' the body of Christ '. Practitioners are very busy people, even in the evenings, as are the clergy, and for these reasons it is difficult to secure good attendances at any meeting.

Although there was previously little basis for any formal meeting, on the one hand, of clergy and church workers and, on the other hand, medical practitioners who restricted their practice to the care of the physically ill, the position is changing rapidly. Now that organic illness is often treated so successfully, the incurable case of physical illness is beginning to stand out. Each one requires support and, in this, prayer and compassion have their part to play. All sorts of organisations are springing up to care for mentally retarded children and adults, the spastics, and those who have some disability such as blindness, deafness or some protracted disease such as disseminated sclerosis. The care of the elderly is an obvious field. There will thus be many meeting points of the Church, the body of Christ, all who have found the faith, and the doctor, the psychiatrist and the nurse, even if these subjects seldom lend themselves to many formal discussions.

THE MEETING POINT IN PHYSICAL DISEASE

When a clergyman meets a medical practitioner and they engage in conversation, this is but the localised and personal aspect of the whole encounter of the Church and of Christian theology on one side and the sciences and practice of Medicine on the other. Let us, however, start on the personal level. The parson meets the practitioner. They discuss a particular person; one calls him a ' parishioner ', another calls him a ' patient '. They represent two different points of view, although both are looking at the same person. We must expect some conflict and disagreement. They can only meet and discuss if each respects the other and both have charity. Fundamental to the problem lies the whole difficulty of communication wherever there is specialised knowledge. This is widest between the humanities (especially theology) and the sciences, but is also becoming acute within any one science. Thus those who engage in experimental medicine have real difficulty in communicating with the general medical practitioner. A large pile of unopened copies of the

Lancet in many a doctor's office bears silent testimony to this.

What is the basis of the doctor's approach to illness? What is his concept of illness? The medical student's first impression of the science of medicine is that it rests, perhaps exclusively, on clearly ascertained objective data which can be grafted on to our knowledge of anatomy, the macabre dissection of a corpse for many hours each week for about a couple of years. This leaves a mark on most men, both in the scientific sense and in other ways; we feel that we understand basically what man is. This is dangerous because it is deceptive. In physiology one feels that one is gazing into the ultimate processes of life itself, that there is little outside, or perhaps that all which lies beyond these boundaries is vague, almost unreal, perhaps even an artefact. In the clinical years in the wards one is introduced to the fundamentals of disease largely in the study of morbid anatomy in the post-mortem room. In other words, one is regaled too often either with classical cases of certain diseases or else with complicated problems involving neurology, biochemistry or endocrinology. The reports flow in and out; the notes pile up. Amidst all the hot debate at the bedside concerning the diagnosis and prognosis, one can almost forget to notice the patient, who becomes a notice board on which a certain number of data are written and graphs charted.

Medicine is a restricted and selected field

Now the truth of the matter why medicine so often appears to be, and actually is, effective is because it works on a restricted field. This happened quite unconsciously largely following the Renaissance, when anatomy became the basic science. Out of the total mass of human misery, medical science restricted its attention and *selected* those maladies which affected the structure of the body, as demonstrated in morbid anatomy, or function as far as this concerned bodily disturbances of physiology. The material of the science of medicine was demonstrable to the senses; the data yielded to measurement, even to statistical analysis and experiment.

The most thrilling change which has occurred in modern times is that doctors are being asked to treat and cure the minor mental disorders. It is really very recent. When I trained at St. Thomas' hospital, some 40 years ago, we dealt only with obvious organic disease, people who had something demonstrably wrong in the body. But now, not only people who recognise that they are not well (the neurotics) but also the criminals and the child delinquents are being referred to doctors. This is almost the greatest revolution in medicine. We can prophesy that in addition to all the knowledge which science and dispassionate observation bring to this subject, there will need to be contacts with the humanities in ethics and philosophy. What after all is the good life? What is normality? There will be contacts too with religion which has long pondered problems of wherein lies excellence, of whether there is a plan and a purpose in life. The great hope is that medical science will at least enter this large field (to which psychology makes a great, but not an exclusive, contribution) with a sincere love of truth and with the humility of the scholar.

The Christian must appraise all this quest of the doctor, both in the realm of physical disease and in the more recent area of mental disturbance. It is through the doctor and the psychiatrist, many of whom are Christian laity, that the Church moves out to heal these people. The doctor has insight into the law of the Lord, even if he only calls it scientific law, and in this law doth he meditate day and night. Much of the Old Testament is saturated with the concept of the law of God; it is true that this later became restricted almost exclusively to the moral law and that in the end this degenerated into the legalism of the Pharisees. Yet, on the other hand, many of the Psalms and the Wisdom literature extol the law of the Lord and speak about the foundation of knowledge. Professor Butterfield (1957) in his book *The Origins of Modern Science* makes the point very firmly that it it was only out of the mediaeval Christian world's employing concepts of the constancy of God's power and love and law that the modern world of the Scientific Revolution could be born.

Apparent conflict between Medicine and the Church

This at once brings a conflict between science and religion, for in the consideration of all phenomena, the doctor must ask whether there is not some law, some scientific generalisation that lies behind every apparent anomaly. From the nature of his training, and from the terms of reference of his task, he will tend to seek some natural explanation for all that appears inexplicable. In his search for a generalisation the doctor cannot certify the presence of the supernatural, at least as regards its effect upon the body, until he can be certain about the boundaries of the natural. Concerning the latter, he must often plead ignorance, or that judg-

M

ment should be suspended. This must often appear blindness or evasion to the theologian and the clergyman, who are always asking if any unexpected recovery is not an answer to prayer? ' Has not God intervened? ' they query. A doctor is embarrassed by this question, for he cannot firmly answer either to the clergyman or to the patient. Neither can he answer the question in his own mind, which is compounded, if he be a Christian, of the religious man who hopeth all things and of the scientist who doubts everything. This might be regarded as philosophic schizophrenia, yet every Christian doctor has to learn to work with it.

The doctor cannot help but have great difficulty in this matter of miracles and answers to prayer. Usually he imagines that he knows the laws of nature, and he thinks he can anticipate what will happen. Then, by his own thought, he selects a certain drug and alters the course of events in the patient's body. The patient may claim that the normal course of his illness was altered in a miraculous manner, a ' miracle of healing '. The doctor knows that he has selected another scientific law, another drug, to modify the course of the illness. He thinks that the natural law of cause and effect still stands intact as an unbroken circle. But as C. S. Lewis (1947) points out in his book *Miracles* it is the *choice* of the doctor, his thoughts, which have modified the course of events, although what happens is, so, the doctor thinks, just the normal working of natural law.

As Christians we believe that the thought and the power of God enter into all variety of circumstances and this as an expression of His love. The thought of God is able to affect human minds, and natural laws, working in them and through them, while we short-sighted humans can see no evidence at all of God's activity. Our desires, our minds, enter by prayer into all this activity of God and are linked with Him.

We certainly must not think that in prayer we dictate to God, although many persons in illness do so. ' I must remember,' said Florence Nightingale, ' that God is not my private secretary '. Naturally, when we are ill, we must ask for recovery and believe that what happens is then what His Will permits. This is the usual way in which God answers prayer. There are at times quite unexpected and spectacular events, such as the recorded miracles in the New Testament. But a spectacular event must from the nature of the case be very rare; if it were common, like the rising of the sun every morning, dull-witted men would not count it a miracle.

Doctors are often, almost every day, being faced with the most unusual happenings. They must explain these surprises in terms of the great variability that disease displays largely because no two individuals are alike, and their diseases are also dissimilar. Very rarely an advanced case of cancer recovers for no apparent cause; this is certainly a medical fact. About 10 per cent. of early cases of disseminated sclerosis appear to make a spontaneous and permanent recovery; others progress steadily to death. Again, how often is the doctor right about the diagnosis? The answer is he can never be certain that he is right, until a full post-mortem is performed; then usually some surprises turn up, things never suspected in life. In a large proportion of cases the final post-mortem diagnosis of disease is usually a long list of defects, not just one complaint and often these differ fundamentally from the illness considered to be present during the life of the patient. There are great uncertainties of diagnosis and there are even greater vagaries of prognosis, that is of saying how any single individual will respond to any one disease. Almost always what the patient alleges to be a good old-fashioned miracle is a mistake in diagnosis or prognosis.

Unless we can have some preliminary agreement about such things, we cannot begin to talk about any formal consultation or study by doctors and clergy concerning the care of the sick. A clergyman must endeavour to understand the mental background of the doctor and his mistrust of quacks and unscientific methods of treating the sick. Unfortunately, some of the work of a parish parson or a hospital chaplain would appear to certain doctors, especially if they are not Christian believers, as partaking of quackery and superstition. Yet a pastor must minister to his flock in times of sickness.

I am opposed to all public services of healing, but there is a place for these private intercessions and ministrations in the case of committed and instructed Christians. In these services of prayer and anointing we place ourselves as creatures once again into the hands of the Creator, telling our heavenly Father what we as children desire. Then we ask that His will, not ours, be done and that He will not allow us to go into any time of 'testing' (Matt. vi. 13, NEB) unless we are eventually delivered from all evil and from the evil one. What happens after prayer, the laying-on of hands, or Holy Unction, is always God's answer—always a miracle of His love. Spiritual blessing is not always accompanied by physical healing. It is of great value in itself. I can think of no better way of starting out on our last journey than after receiving the Communion of the Body and Blood of our Lord.

MEETING POINT IN MENTAL DISORDERS

From the theological point of view there can be no doubt at all that the record of ' demon possession ' in the New Testament is the basic problem in the ministry of the Church to those who are sick. For those who are sick in body the clergy have their usual pastoral ministry, for many of these patients will be anxious about themselves and their illness; there will be fears of a continued disability or even death itself. When, however, the disorder lies primarily, or even entirely, in the mind and spirit of a man, then it is felt that the Church ought to be able to make a vital contribution. The most fundamental miracles performed by Christ were the exorcisms of ' demons '. This was far more basic to the Christian *Kerygma*[1] than the cure of any physical disorder. Embedded in the Marcan narrative, it was this authority over ' evil spirits ' that was to be the hallmark of the disciples. Likewise, the seventy were given power over ' demons ' and reported that they had subjected them.

It is clear that in the time of Our Lord all mental disorders were ascribed to evil spirits. In addition, a person with a spinal deformity was also stated to be possessed by a demon. Our Lord appeared to accept this outlook and to cure persons by casting forth ' the evil spirit '. On one occasion, they were many and they entered some swine, who then raced down the hillside to their death in the lake. All this sounds so strange to modern ears as to suggest a ' scandal ' and a ' superstition '.

It must first be recognised that there has been a widespread belief in evil spirits in every country and civilisation of the ancient world. All forms of mental disorder and much bodily ailment were ascribed to them. In some countries much of the physical illness was attributed to them. The priests and their temples were the natural places at which cures were performed. Thus in the Greek world excavations of the temples reveal many records of miracles performed and evil spirits exorcised.

[1]Gr. Kerygma=the proclamation of a herald, the message.

By the time of Our Lord it is clear that all mental disorders and some physical disorders were being ascribed to evil spirits in Judea. As already indicated, this belief was shared by every civilisation this world has known and was universally held in Europe until the scientific revolution of the seventeenth and eighteenth centuries.

Antagonism between Christianity and Psychiatry

The history of the association of the Christian Church and the treatment of mental disorder has been characterised by centuries of superstition and crude treatments; only recently has it been redeemed by measures of compassion. When psychiatrists began to investigate these disorders a century or two ago, they came into violent conflict with many of the practices and attitudes of the Church. A deep antipathy developed between psychiatrists and Christianity, and it will be a long time before there can be considerable rapprochment. There is a long history of deep antagonism so that the attitude of the Church should be largely that of repentance. Added to this, most of the contributions to psychiatry and psycho-analysis have been made by agnostics, and the temper of the whole science is still largely rationalistic. The whole of the influence of psychiatry, psycho-analysis, indeed sociology and much of science is to challenge the validity of religion, especially revealed religion, which is airily dismissed as a special form of illusion.

Compassion for the mentally sick remains a strong motive in a Christian. But studied antipathy, if not disdain, will continue to be the attitude of many psychiatrists to the Christian attitudes. There are, however, certain hopeful signs. Briefly speaking, psychiatrists have always had a far more difficult task than physicians. The latter are able to study the normal anatomy and physiology in health, and then the changes which occur during disease can be assessed by many exact techniques. A scientific classification of diseases of the body has been elaborated and precise methods of investigation have been found.

This is not so in psychiatry. It is only possible to examine small parts of the normal healthy mind by scientific methods which involve experiments and measurement. Small aspects, such as the rate at which mental fatigue occurs, may be studied; but it is still impossible to examine in a precise, objective and experimental manner most of the conscious and unconscious mind either in health or in disease. Psychiatry has, therefore, not advanced in an orderly manner comparable to that encountered in medicine and the study of physical disease of the body.

Thus attempts to define a clearly marked disease in the mind, comparable to the precise picture of diabetes in the body, is doomed to failure. The psychological outlook changes radically from time to time. Thus many cases of ' hysteria ' as diagnosed at the beginning of this century, would now be called ' schizophrenia '. The boundaries between one disease and another are not distinct.

Severe mental disease

At the present time mental disorders fall roughly into two categories ; those which are sufficiently severe to require treatment in a special institution and those which are less severe and can be treated while the patients are still at home. The former are considered to have a psychosis and to have little insight into their condition. Modern treatment in mental hospitals consists in making life as interesting and rich as possible. There are very few locked doors and physical restraint is reduced to a minimum. Modern drugs are used to quieten violent patients and there are hopes that other drugs may be able to decrease depression and alter the mood of the person. Electroconvulsive therapy has also made a big contribution, chiefly in depressive states.

Treated along modern lines it is found that a large proportion of mental disease will improve, and that the outlook is not as hopeless as had earlier been considered. Every effort is made to prevent patients from becoming habituated to an institution and to solitude, for under such conditions many deteriorate. Many of the elderly patients in a mental hospital have become institutionalised and will never be able to leave; it is hoped to prevent this state of affairs among new admissions. As soon as possible these will be returned to the community.

The whole tendency will be to discharge mental patients as soon as possible from the mental hospitals to the community. This may mean that they return direct to their homes or spend some time first at an intermediate institution which is run more like a convalescent home or a hostel. There will certainly be a growth of these after-care institutions and arrangements, each probably with some kind of committee, and possibly with some paid and some voluntary workers. There will be endless opportunities for co-operation here, not so much between the psychiatrist and the pastor, for both of these figures will be rather in the background, but, it is to be hoped, that many of the psychiatric social workers and the voluntary workers will be Christians and activated by Christian motives.

Minor mental disease

We must also bear in mind that, especially in modern secular society, a large number of persons use their doctors, solicitors, bank managers, and even ladies their hairdressers, as persons to whom they turn for advice, counsel and a good chat. In any doctor's surgery there will be from about 10-30 per cent of persons who have something wrong more with their minds than with their bodies. In a few of these patients a mental state, such as anxiety, has been an important factor in producing bodily illness. The psychosomatic group of diseases is poorly defined and most of them have many factors in their causation. Thus migraine occurs more commonly in certain types of personality; attacks may be provoked by mental strain, but also by travelling and by eyestrain. Certainly, giving any sufferer from migraine the peace of God will not prevent all the attacks. In such an area the pastor can do no more than perform his normal spiritual functions; he cannot co-operate in any technical sense of the word with the doctor.

How does a practitioner treat the large number of neurotic persons who come to him? His first care and his continued anxiety must be that he is not missing the early stages of serious physical disease. Thus someone may consult him who has lost his appetite and is losing weight, and examination, including the X-ray examination of the stomach, reveals nothing abnormal. The patient continues to lose weight, a second X-ray examination is conducted and now evidence is obtained which suggests, but does not prove, that cancer of the stomach is present. This is a common state of affairs and it makes a medical practitioner very cautious before he establishes a firm diagnosis of the absence of all physical disease and the presence of neurosis.

Doctors of the older generation were not trained at all in the minor mental disorders, which constitute however about a third of our patients. A great change is now occurring in the medical profession. Lectures in psychology are given to medical students while they are studying anatomy and physiology. During the three years of hospital teaching they are given a few lectures on the common minor mental disorders. These are usually delivered by psychiatrists, who however may seldom see and treat a minor disorder. Actually there is very little known about these disorders, such as insomnia, anxiety, and so on. It is very difficult to study them in a scientific manner.

In a similar way doctors are being encouraged to regard delinquent children and adults as their problem. This is a new attitude. These subjects are still not well-taught at a teaching hospital where few of these cases are seen. However, a real concern is working up among general practitioners. It is one of great promise. It is one in which the Church can directly or indirectly play its part. The medical profession is only just beginning to turn its attention to this enormous challenge. There will be an increasing number of meeting points in this field.

REFERENCES

BUTTERFIELD, H. (1957). *The Origins of Modern Science*. London: Bell.
LEWIS, C. S. (1947). *Miracles*. London: Geoffrey Bles.

CHAPTER XI

MEDICINE AND THE UNITY OF MAN[1]

ANDRÉ SCHLEMMER[2]

For the past hundred years medical science has tended increasingly to view and treat the human being as a collection of various organs, systems, tissues, functions and faculties. The purpose of this chapter is to examine the implications of this tendency in the minds of both doctor and patient.

It is a tendency which can be seen in the ever-increasing number of specialties and specialists, and this reflects the tremendous expansion in the medical sciences, with the result that no one mind can cover the whole range. Again, it reflects the increased number of medical and surgical techniques which makes it impossible for any one person to know how to operate, let alone possess, all the available diagnostic and therapeutic expertise. It is now necessary for some doctors to specialise in one branch of medicine as it is no longer possible to be an expert in them all. The specialist looks after one part of the body, his specialty receives a particular Greek name and he may be primarily interested in only one type of illness. He has deliberately reduced the range of his activity in order intensively to study a limited part of the whole.

This necessary subdivision of work in dealing with the patient's body and its illnesses has accordingly become more widespread. The decision to consult a specialist satisfies the patient who is reassured by the impression that he is benefitting from greater competence and superior treatment. The doctor himself in specialising gains assurance by the feeling that the more a discipline and the tools of that discipline are circumscribed, the more completely he can master them. This feeling of security and confidence is reflected in the relatively higher fees of the specialist as compared with those of the general practitioner, who is looked upon as being a ' Jack-of-all-trades' but master of none.

[1]This chapter has been translated, by permission, from the French original in Philosophy and Christianity, Essays dedicated to Professor Herman Dooyeweerd, 1965. Uitgeversmaatschappij J. H. Kok N.V. Kampen Amsterdam: North Holland Publishing Company. The thanks of the Editors are due to Mrs. Rosemary Barker of Dundee for her translation.

[2]André Schlemmer, M.D., Physician, Paris.

Some remarkable results have been obtained by specialising, some of them life-saving, such as the early diagnosis and operative treatment of tumours. But there is also a darker side to the picture. Experience and mature thought have brought to light the dangers of certain treatments when applied universally, for example, the indiscriminate removal of tonsils and adenoids, the application of antiseptics to the roots of devitalised teeth, the abuse of topical antibiotics, gastrectomy with its late complications, the dilemmas of steroid therapy, the unforeseen sequelae of psychosurgery, the disastrous surprises resulting from ' promising ' hormone therapy. How many patients are shuttled from one specialist to another, each claiming to have diagnosed and to be able to treat the cause of all their ailments, when the only result of this search for the root cause is further setbacks or even unnecessary mutilation.

Whereas one patient may take the advice and follow the treatment of all sorts of specialists, another may remain faithful, if not to the same specialist, at least to the same speciality. In either case, despite all the treatments, the illness clings obstinately to him, unless it is a case of his clinging to the illness.

THE UNITY OF THE BODY

In fact the movement towards specialisation in medicine tends to deny, or at least to forget, the unity of the human body. From the scientific point of view, one can consider organs and functions in isolation; but it is important to remember that this is an intellectual exercise, a working hypothesis, which leaves out one aspect of the truth, namely, the unity of the body in illness as in health. The body is not a collection of different units, a cluster of cells, tissues or organs. Every element, every tissue, every organ in the body makes up the whole, and only has significance in relation to the whole. It is true that separate organs may be kept viable outside the body, such as tissue cultures and the perfused heart. But compare this artificial, complicated and precarious existence with the facility of existence within the body. Further, the prolonged life of such a disembodied organ has no meaning, because it is only in contributing to the activity of the whole body that it achieves its meaning.

Moreover, this unity does not derive from any one dominating organ, as if there were a hierarchy within the body. It is not a case of an organisation but of an organism, in which the unity evidenced by normal growth, harmony of function, adaptation to changing environment, repair of trauma, and recovery from illness is obvious yet cannot be pin-pointed. Although it keeps the same constancy of form and composition, the body is not merely the sum of its physiochemical elements; these are continually changing, whereas the body remains, at least until death, when the elements degenerate and disintegrate. Thus the body is, in a sense, a vital whole. Its reality is undeniable, yet cannot be measured or weighed.

Accordingly, whoever cares for the body cannot lose sight of its unity without his perspective of the truth being distorted, and the attitude which treats separately symptoms, syndromes, infections and organs can only correspond to part of the truth. Paul Carton expressed a broader view when he said: ' There is no such thing as a localised illness.' He has expounded this adage well and there is no need for us to dwell upon it. Once this unity has been understood it is self-evident.

Moreover, the reality of the body is not only spatial, it is also temporal; its unity expresses itself not only in the body's harmony of function, but also in its continuity. The body in fact has its ' memory '; the antibodies which it has acquired by illness or vaccination, the allergic reactions to previously encountered noxious substances, the conditioned reflexes which it has accumulated, the sensorimotor patterns which make up the skill and facilities of its movements, and the adaptations which it has made to its environment, are the expression of this sort of ' memory '. To some degree this ' memory ' transcends the individual and reveals itself in behaviour, in purposeful instinctive reactions, and, more purposeful still, in the achievement of reproduction and growth it is handed on from one generation to the next in the factor which we call heredity. From the moment of conception a new individual with physical form is fixed, an individual being, single and complete in itself.

At heart every doctor (by the very nature of his vocation) has a sense of this unity and this completeness, unless the demands of a narrow specialisation have, for neurotic reasons, taken hold of him, forcing him to avoid a wider approach. His own neurotic problems can also cause him to fear, in the practise of his work, every flash of intuition. This approach is the result of obsessional tendencies which he can only satisfy by using clear and limited concepts. These lead him to diagnoses and treatments which sound like mathematical equations, such as a computer might give, without that computer, of course, being involved in any responsibility. This is why the underlying presuppositions of a narrowly materialistic view of medicine are often just as cramping for the Christian as for the agnostic doctor.

It is a strange thing, however, that it is often the patient who speaks of one of his organs as an object or as having being. He remarks—' It is my liver which is playing me up '—' It is my nerves that are on edge '—' It's my leg that just won't go ' and he asks the doctor, as he would his watchmaker or his garage mechanic, to repair the thing that is out of order. At other times the patient refers to his illness as a visitor. He personifies his sciatica, his ulcer, his angina or his wound. He himself is responsible for this objectivity. He claims to have identified the culprit, and he no longer sees his body and what is going on in it as a whole, sometimes even speaking of his body as if it were not himself but an outside object.

THE DIVORCE OF MIND AND BODY

At this point we reach a division of the human being which is even more serious and more artificial, the separation between body and mind, between the soma and the pysche. Among the medical specialties is one which intentionally has not been mentioned so far, namely, psychiatry with its different components, classical psychiatry, psychopathology, the various forms of psychotherapy and psycho-analysis.

The human being is aware of having a space-time reality, of having a body which is investigated scientifically in anatomy, physiology and biochemistry. During the past three generations the physical sciences have made unprecedented advances by means of the use of the light microscope and then the electron microscope along with the development of stereochemistry. The body indeed has its complaints, its disorders of function, its anatomical lesions, objects of a science called pathology, a science practised by the doctor or, should we say, doctors, if we are considering the body as a collection of parts, each with its own pathology.

THE GROWTH OF PSYCHIATRY AND ITS EFFECTS

The human being, however, is also aware of having a reality which is essentially psychic, and therefore chiefly temporal, and this is the realm of psychology. In the past two generations this branch of knowledge also has explored a vast new region. The mind also has its sufferings, its functional disorders, its illnesses, and these are the concern of a further specialty, psychiatry—the pathology of the mind.

In the past century psychiatry was at first the realm of clinicians who simply identified and described the main symptomatic entities of each of the more common mental illnesses. Then they were influenced by the organic approach and dominated by the powerful thinking of Virschow and Pasteur. Psychiatry has tended, therefore, to be the study of the mental aspects of neurology and particularly of brain disease. This has led psychiatry to the localisation of the various abnormalities to different physical areas of the brain. For example, the alcoholic psychoses, the exact anatomical siting of the lesion in epilepsy (that most psychogenic illness) and, at the turn of the century, syphilis as the cause of general paralysis of the insane.

For the past 50 years this form of psychiatry which regards mental function as having a physical basis has not greatly extended its domain, except in the discovery of certain groups of drugs which certainly are very effective. This is its great consolation, because the vogue of its three other therapeutic discoveries, i.e. psychosurgery, electroconvulsive therapy and sleep therapy, has greatly declined.

The temporal unity of the human being is the work of his memory. In this sphere the great discovery of our century in psychology is that the human being possesses a clear awareness of only a small part of his psychic being. Only a fraction of all that his memory has recorded is available to him. The rest is not entirely obliterated but is hidden. Certain associations and events can recall it for him. Most important, certain of the most unwelcome emotions which have been repressed are none the less present and active—revealing themselves by symbols, attitudes and acts that are all the more powerful because their true motivation is hidden and he is able to give them different meaning.

Furthermore, since the exploration of the vast realm of the unconscious, which gives the psychoneuroses a basis that is essentially effective and emotional (in a word, psychic), inspired by the work and concepts of the psycho-analysts, psychiatry has made great progress. It has not only transformed psychology and psychic therapy, but has also influenced contemporary humanism. The psycho-analyst refrains from treating the body and does not prescribe drugs or diets. His therapeutic activity is essentially verbal and consists chiefly of the conclusions to be drawn for the patient from his own words, from the free association of his own ideas and from the dreams which he recalls. The psyche is in this way considered as independent of the body, but not the body of the psyche; for the physical manifestations which appear are often interpreted as the expression of the unconscious mind or a means of flight from it.

Thus medicine is divided into two schools of thought. For the one, reality is to be found in physiochemistry, while for the other, it is essentially an affair of affect and emotion. Each type of doctor declares that he is incompetent in the other's field, which does not concern or interest him and which may even frighten him. In both cases the doctor abstracts, separates, dissects something from the unity of the human being. At least, this is what he claims to do. And yet, in the realm of even the most organic medicine, what treatment can avoid being at least partly psychological, whether the doctor is aware of it or not?

MAN IS A SOCIAL BEING

Finally, the human being is also a social being. That is a part of his unity. For the reality of love, the family and the environment (scholastic, professional, social, national, religious) is also part of his make-up, as is his cultural life. Barres, who saw reality only in the self, was nevertheless found to recognise in that self the essence of his race which led to his becoming a nationalist; and Jung recognises in the 'collective unconscious' the relics of ancestral myths.

The picture of the human race as presented by the sociologists and ethnologists is not entirely foreign to modern man. Medical practice, which does not take into account this dimension of the human being, rejects part of his totality. The cachexia described by Spitz in infants brought up in institutions, however well they are looked after on the material level, shows that the natural emotional relationship between mother and child is essential for the young child, even if he has never known it. It is therefore an inborn reality. We also know how much difficulty in adapting to life is experienced by children who have never been to school. We know how difficult to follow, how ineffective and even dangerous sometimes, the most logical medical prescriptions can be when they force the patient to go against what he feels to be the social conventions. Medical care must take into consideration what is possible from the familial, professional and social point of view.

Moren has shown clearly in his sociological researches and in his psycho-drama therapy the importance and the power for good or ill of the group relationships. In contrast we see how inhuman and mutilating is medical care which reduces a man to being no more than a cell in the organism of society. The sick it forces uniformly and inexorably (as would a computor) into diagnostic pigeon holes, each with its own textbook treatment. To the well it applies epidemiological, sanitary and hygienic rules which have been worked out scientifically for the good of the species and the benefit of the human herd! The observant young practitioner very soon learns how rarely the cases which he meets in his practice correspond to the descriptions which he has learnt from books, and how rarely he has the opportunity to make one of the beautiful diagnoses which were shown him on the wards.

THE IMPORTANCE OF THE PERSON

In reality, in order to approach the human being as a unity, we must not only avoid removing anything from his totality by considering him truly as an individual, but we must also view him as a person. He must be treated in the role (*persona*) which he is called upon to play, and this has its own finality and particular significance for him and for others, and makes up his uniqueness.

The veterinary surgeon, when he is deciding whether to treat or destroy an animal must take into account the wishes of his client or of the owner of the animal. In other words he compares its potential value as egg or meat producer, or as draft animal, with the cost of treatment, unless the animal is the object of human affection, when it has a special personal value. The horrors of the concentration camps have shown the monstrosities that result from considering man purely in terms of his economic usefulness.

Instinctively, by virtue of that grace which is inherent in his calling, the doctor becomes part of the ancient pre-Christian tradition which considers the patient as a person of value because of his uniqueness, whose health—which means his life—has been entrusted to him. The tradition is clearly expressed in the Hippocratic Oath, written by a contemporary of Socrates, but pronounced to this day by candidates for a doctorate in medicine in certain faculties (in France), for example, Montpelier. The essential principle is there:

'I swear by Apollo . . . I will use treatment to help the sick according to my ability and judgment, but never with a view to injury and wrong-doing. . . .'

THE UNITY IN TOTALITY

This reminder of the unity of the human being, in illness as in health, does not aim at reassessing the place and training of the general practitioner. The latter should be at the centre of all specialised investigations as is a conductor in an orchestra, and should set aside the necessary time for general examinations and therefore receive appropriate fees; nor does it aim at sentimentalising over the virtues of the old-fashioned family doctor. Rather it aims at bringing to the medical profession and to thoughtful members of the general public, an awareness of the Copernican revolution which is accomplished when our conception of medicine encounters this idea of unity in totality. The patient believes that the doctor knows what is wrong with him, and that to name his illness is to have it under control. The doctor knows better than to entertain any such magical notions.

The aim of the consultation should no longer be merely to establish an exact diagnosis, however essential this may be, nor to institute the appropriate treatment. This would be a counsel of despair because in reality the complaints met with in any practice refuse to be classified according to the lists in the textbooks, and also because we know too well the poverty of the forms of treatment which make up the final chapter of each illness and which change with every new edition. The aim of medical treatment must be to understand the meaning of clinical signs and the significance of the illness itself. It must in this view be far reaching and purposeful, because one is dealing with a living being, whose continued existence, whose homeostasis and whose response to attack are all purposeful and ultimately characteristic of life.

In the seventeenth century Sydenham, the English Hippocrates, expressed this very well when he wrote:

'A disease, however much its cause may be adverse to the human body, is nothing more than an effort of Nature, who strives with might and main to restore the health of the patient by the elimination of morbific matter'.

All that a person feels, thinks or desires tends to show itself in and through the body. It is only by bodily expression that he reveals himself to others and becomes aware of what is within him. Symptoms and illnesses are meaningful. They are the language of the body. To understand and obey this language is the work of that doctor who respects Life and whose healing work responds to the language of disease by reorganising the way of life of the patient.

Above all, when it is no longer a case merely of the unity of the living body but of the unity of the whole being, body, mind and spirit, the concept of the significance of symptoms and disease takes on a new dimension. The question is no longer ' What has he got'?; but ' Who is he '? What is the meaning of this crisis in his life? What is his being trying to express through this suffering, this distress, this powerlessness? How many complaints are, at least to begin with, both the disguised expression and the unloading of emotional suffering or conflict. Moreover, these mishaps are interpreted by the patient all the more emphatically as physical ailments because they constitute a sort of escape, making the unbearable bearable. Such then is the hidden meaning of most of the illnesses which the patient brings to the general practitioner.

The patient fears or rejects this revelation and yet in his heart he is longing for it. Nothing is more significant or more moving than this opening-up of the patient to his doctor, and the relief which accompanies it. It appears at the first consultation, if one is really ready to listen, except in a few cases, where—to defend his position—the patient keeps a third person (mother or spouse) between himself and the doctor.

This opening-up not only has a value essential to the correct orientation of treatment. It also has on its own a therapeutic effect. This is a fact of experience. As Michael Balint has said— of all the means of cure which a doctor has at his disposal, the most important is himself. Yet, too often, he knows neither his power, nor his limitations; neither the indications, nor the contra-indications; and he is ignorant of the dangers, the dose, and the method of use. Certainly this method of treatment can enter to a greater or lesser degree into the doctor-patient relationship under the guise of a diagnosis or a drug. Every doctor in this sense practises psychosomatic medicine, but unwillingly and unconsciously, and therefore very inadequately and very blindly.

Each person who seeks medical help brings to his doctor an emotional reality (more or less intense), assigns to him an important role and establishes with him, as long as the doctor does not reject

N

this, a very special relationship. This is a psychological fact. One can either close one's eyes to this reality or one can observe what is happening in the patient, in the doctor, and between them both. In this latter case, one can take it into account if one wishes to use it to the good of the patient. For every investigation which modifies the observed data is blind, if the investigator is not aware of it. Now experience shows how much the fact of being doctor of the whole of the person—both mind and body—allows the practitioner to make a prompt and effective approach, which the specialist psychiatrist does not always find.

THE BASIC QUESTIONS

The more one considers medical work as applying to the whole person, the more the question on which it depends ' What is the meaning of this patient's condition? ' is related to a deeper question which is still more total:—' What is the meaning of human life? ' Whether the reply to this question springs from faith or agnosticism, it reveals a fundamental choice of a religious nature. For there is so much that could be said about the philosophical (and basically Christian) presuppositions which are the background of the concepts and practices of the art of medicine, when it divides or amputates the unity of the human being! ' What is man? ' remains the basic question of every philosophical enquiry.

Material monism sees in a man a collection of cells grouped in organs, the fortuitous product of evolution from the primitive protozoa. Idealistic monism of which solipsism is the ultimate form, believes the body to be a presence, cloaking an illusion. This latter is the concept of a great part of Indian philosophy expressed in the theories of Buddhism and of Schopenhauer.

That in earlier centuries there was a dualism consisting of a mortal body and an immortal soul is attested by prehistoric funeral rites and in the well-known Book of the Dead of Egypt. Plato, then later Aristotle, introduced it into Western philosophy. Its Christian forms arise on the one hand from St. Augustine and, on the other, from Thomas Aquinas. Dualism may have two different end-results. It can end in disgust for the body and for life, and thus in the negation of all medicine. It can also lead the Christian doctor to a medicine of the body, which is rationalist and materialistic, his Christian faith finding expression only in his teaching and his sense of duty. Sensualists tend to make of the body a subject, idealists an object. The spiritualist says ' I have a body'; the Materialist ' I am a body '; the Buddhist ' my body, this illusion . . .'.

Philosophers of the phenomenalist school have rejected both concepts and yet have remained hesitant or equivocal on the question, except perhaps Merleau Ponty, who has devoted to the study of the value of the body half of his *Phenomenologie de la Perception.* It is one of the focal points of his doctrine of being. He concludes his study with these words:

' If now, as we have seen, the body is not a transparent object, and is not given to us as the circle in geometry by the geometrical constitutional law, if it is an expressive unity which one can only learn to know by *assuming* it, this structure is going to communicate itself to the feeling world. The theory of the bodily schema is implicitly a theory of perception. We have learnt again to feel our bodies, we have rediscovered beneath the objective and distant knowledge of the body that other level of knowledge of it, which we have because it is always with us and because we have bodily form. Now we need in the same way to awaken to the experience of the world as it appears to us, in as much as we perceive the world through our bodies. But in regaining contact with the body and with the world we will also be re-discovering ourselves since, if one perceives with the body, the body is a natural self and like the subject of perception '.

MAN AS TRINITY

If the materialistic and idealistic conceptions of the human being mutilate him, and if dualism divides him, what can be said for a conception of man as a trinity which distinguishes spirit, body and life with its instincts? Theosophical and occultist doctrines have rallied to this position. That great French doctor, Paul Carton, found in it the necessary conditions for accommodating his clinical observations; control of hygiene and diet for the body, guidance of temperament for vitality, correction of character for the mind, constituted three foundations of his therapy. When he wrote that at death, life having fled, the body dissolved and the spirit remained eternally, he was not concerned with a mere working doctrine of this division into three unities, but he characterised to some extent its constituents.

It is true that he was quoting a phrase of the Apostle Paul (1 Thess. v. 25), but surely it is forcing the text to see in it a fully-developed anthropological doctrine. It is not affirming the division of the human being in death, but its unity and totality in life and in the resurrection. In no place does Scripture discern in the human being separate entities capable of existing apart, deprived of the support of God, for without this support there is only nothingness. The valid contribution of occultist research to

Western thought is to be found rather in the doctrine of the micro-cosm, at the heart of the macrocosm. This was indeed borrowed from Plato, who himself received it from the Ionian school, and in particular, from the Pythagorians. Every man is a complete micro-universe related to the cosmic universe, each of them created in order to glorify their Creator.

The unity of the human being in his totality and his uniqueness cannot be established as a scientific discovery or as a philosophical speculation. It is in reality a religious choice. It is not only Christian. The Christian, however, is unable to think otherwise, if he recognises each man as being the object of the love of God in Jesus Christ.

From the moment when he has received insight into this unity, this totality, this uniqueness, the doctor meets each of them throughout his professional thought and action. Medical thought must essentially cover all the factors that go to make up the human being. It must apply itself to all the facets of that being. Yet these various applications must be synthesised into a single unity.

Let us not, however, confuse the vocation of the Medical Practitioner with the Christian Minister. To see men as unique beings does not mean that the doctor will seek opportunities for proselytising or for the ' cure of souls ', which is not his role. It means rather that he will give his attention and his care, simply and to the best of his ability to the health and the life of his patient, that unique human being who entrusts himself to him as a doctor.

REFERENCES

BALINT, M. (1957). *The Patient, his Doctor and the Illness.* London: Pitman.

BALINT, M. *Psycho-therapeutic practise in médecine.* London: Tavistock Publications.

BAYLE, F. (1950). *Croix gammée contre caducée. Le experiences en Allemagne pendant la 2e guerre mondaile,* p. 1521.

BOSS, M. *Introduction a la médecine psychosomatique.* Paris: P.U.F.

CARTON, P. *L'art médical, Diagnostique et Conduite des Tempéraments et Traité de médecine Naturiste.* Paris: Le Francois.

DOOYEWEERD, H. *A New Critique of Theoretical Thought.* Amsterdam: Kok.

MORENO, J. L. *Who Shall Survive?* New York: Beacon. (translated from *Sociometrie.* Paris: P.U.F.).

PONTY, M. MERLEAU. *Phenoménologie de la Perception.* Paris: Gallimard.

CHAPTER XII

MAN HIMSELF—THE VITAL FACTOR[1]

Man is a complex creature. It is obvious that he cannot be explained from a single angle and in only one way. New facts concerning his physical constitution are still regularly being gathered by scientific observation. These he is found to share in many respects with the animals. In addition, however, there are various other considerations which arise from a scrutiny of his intellectual pursuits. The kaleidoscopic inter-relationships which he has with his fellow humans are of first importance; they are found to be influenced, or determined, by a sequence of personal choices. These in turn arise out of different temperamental and educational backgrounds. They are controlled by a variety of motivations. His behaviour is, therefore, far more complicated and unpredictable as compared with that of other living creatures.

There is one basic observation about Man which is continually thrust to the forefront of our thinking. In him there is an additional factor, which is absent, or certainly not evident, in the case of the highest animals. He has a unique ' spiritual ' constituent, that is an awareness of reality in the unseen world of his spirit. It is a matter which has been debated for many centuries. No final ' scientific ' explanation has made it any less demanding. Indeed, Man's own growing discontent with his environment and his efforts to penetrate the mysteries of space have heightened the tension. In trying to probe into this baffling problem he immediately meets the difficulty that the human mind is called upon to undertake a process which, in some respects, resembles the attempt of the inner chamber of a camera to take a photo of itself. Self-consciousness and self-analysis have their limits. The basic question thrusts itself to the forefront—who and what exactly is Man?

THE IMPORTANCE OF CORRECT ASSESSMENT

The problem has become the more urgent at the present time because various palliatives for our social disorders, which are prescribed by politicians, sociologists, industrialists and ' planning

[1]This chapter is based on a talk to a Discussion Group by the Rev. D. Martyn Lloyd-Jones, M.D., M.R.C.P., Minister of Westminster Chapel, and it is published by permission.

controls ', are becoming increasingly based upon the trends in the newer sciences of Psychology, Anthropology and Behavioural Studies. That such far-reaching measures should be well-founded and truly effective has become—whether he realises it or not—the concern of every adult in the country. All such planning alters the immediate situation far more than in primitive conditions when the individual was able to conduct his affairs within a few comparatively simple relationships. In earlier environments good effects or unwelcome mistakes, mostly affected little more than each man himself or his immediate neighbours. Today, erroneous planning, when it is applied by a modern government on the grand scale, can swiftly alter the lives of millions for good or ill.

That such assertions are relevant and justified may now be seen from the history of Medicine (Hobson, 1963). At points during earlier centuries the truth was obscured by the simple personal relationships between an individual practitioner and his one particular patient. Today the world application of Preventive Medicine highlights the importance of the need for the validity to be assured for all prophylactic measures before they are widely applied in the community. This branch of the Profession has long outgrown its early status as the hobby of a few devoted pioneers. The departments of Public Health and Tropical Medicine are in the vanguard of medical progress largely as a result of the beneficent work done by the World Health Organisation. Each medical observation in the aetiology, diagnosis and treatment of disease must, therefore, be carefully scrutinised. Each accepted ' fact ' must be substantiated by the fullest available confirmatory evidence, before it passes into currency. For any one of these ' facts ' may tomorrow be taken up by some ' planner ' and applied on a universal scale. It is, therefore, of the greatest moment that before whole populations are manipulated, the planners should be sure concerning the nature of Man and what is ' right ' and what is ' wrong ' in dealing with him and his needs.

THE MEANING OF ETHICS

In earlier centuries such a question would have been posed and debated within the framework of a prevailing philosophy or theology or total explanation of the Universe.[1]   The discussion of Man's conduct and obligations in social relationships was known

[1]The dominant philosophy or religion of an epoch was called by nineteenth century German scholars its ' weltanschauung ', or ' world view '.

in the Greek and Roman world as ' Ethics ' and ' Morals ' respectively.[1] Obsessed today by the importance of the individual and his comfort, our ' atomised ' view distorts the perspective. Such concepts as those of a ' world view ' and ' a science of ethics ' have lost their clarity. This is due to the great transformation in the attitudes and working methods of philosophy and theology resulting from the triumph of the ' scientific method '. They have been pushed into the background and treated as the hangover of primitive speculation or religious sentiment. That this should be the case is to be regretted on several grounds—not least because of the unsatisfactory substitutes which are offered, or the virtual absence of such.

It needs to be emphasised that it is a disaster that so many educated people uncritically accept the view that because the assumptions and methods of the natural sciences are so successful in their proper spheres, they are, therefore, applicable to all aspects of human experience. Such a notion leads to a misleading and self-imposed limitation of which its advocates are contentedly unaware. It inhibits them from further enquiry from other angles at important points where the scientific method does not help them.

Very early in the history of thought, Aristotle gave a great deal of his attention to the strange fact that Man had the haunting awareness that he ' ought ' or ' ought not ' to do this or that. The problem remained to challenge thought until the eighteenth century. when the philosopher Kant busied himself with this mysterious ' oughtness ' in Man's inner consciousness, and for which he coined the term ' the categorical imperative '. Much current thought, however, quietly sidesteps the question. In the present climate of opinion it is usually preferred that the question be not posed.

SOME CONTEMPORARY VIEWS OF MAN

Current discussions of the problem of human conduct are frequently confusing and unsatisfactory because speakers and writers persist in asking what a man *does*, rather than—in the first instance—what he *is*. The modern approach is incurably subjective. It fails to examine Man as an individual or Mankind in the mass in such a way that his origin and nature can truly be

---

[1]The Greek plural ' *ta ethica* ' (Latin: *morales*) literally meant the ' customs ' of a tribe or nation. Later, the term became extended to describe the plexus of the formal problems of personal and social relationships.

adequately determined. As a result, certain attitudes, methods and rules become adopted which often apply only to some specific facet of his total activity. The tendency is to discuss the results, rather than to endeavour to assess the *person* who is responsible for them. Yet, the fact is that before any legislator or administrator can rightly lay down rules of conduct, it is imperative that an answer to the fundamental question ' What *is* Man? ' should be found.

In the history of thought there have been numerous divergent suggestions to account for Man. They may be conveniently summarised in the following broad terms. The biologists have suggested that, in the last analysis, Man's behaviour is the outcome of the interplay of hereditary and environmental influences. In particular, it is the resultant of a biochemical system, itself controlled by a delicate balance amongst the endocrine glands, which in turn preside over a complex chemical process. This view has been supplemented by that of the psychologists and psychiatrists who regard Man's conduct as the end-result of the integration of a number of fully developed instincts, which have been common, in simpler form, to the whole animal world. Man's day-to-day activities were, from this point of view, determined by the relative preponderance of one or more of his ' drives '.

Economists have explained Man in terms of a dialectical process which it was claimed could be discerned at various stages in the course of history. Man and his activities are said to be the products of the continual clash between economic forces such as those of supply and demand. Periodic conflicts have from time to time thrown up a series of partial solutions, only to be followed by a repetition of the conflicts. Historians have differed in their view of the results. On the one hand are those who, with Professor Toynbee, would describe them in terms of the rise of a new dynasty or new collective authority. Others would claim that the process has thrown up new economic trends and types of person until the rise of the fully developed Marxist ' economic man '.

The current views of the scientific humanist represent an attempted synthesis of the results of applying the scientific method to all aspects of life, including those in which it would earlier have been thought irrelevant. Man is the dominant animal in an evolving expanding universe. He is the resultant of the natural forces, which have conducted him through the earlier stages of animal development to full self-consciousness. He is now powerful in relation to his environment and responsible for guiding his own destiny. Master of his world, he is responsible only to himself for his future.

The list could be extended. Such brief statements do not, of course, do justice to the arguments in their favour which would be advanced by their supporters. In their own limited contexts these views have considerable areas of truth, which account for their popularity. Each, however, throws light on only one aspect of the complex personality of Man as we know him. In his totality he remains unexplained.

THE FOCUS OF THE DIFFICULTY

There is a crucial test to be applied to all such explanations. The question is—' What is the reason for Man's recurring crises in so many spheres of his life today? ' It is not sufficient to reply that they are due to Man's failure to continue to develop biologically in smoothly articulated stages, or to some imbalance which has occurred in his biochemical make-up, or to an arrest in his further mental development which had not been anticipated. Nor will it do merely to say that there has been a hiatus in the measures designed for the completion of human education, or that, for some reason, Man has failed to continue his natural social development and, in particular, has been unable fully to integrate religion into this process.

Some have advanced a theory that various stress-diseases in modern life have caught up with responsible statesmen and key industrialists. They point out how, in times of crisis, a key person may suffer from incipient disease, for example, Chamberlain at Munich, Roosevelt at Yalta and Dulles during the Suez crisis. In each of these cases, there was an unsuspected pathological condition, which subsequently disclosed itself. It is suggested that these physical defects influenced the statesmen's reactions and they were betrayed into making major mistakes. But here, again, the explanation is relevant to very limited aspects of Man and his history.

There is a universal call for more education and more knowledge. Further research, it is hoped, will dispel our present uncertainties, and enable vigorous and accurately directed measures to be applied more effectively. Yet some would advocate a course which is, in fact, the exact opposite.

' Let us go back to nature ', they say, ' for most of our trouble comes from the unnatural and artificial lives which we are now living. Man was much happier in his pastoral communities and can only find his true self by returning to a life which is nearer to the soil.'

Others are calling for more intensive medical research, especially in the sphere of genetics. Their aim is to secure the widespread application of eugenic measures in the hope of breeding a nobler and stronger race. Finally, there are those who are convinced that the essential trouble lies in man's need for greater opportunities for self-expression in all its forms. He needs to be able to escape the many unnecessary frustrations which have dogged his steps in our present type of civilisation. The appropriate liberalising measures are advanced. Such proposals, however, are, again, found to be very limited in scope.

Each type of specialist has his panacea only for the part of the problem he sees. Much that is important to the individual is omitted. For example, the sensibilities and emotions of the average man are widely forgotten. His poetic imagination, his capacity for true love and the activities of his inner consciousness, with its sense of the ' ought,' are minimised or omitted. No explanation seems to be offered for man's demonstrable possession of this last-named faculty and for all that is comprised under the term ' conscience '. Again, none of these schools of thought really do justice to man's self-consciousness. There is no real explanation for ' self-hood ' as commonly understood. The analysis is not radical enough. For the total make-up of Man is insufficiently accounted for just at those very points in which human reflective self-consciousness differentiates Man from the animals.

There is a further objection from the point of view of ethics. All the usual explanations tend to whittle down, or to ignore Man's responsibility for his own actions. If he is no more than the end-result of a balance (or imbalance) in a series of biochemical products, or the resultant of mutually conflicting psychological ' drives ', or the mere plaything of blind historical and economic forces, it is clear that no person can be regarded as actually *responsible*, either for ' right ' or ' wrong ' or ' good ' or ' evil '. If the above views be true, then certainly the Law and the processes of justice are continually and flagrantly unjust. The thought of moral ' responsibility ', in any meaningful personal sense, must be greatly reduced or excluded.

There is a final criticism which needs to be honestly faced .

Several of the current explanations of the nature of Man are in complete opposition to each other. Both groups of opposites cannot equally be right or be accorded equal consideration. The fact is that, as things are developing in the world today, the Christian Church has every right to claim that, if the Bible's explanation be rejected, there remains no adequate alternative explanation of the personality, thought and action of Man.

THE HEBREW-CHRISTIAN RELIGION

It is therefore relevant, at this point, briefly to summarise the Hebrew and Christian view of Man which is derived from the teaching of the Bible. As soon as we examine this Book it becomes clear that each part of its description of Man is in the perspective of his relation to God as his Creator. Throughout all the sections which comprise the Bible, this basic concept controls all else. It is explicitly taught that Man is a special creation and not simply a superior species amongst other animals. Whilst the human race and the animals are all described as living together in the same natural environment, and there are physical similarities between them, yet Man is consistently regarded as unique.

At the beginning of the Bible, Man is described as created in ' the image and likeness of God ' (Gen. i. 26-28; ii. 4-7). One of the most penetrating discussions of this phrase is found in the writings of the eighteenth century American writer, Jonathan Edwards. He distinguished between a ' natural image ' and a ' spiritual image '. By the former term he understood that Man is to be distinguished from the animal world because he is capable of ' moral agency '. By the latter is emphasised those higher spiritual capacities which, in common speech, are regarded as ' god-like ' (Cf. the English adjective ' godly '). It is possible for an individual to lose the latter features, and yet still retain the essentials of the ' natural image ', that is, still to remain essentially a Man. At an earlier date the Swiss Reformer, John Calvin, had similarly taught that ' the image of God extends to everything in which the nature of Man exceeds the animals '. There is no evidence in animals of ' spirituality ' in the above sense, or of those ' psychical ' powers which entitle a man to be considered a free ' moral agent '. There is similarly no convincing evidence that animals have the endowment of self-consciousness or ' self-hood ', which enables them to carry out self-criticism and self-analysis. It is a feature of biblical thought that Man is always capable of exercising these particular powers (1 Cor. xi. 28).

Differences of opinion exist amongst theologians whether the Bible teaches that Man is to be regarded as comprising two major constituents or three. Because of several more complex descriptions (which occur, however, in only two contexts) the question is discussed whether he consists of ' body, soul and spirit ' (1 Thess. v. 23; Heb. v. 12) or of two elements ' body-mind ' and ' spirit '. The textual evidence is difficult to interpret with precision, because the Hebrew and Greek terms for ' soul ' and ' spirit ' are apparently interchangeable in a number of the relevant contexts. A mediating solution is to regard Man as a conjunction of (a) a body-mind element with (b) a soul-spirit element which together make up his total personality, described in the Bible as ' a living soul '. The important fact is that throughout the books of the Bible Man is very specifically regarded as possessing, besides his physical constitution, a self-conscious moral or spiritual nature. This ' spiritual nature ' is the essential part of him. It is, also, taken for granted that Man can communicate with a spiritual world outside of himself.

The possession of this faculty for communication with the unseen, or—to put it at its very lowest—a wistfulness concerning the possibility of such communication, is of the first importance. The reformer Calvin states: ' Even primitive peoples have the sense of a God above all gods '. Modern ethnographical research has confirmed, rather than weakened the grounds for this statement. In a number of the polytheistic tribal religions there is found to be one of the gods who is pre-eminent. We must note, therefore, that besides his self-consciousness, Man possesses a central awareness of God and the power of communicating with Him. The Bible from its first page is interested in this fact. We are told that Man is not only able to, but in the early days of our race he in fact *did*, communicate with the Divine. ' God walked and talked with Man in the cool of the garden ' (Gen. iii. 8). Hence, in the thought-structure of the Bible, Man originally functioned appropriately and efficiently both in relation to God and to the rest of creation. Augustine's well-known affirmation is based upon this fact and is still as relevant as ever—' Thou hast made us for Thyself and our hearts are restless till we find our rest in Thee '.

The Bible further constantly assumes that Man is morally ' *responsible* '. That is, when at the outset he made a convenant with him, God treated him as a fully responsible person who had the power, if he wished, to keep his side of the agreement. There was also the possibility of progress. Man was made responsible for the other living things and put in control of the rest of the creation. Man therefore could only function properly if he remained aware of his status and duty. From the thought of the Bible, he was clearly bound to act in conformity with the purpose of his life and to make appropriate use of God's gifts.

MAN'S PRESENT STATE

As we find him today, however, Man is not like this. He is not faithfully and responsibly functioning as a good steward of God's property. He is either a complacent materialist busying himself in what he can acquire for his own advantage, or he is restlessly dissatisfied both about what he himself is, and what his primary task should be. What is basically wrong? It is basic to the thesis of this chapter that it is impossible satisfactorily to account for modern Man, and the observed facts about him, other than in the way in which the Bible has done. The teaching there constantly asserts that Man has rebelled, broken the covenant and fallen from his original fellowship with God. As a result, he has plunged his race into a series of unwelcome consequences. History supplies ample illustrations of the legacy of this rebellion. The sequel continues to work itself out in succeeding generations and in ways which the Bible has penetratingly anticipated for us. The Bible's analysis of the result of Man's estrangement from his Source is astonishingly accurate. An honest observer need not fail to recognise their contemporary expressions. Amongst the chief are:—

1. An awareness that the Divine Law has been broken, accompanied by a sense of guilt, however unconscious or suppressed it may be. It is a universal phenomenon, as witness the pathetic attempts made by some of the primitive peoples to hide from and placate the offended Deity.

2. A certain ' fear ' at the mention of God's Name. It may be expressed by determined opponents in the form of hatred. The Bible clearly describes this ' enmity against God ' (Rom. viii. 7) which is as widespread as it is irrational. Why is so much heat engendered? Its origin seems to be in Man's difficulty of repressing the knowledge deep within him that there is a God and that all is not well on the human side.

3. Again, the biblical diagnosis is that humanity in the mass has become spiritually ' dead '. Man no longer retains the intimate knowledge of God which was his original privilege. He is, therefore, not properly functioning at the most important level of his personality.

4. He has also become subject to a shortened life-span and death. ' Through fear of death ' he has become ' subject to life-long bondage ' (Heb. ii. 15, NEB; Rom. v. 12). There is a universal awareness of a haunting fear of death in greater or less degree. Man may contrive to suppress it. He may seek to distract his mind from the stark realities by beautifying death in literature and fine arts, but the sober truth remains that everywhere man is disquieted by it.

5. In everyday experience, and spoiling his highest aspirations, Man has become conscious that in a curious way he is constantly the victim of a lower nature. This is not his physical body[1] but rather a down-drag and bias in his inner being which causes him to fall below his ideals, and for this the Bible uses the word ' flesh '.[2] The Bible writers are careful to distinguish this ' lower nature ' from Man's physical body and ordinary powers of thought, which are both morally neutral.

6. Again, man and woman have become self-consciously ashamed of their sex (Compare Gen. ii. 25 and ii. 7). Whilst the description has been satirised in literature, the account in Genesis of the fig-leaves is none the less a realistic portrayal of something which is universally present amongst all races. It survives in various forms even amongst very primitive tribes where clothing customs have not assisted in its perpetuation.

In any case, Man's sexual and instinctual capacities were certainly not designed to control him; but rather the reverse. He should be governed by his higher rational and spiritual powers. But the balance has been lost. He no longer gives evidence of successful spiritual and rational control over his lower nature. The ' flesh ' i.e. ' sarx' not ' soma ' (Rom. vii. 14-25) has taken command. The animal appetites, instincts and urges have constantly proved more powerful in controlling action than his rational powers. He endeavours to do better and as often fails. It is

[1]Greek: Soma indicates the physical body.
[2]Greek: Sarx is used for the self-centred indulgence of mankind.

not simply a matter of individual wrong acts, but the same in-
capacities have invaded all his faculties and potentialities. In
spite of talk of ' progress ', which is largely superficial and materialistic, Man feels starved of those very spiritual qualities which he
naturally covets. A feeling of moral defeat makes itself felt at
some time or other in all departments of his personal life.

SOCIETY IN GENERAL

The same basic facts account for the majority of our social,
national and international problems. They explain our inability
to achieve a better state in industrial affairs through rational and
peaceful negotiation. Man plans for his own advancement,
indulges his own desires and hates restraint, including God's.
Inevitably, therefore, we have class-hatred, international jealousies
and, finally, ruinous strife at all levels. One biblical writer,
St. James, comes straight to the point: ' From whence come wars
and fightings among you? Come they not hence, even of your
lusts that war in your members '? (Jas. iv. 1).

The lessons of history emphasise that whilst Man may be
able to reach a certain degree of palliation of the chief disorders
of society and maintain the *status quo* for a time, yet he has always
been incapable of securing any radical and lasting correction.
All the while he persists in his estrangement from God, he remains
spiritually ' dead '. Only from the divine Source can he derive
power to recover his original state at the spiritual level. If he would
set himself to find this Source, however, he could restore the
position. His restoration must come from ' Above ' downwards.

THE ROAD TO RECOVERY

What can and should be done? Some advocate as correctives a
radical revision of the Law, a more extensive development of
scientific education and appropriate cultural improvements. It
would be necessary, of course, that these measures be thoroughly
applied on a world scale. Current world trends, however, do not
encourage optimism at this point. It must surely be plain to most
observers by now that, even at their best, such measures can only
act as temporary restraints on evil. Their effect is largely of a
negative character, operating by localising and reducing the worst
symptoms. They tend to deal with the effects and manifestations
of social or individual sin; but their beneficent influence tends to be
superficial and evanescent. In spite of the fact that there is very

much more education on every hand, the world continually stumbles into further new evils. The moral problem is increasing. The restraining influences of law and education do not exist in their own right. They are simply a means. We must ask—' Lawmaking, educational activity and cultural endeavour? Yes. But for *what*? ' To what end must all the beneficent activity be directed, and what will be the authority behind them?

The Bible is in no doubt about the treatment. It contends that the primary need for Man, both individual and collective, is to be reconciled to his Source. He has not been so constructed that he can happily or successfully exist as an autonomous being. Awareness of his dependence on the Creator is vital to his true character and functioning. As soon as any individual awakens to this fact, he is at once conscious that he first needs God's forgiveness. He is also aware that he must gain a new nature if he is to enjoy fellowship with the Divine Being. Radical enmity against God must be replaced by a return to the right spirit. He needs a recovery of his original knowledge of God and ability to obey His commandments. The Bible's persuasive message is that he who comes to God in sincere faith and obedience receives the gift of the Holy Spirit Whose function is to renew what was lost by the rebellion, and to restore ' the knowledge of God, righteousness and true holiness ' (Eph. iv. 24).

THE GOLDEN RULE

It is only in such a context as the foregoing that Christ's ethical teaching is seen in true perspective. Not only is the individual's basic problem removed by the process of Christian renewal, but— rightly understood—so are those of the community. Christians finding themselves restored to a ' knowledge of God ' are able to recognise ' the Golden Rule ' (as laid down by Christ) as the epitome of the whole ethical teaching of the Bible. It states:

' Thou shalt love the Lord thy God with all thy heart,
and with all thy soul, and with all thy strength and with
all thy mind; and thy neighbour as thyself ' (Luke x. 27).

Again, it must be insisted that this command was not given in a vacuum. It is only truly appreciated if seen against the dark background of the Bible's teaching about Man's true nature and his profound need. It was not designed as some ' patent remedy ' which automatically works, as if by magic. There have, indeed, been too many examples of defective forms of Christianity and many misguided attempts at practice to permit any facile optimism in seeking to treat the essential needs of Man. True Christians have so often existed in relatively small numbers and have exercised pervasive influence in only a few countries. Fewer still of them have been in a position, nationally or internationally, to control the whole situation. Yet wherever the teaching of Christ has been freely and fully practised, it can be shown to have produced the characteristic results which are claimed for it.

THE BASIC ISSUE

Modern thought must be confronted with the fact that the ultimate sin is intellectual pride. Man is not, and has no right to be, autonomous. The moment a man makes a virtue of his claim to autonomy, there is war on a scale commensurate with the bounds of his influence. He will decline to listen to anyone else, he will endeavour to erect his autonomous world around himself, and seek to conquer as much of the neighbour's territory as he can. Many intellectuals in different parts of the world have recently become seriously concerned at just this fact. It is, therefore, relevant to point out that Man is at all times unable to rectify his life unless he is ready to welcome God's initiative in revealing His Will and effecting the recovery. An honest man, facing this matter radically, must surely concede that Man's plight is basically a spiritual one. The antidote offered by the Bible is spiritual, rational and, when properly practised, effective.

THE RELEVANCE OF ETHICS

The considerations which have been advanced above have both a direct and indirect application to medical ethics. Medical practice makes many demands upon the abilities, special training and character of its practitioners. In the earlier centuries when available therapeutic measures were comparatively few, Medicine was regarded as an ' art '. Indeed, in the doctor-patient relationship at its best, there is necessarily an element of ' art ' and this will always be so. During the Mediaeval period when the prestige of the Profession was low, it could be little more than an art, for the status of physician, apothecary, and surgeon differed little from those of any other guildsmen and craftsmen of a great city. In the seventeenth and eighteenth centuries, however, individuals such as Boerhaave, Sydenham, John Hunter and Jenner emerged as marking advances towards a scientific approach to clinical

o

Medicine and Surgery. It was not, however, until the early twentieth century that it became really meaningful to speak of the ' Science of Medicine '. Today, Medicine comprises several elements, it is a ' Profession ' as distinct from a trade, it is an ' Art ' to which are added elements of administration and community service, and it is an applied ' Science ' which yearly grows in significance and the scope of its powers.

We need to enquire, therefore, how far the ethical considerations which arise in the course of practice will be affected by such views of Man as have been outlined. Clearly the technical performance of any given individual will depend primarily upon his natural endowments, the quality of his training, his degree of experience and the conscientious application of his skills. His philosophy of life or religion will be of importance only in so far as it reinforces his conscientious pursuit of his duties and tends to encourage or discourage him in making further efforts to achieve scientific and technical advances. We would not expect his view of Man to affect the application of his scientific training to the elucidation of the etiology, diagnosis and treatment of disease.

However, in the second place, the doctor's philosophy or his ' world-view ' will certainly affect his personal outlook and his total interpretations of the facts and phenomena which daily confront him. The doctor's fundamental outlook at this point makes a real difference. It will appear chiefly at those points where there are important ethical relationships and interactions in the doctor-patient relationship. For example, a non-religious man (who does not believe in a Supreme Being and who is convinced that Man is only a superior animal) of necessity will approach the ultimate issues of life and death in a manner different from that of a deeply religious man, whose view of their meaning is so divergent. No good purpose is served either for Medicine or the community by evading or glossing over this fact. Since those who do and those who do not adhere to the Christian outlook have to live together, and co-operate in the community's medical services, nothing but good should come from a greater effort of the two groups to understand one another. At least, it should be emphasised that both the ' ethics ' and, to some extent, the ' etiquette '[1] of the Profession are at these points affected.

[1]This term is commonly used for the professional relationships between two doctors, as distinct from the more general principles which bear upon the moral problems involved at some points in practice.

FIRST CLAUSE OF THE GOLDEN RULE

The Christian who sets out to apply the Golden Rule to his daily work is at once confronted with the searching requirement that he must ' love the Lord his God with all his heart, soul, strength and mind ' (Matt. xxii. 37-40). It is for this reason that he seeks to approach Medicine as a ' profession ', or ' vocation '. It is a measure of the degree of secularisation and lowering of meaning which the English language has undergone in recent years that the word ' vocation ' has so largely lost its original meaning. Most men derive their means of living from what are essentially ' services ' to their fellows. The word ' profession '[1] is itself derived from the terminology of the Mediaeval religious orders. The new member of an order ' professed ' to follow the religious life. The word ' vocation ' was also given currency and a special meaning by the Protestant reformers in their teaching of the importance of ' secular ' activity. The underlying concept is that the truly religious man's motive in daily work shall be his love for God. In this view, if a man is serving in his right place, ' secular ' work is to be regarded as much a daily service to God as any ' religious ' activity.

Similarly, if any one is convinced that the world ultimately exists for the purposes of God, and that Man has been given delegated authority to administer, control and develop world resources in line with God's purpose, then he cannot help but regard life as a ' stewardship '. To borrow the poet Milton's words, he will carry through his daily tasks ' as ever in my great Taskmaster's eye '. It follows that the religious man will tend to be a conscientious and industrious worker. A Marxist is pleased to call this ' the slave mentality '. It is, however, a strange misunderstanding that there is anything slave-like in a man's working in responsible partnership with his Maker! It is also significant that in just those countries in which Marxist's principles have had the greatest application is to be found the slave mentality on the grand scale!

The paradox of history is that wherever the true Christian obedience has been allowed free practice, the greater has been the degree of stability, progress, sense of freedom and inner peace. The decline in the influence of Christianity and loss of awareness

[1]The S.O.E.D. gives the definition of ' profession ' as ' A vocation in which a professed knowledge of some department of learning is used in its application to the affairs of others in the practice of the art founded upon it.'

of being committed to a Divine purpose has brought nothing but loss and inner uncertainty to Western society.

The Christian principle favourably influences the medical practitioner's attitude by its salutary reminder that he is exercising a ' stewardship ' in practising Medicine. It also reminds him that the patient belongs to the Creator and is made in His ' image '. However marred that ' image ' may have become through human sin and folly, God is still interested in the individual. The practitioner must therefore exercise responsible stewardship on the latter's behalf. There is more to it even than that. Each sick person has a spiritual nature and a destiny. Whilst the Christian ministry has a special duty in this matter, and it is not the doctor's primary concern, he cannot remain disinterested.

THE SECOND CLAUSE OF THE GOLDEN RULE

The second clause of the Golden Rule is as searching as the first—' You shall love your neighbour as yourself '. As things are, this is virtually impossible to achieve. It only comes within the bounds of possibility after one has, with the help of God's Spirit, begun in practice to know something of the Rule's first clause. Practised on the grand scale they could prove the lubricant which would lead to the smooth functioning of human society.

The pioneer of modern surgery, Joseph Lister, paraphrased the second clause of the Golden Rule for the context of Medicine, when he declared that ' There is only one rule of practice, put yourself in the patient's place '. It is not easy to put ourselves at all times in the patient's place. Persistent endeavour to do so, however, on the part of the great exemplars of the Profession have been of incalculable value for the doctor-patient relationships and the prestige of Medicine as a whole. Honest attempts alike by Consultant and General Practitioner to make such attitudes habitual, is rarely overlooked, or unappreciated, at the receiving end. It often has a therapeutic value. The contrary evidence seems also clear, viz., that dislike, resentment or coldness between doctor and patient not only does not assist recovery but, in some situations, is positively harmful. This is so—if for no other reason than the reluctance of the patient to co-operate or to seek further advice.

There are, of course, not wanting those who regard all such attitudes as arising from sentimental idealism. They consider it has little bearing upon the ' scientific ' practice of their Profession.

Yet nothing could in general be more wrong-headed. It is not seldom those very persons who, by their monolithic impersonalism, are the most responsible for worsening relations and the lowering of the public image of the Profession. Willingness to accept medical advice—especially in the crucial early stages of disease— still depends to a considerable extent upon the degree of confidence which a patient has in the disinterestedness, integrity and friendliness of his adviser. It may mean all the difference between an early, or a late, diagnosis of serious conditions. It may lead to steps which by-pass the specialist (who may be highly skilled, yet is the personification of aseptic frigidity) for the warmer human sympathies of the unqualified and the quack.

Where there is room for discretion and choice, true love for one's neighbour will prompt the giving of advice in a form which one would, in the same circumstances, desire for oneself. It is no easy-going ' rule of thumb ' which is being advocated. On the contrary—there is constant need for responsible thought and action on the part of the practitioner. A big step forward is taken whenever he can begin by honestly trying to put himself in the patient's place. There is ample opportunity in practice for the application of the Christian principle of love for one's neighbour. To be at its best, however, and fully effective, it must be applied in close association with its complementary principle of wholehearted love for God.

REFERENCE

HOBSON, W. (1963). *World Health and History*. Bristol: Wright.

INDEX

Abortion, 62-66, 73-78
Alcoholics Anonymous, 115, 130
Alcoholics' Treatment Centres, 108, 110, 114
Alcoholism, 108-116, 129-132
Animal Experimentation, 3-6, 54
Anthropology, 13-14
Aristotle, 67, 178, 183
Artificial Insemination, H., 80, 81
    D., 81-84
Attempted suicide, 126-128
Attitude, of Doctors, 24-26, 31, 55, 56, 81-84, 118, 125, 130, 141, 160, 171, 175-178, 194, 196
Augustine, 67, 127, 178
Authority, 36, 69, 75
Ayer, A. J., 47

Balint, M., 177
Behavioural studies, 4-6, 9
Behaviourist views, 35, 68, 100, 184
Beliefs, 34, 39
Biblical principles, 48, 49, 64, 127, 146
Bibliographies, 21, 40, 70, 87, 99, 107, 116, 134, 168, 180, 197
Bill of Rights, 27
Birth rate, 78, 79, 90-94
Bourne case, 73
Brain, R., 101
British Medical Association, 114, 131
Butterfield, H., 161

Calvin, J., 67, 187, 188
Cambridge-Sommerville project, 12
Certification, 81, 82
Character, 119
Children, studies of, 10-12, 16
Christ's teaching, 21, 27, 49, 52, 55, 56, 68, 84, 89, 121, 149-152, 192
Christian principles and teaching, vi, vii, 14, 20, 34, 39, 42, 43, 48-52, 55, 60-70, 72, 73, 84, 99, 114-117, 120, 121, 125, 127, 132-134, 146, 147, 152-168, 179, 180, 187-197
Church, and Medicine, 99, 126, 132-134, 147, 148, 152-154, 161-164
    and Psychiatry, 164-168
    and Tradition, 50, 51, 55
Clinical experience, 2, 7-9
    medicine, 22
    research, 22-26
    trials, 25, 26, 30, 31
Codes of ethics, vi, 27, 37
Commandments, biblical, 49-51, 59, 69
Compulsion, 136-140, 143-145
Conditioning, 4-6
Consent, v, 28-31
Contraception, 67, 78-80, 85, 95-98

Contract, v
Co-operation of patient, 28-31
Criminal abortion, 77, 78
Criminals, study of, 10, 11, 13-17, 119

Death, 55, 61-62, 153, 163, 164, 190
Death rate, 91-94
Declaration of Independence, 27
    Rights of Man, 27
    Helsinki, vi, 37
Definition, of Man, 42, 43, 181-189
    of Life, 52, 53
Delinquency, 9-12, 15
Denning, Lord, 66, 67
Determinism, scientific, 18-20, 35, 100, 104-106, 118
Devices, 50, 63
Devlin, Lord, 67, 120
Diminished responsibility, 1, 2, 13-16, 118-121, 129-131
Divine mandate, 26, 27, 43-45
Doctor-patient relations, v. (See also Attitude of Doctor)
Doctor-clergy relations, 132, 156-168
Double effect, 49, 86
Drug addition, 110, 111, 113

Edwards, Jonathan, 187
EEG, abnormal, 9, 10
Eichman trial, 2
Einstein, A., 39
Elderly patients, 57-59, 128, 159
Emotional studies, animal, 3-6
Engels, 12
Equilibrium, disturbance of, 88-90
Ethical principle, 33, 37, 41, 47, 65-70, 120, 121, 127, 158, 182, 183, 193-197
Ethics, neglect of, v, 160, 161, 183
Ethics of clinical research, 22-40
Eugenics, 74-78, 85
Euthanasia, 59-62, 65
Expedience, 44, 45, 50
Experimentation, 3-6, 22-24, 28-31
    W.M.A. Code, vi

Facts, importance of, 2, 3
Family Planning, 79, 95-98
Fertility, 79, 80
Fluoridation of water, 140-145
Foetus, life of, 49, 54, 62, 64, 66, 72, 73, 76, 77
Food supplies, 89, 94
Fox, R., 64
Freedom, Limitation of in Preventive Medicine, 136-147
Freud, S. (Freudian), 9, 19, 100

Genetic studies, 7, 8
Geneva, Declaration of, vi, 27

198

General practice and research, 25, 26
Golden Rule, vii, 192, 195-197
Green, Canon P., 44
Guilt, 15-18, 119-121, 127

Halevi, Judge, 2
Hammond, T. C., 44, 45, 51, 68
Hart, H. R. A., 121
Hartnup disease, 8
Helsinki, Declaration of, vi, 37
Hippocratic Oath, vi, 37, 175
Homicide Act, 2
Homosexuality, 121-126
Human behavioural studies, 6-8, 10-12
Humanism, 39, 48, 69, 134, 184
Hungary, abortion rate, 77
Huxley, Julyan, 48, 55, 80, 82

Illness or wickedness, 15, 16
Image of God, in Man, 44, 72, 187, 196
Improvement of human nature, 11-13, 191-193
India, 86, 94-98
Individual, the, 20, 26-28, 141
Infant mortality, 79, 80, 90-94
Inferences, 49-51, 55, 65, 69
Inner moral compulsion, 120
Insemination, A.I.H., 81-84
Intra-uterine contraception device, 96-98
Interpretation, 5
International Code of Ethics, vi
Investigator's training, 33-39

Japan, and abortion, 78
Jewish (Hebrew) religion, 21, 26, 43, 45, 122, 125
Joseph Rowntree Social Service Trust, 110, 131
Judicial execution, 45, 51

Kilmuir, Lord, 123

Law, Divine, 46, 50, 77, 125, 145, 146, 161, 189, 192, 195-197
in principle, 37, 64, 66-70, 117, 120, 121
state, 15-19, 28, 50, 60, 73, 77, 78, 82, 86, 119, 122, 123, 137-140, 142, 191
Lewis, C. S., 162
Liability, 6
Liege trial, 17
Life, 42, 51-54, 65
Limited responsibility, 2, 6, 13-18
Limits of scientific method, 4-6, 13, 18-20
Logical positivism, 47, 67
Love, principle of, 46
Luke, St., 153-156

McCance, R. A., 25, 32, 33, 37
Machines, preservation of life, 56
Macnaughton, Mr. Justice, 73
Malthus, 92
Man himself, 26-27, 41-45, 181-197
Man's unity, 169-180
Marriage, 73, 79, 81, 84
Marx, K., and Marxist, 12, 184, 195
Mass advertisement and medication, 141-143
Materialist view, 68, 69, 72, 178 and 179
Maternal mortality, 79
Matthews, W. R., 46
Medical Officer of Health's duties, 139-140
Medical Research Council, vi, 37, 39
Meeting points of Church and Medicine, 148
Melanesian tribes, 13
Mens rea, 16
Mercy killing, 43-46, 59-61
Mill, J. S., 120
Mind, effects of disease, 8, 9
Miracle, biblical, 148-156, 161-163
Moral law, 44-46
Motives, 34
Murray, John, 45, 46, 51

National Health Service, 22, 75, 114, 131, 139, 157
Natural law, 67
Norms of behaviour, 13, 14

Open door policy, 102, 103

Pascal, 7
Patient's consent, 28-31
Paul, St, 14, 68, 125, 153-157, 179
Pavlov, 3, 4, 5, 19
Personality, 52, 53, 56, 58, 59, 63, 65, 101, 107, 114, 119, 128, 132, 175-6, 186, 188
Phenomenalist view, 179
Phenylketonuria, 7
Physician—friend, 24
Piper, O. A., 55
Plato, 67, 178, 180
Population control, 88-99
explosion, 78-80, 86, 91
Positivists, 47, 67
Predictability, 3, 4
Preservation (prolongation) of life, 43, 51-53, 55-58
Preventive medicine, 65, 136-147, 182
Primitive behaviour, 13
Private and public morality, 120
Professional responsibility, 15, 16, 36-40
Progress, 24, 25
Psychiatry and abortion, 73, 75, 76

Psychiatry and responsibility, 100-107
Psychopaths, 15, 16
Psychosomatic disease, 167, 168, 170-172
Punishment, in relation to responsibility, 16-18

Rape, 73-75
Religion and behaviour, 12, 66-70, 134, 161
Research, nature of, 22-24
Respiratory failure, and life, 56
Responsibility, investigator's 28-31, 33-36
   Nature and norms, i, 1, 13-14, 118, 119
   Personal, 2, 7, 16-18, 19, 101-106, 118, 119, 186-188
   Preventive medicine, 88-98, 136-147
   Psychiatric care, 100-107, 119, 130, 131, 166, 167
Responsiveness, tissues and emotions, 3-5
Revealed principle, 43, 44, 49, 64, 67, 69, 121, 134, 145, 146
Reverence for life, 42, 43, 51, 59
Risk, v, vi, 28-32, 38
Roman Catholic views, 44, 49, 62, 67, 76, 79, 86
Rubella, 64, 74

Safeguards, 36-40
Samaritans, 128
Sanctity of life, 25, 28, 39, 40, 60, 68, 70, 72-86
Schweitzer, 42, 43, 54
Scientific method, limits of, 13, 18-20, 169, 170
Self-consciousness, 172, 173, 186
Sexual offences, 120-126, 190

Sin, crime or disease? 117
Sixth Commandment, 45, 46, 51, 60, 76
Social aberrations, 117
Society and ethics, 66-70
Sociological studies, 10-12, 82, 83, 174, 175
Specialisation, 169, 170
Sperry, W., 43
Standards, vi, 13, 14, 27
State and Medicine, v, 145-147
Statistical studies, 4-6
Sterilisation, 84-86, 98
Stevas, N. St. John, 44, 51, 66, 67, 127
Stress diseases, 185
Suffering, 38, 39, 45, 54, 60, 61
Suicide, 44, 52, 59, 60, 102, 106, 126-128, 133

Thalidomide, 17, 74
Temperament, 119
Therapeutic abortion, 63, 73-77
Therapeutic community, 103, 104
Tissue response, 3
Trials, new drugs, 23-26, 30
Trust, 24, 29-31, 36, 38, 57

Unity of man, 52, 169-180
Utilitarian views, 35, 47, 60, 61, 68, 69

Variability of tissues, 4

War Crimes, 2, 37, 39, 67
'Wedge' principle, 43, 45, 49
Williams, Glanville, 50, 61-63, 68
Wolfenden Report, 123
Wootton, B., 1, 2, 10, 14, 16, 17, 118, 134
World Health Organization, 88, 90, 97, 110, 130, 182
World Medical Association, vi, 27, 37

Printed by George Outram & Co., Ltd., Perth.